ALTERNATIVE RHETORICS

ALTERNATIVE RHETORICS

Challenges to the Rhetorical Tradition

EDITED BY
Laura Gray-Rosendale
AND
Sibylle Gruber

STATE UNIVERSITY OF NEW YORK PRESS

Published by
State University of New York Press, Albany

© 2001 State University of New York

For information, address State University of New York Press,
90 State Street, Suite 700, Albany, NY 12207

Production by Cathleen Collins
Marketing by Michael Campochiaro

Library of Congress Cataloging in Publication Data

Alternative rhetorics : challenges to the rhetorical tradition / edited by Laura
Gray-Rosendale and Sibylle Gruber.
    p. cm.
  Includes bibliographical references and index.
  ISBN 0-7914-4973-4 (alk. paper) — ISBN 0-7914-4974-2 (pbk. : alk. paper)
   1. Rhetoric. I. Gray-Rosendale, Laura. II. Gruber, Sibylle III. Title.
  PN175 .A44 2001
  808—dc21

                              00-056338

10 9 8 7 6 5 4 3 2 1

We dedicate this book to Alex Weirich,
one of the most remarkable students
we've been fortunate enough to teach.
We will always remember you—
your intelligence, kindness, and willingness to learn.

Contents

PART III
RESISTING LABELS, PROMOTING CHANGE:
TAKING A NEW LOOK AT RHETORICS OF RACE AND
ETHNICITY IN LITERATURE AND FILM

PART IV
OTHER PEOPLE, OTHER CUSTOMS:
DEFYING TRADITIONAL RHETORICS OF GENDER
AND CLASS IN ASIAN LITERATURES AND CULTURES

Acknowledgments

We thank Priscilla Ross, our editor at SUNY Press, for her support of this project. We are glad Priscilla, and with it SUNY Press, was willing to advance a conversation about rhetorical concerns that have not received the attention they have deserved in the past. We also express our appreciation to the contributors from whom we learned a great deal during the experience of writing and constructing this book. Their ideas took our own thinking in critical new directions. We thank them for their patience and diligence as they redrafted and reconceived their own ideas in terms of our vision for this volume. Additional thanks go to Cathleen Collins for her excellent editorial suggestions in the later stages of the project's development. Finally, we thank each other for the chance to work together on an extended project of this kind. We have learned much from each other, from the opportunity to collaborate with each other on this project, and from the hikes we took together during which the ideas in this book have taken shape, been altered, and finally been allowed to take their present form.

Introduction

Moving Beyond Traditions:
Exploring the Need for "Alternative Rhetorics"

LAURA GRAY-ROSENDALE AND SIBYLLE GRUBER

When we talk about rhetorical theory, many of us think of classical rhetoricians such as Aristotle, Isocrates, the Sophists, Plato, Gorgias, Cicero, and Quintilian, and modern rhetorical theorists such as Richards, Weaver, Burke, Toulmin, Perelman, Habermas, Bakhtin, and Foucault. Others refer to specific landmark essays in rhetorical theory, critical essays that interpret or challenge these essays, and texts that present biographical information about these major rhetorical theorists. These theorists, as the list shows, are comprised of well-known and well-respected representatives of a long and prosperous tradition in rhetorical scholarship. To receive a valid and valuable education in rhetoric and composition for many means to know the traditional canon and to be able to apply this knowledge to scholarship in the field.

However, although the traditional texts are an important part in every rhetoric and composition scholar's repertoire, we know that the modern rhetorical canon is constantly expanding and unfolding far beyond the traditional texts with which we have become familiar. Certainly, our need to legitimize the field of rhetoric and composition as a viable academic discipline seemed to necessitate a corpus that could be touted as authoritative, meeting our professional and intellectual needs as scholars in a newly developing field. After several decades of successful programs in rhetoric and composition, though, scholars have started to move beyond what Cheryl Glenn (1997) calls a "canonized, masculinized map" and have begun to engage in critical

1

conversations about the importance of creating new and reconceptualizing old bodies of knowledge. Explorations of rhetoric, race, and ethnicity (Olson and Worsham, 1999; Gilyard, 1996; Smitherman-Donaldson, 1994; Villanueva, 1993, 1997) have become important topics for discussion, and identity construction, gender, and rhetoric (Hesford, 1999; Jarratt and Worsham, 1998; Glenn, 1997) are part of many composition and rhetoric curricula. Exploring the impact of political, economic, and social forces on our value systems has allowed us to begin to challenge the very boundaries of what constitutes rhetorical discourse in a technological world (Warschauer, 1999; Hawisher and Selfe, 2000; Blair and Takayoshi, 1999).

Looking beyond the narrowly defined borders of the traditional canon makes it possible to see rhetoric, and with it the study of rhetoric, not as a remote body of knowledge but instead as part of professional and personal value systems. As James Berlin points out in "Rhetoric and Ideology in the Writing Class,"

> Instead of rhetoric operating as the transcendental recorder or arbiter of competing ideological claims, rhetoric is regarded as always already ideological. This position means that any examination of a rhetoric must first consider the ways its very discursive structures can be read so as to favor one version of economic, social, and political arrangements over other versions. . . . A rhetoric can never be innocent. (477)

Berlin's 1988 proclamation that "rhetoric can never be innocent" has contributed to a new line of inquiry that takes into account that the study of rhetoric is influenced by scholars' perceptions about what is and what is not important. Furthermore, we have become more sensitive to admitting that research questions depend on the scholars who ask them. By including or leaving out questions—wittingly or unwittingly—researchers can grant or deny admission into a rhetorical canon. Thus, ideology, as Berlin says, is always already a part of rhetoric. Or, as Glenn puts it, "rhetoric always inscribes the relation of language and power at a particular moment" (1).

If we look at the beginning of the new century as a particular moment in the history of rhetoric, we can see that the composition of scholars in the field is changing, representing a wider array of cultural, political, ideological, economic, and social backgrounds. This change makes possible and promotes scholarship in rhetoric and composition that includes instead of excludes. The widely varying interests of scholars from, or interested in, different ethnic groups, and scholars exploring women's contributions to the field of rhetoric, for example, have made significant inroads in changing our perceptions of the major players in the field. The rhetorical canon, then, is moving away from being traditional to being open and accepting of different and alternative presentations and representations of the study of rhetoric.

An interesting example of such scholarship is Cheryl Glenn's study of women's contributions to classical and Renaissance rhetoric. She remaps rhetorical territory in *Rhetoric Retold* by disrupting what she calls a "seamless narrative we have for too long been willing to accept" (15). In this traditional narrative, she points out, "not a single woman has appeared in the indices of the most comprehensive histories of rhetoric" (15). Her work provides an alternative to traditional studies of male discourse strategies by discussing such rhetors as Sappho, Aspasia, Cornelia, Hortensia, Julian of Norwich, Margery Kempe, Margaret More Roper, and many others.

In addition to including women in the canon, scholars are studying the rhetorics of race as theoretical constructs, impacted by issues such as history and economy. Keith Gilyard's recently published collection, *Race, Rhetoric, and Composition*, for example, focuses closely on what Gilyard calls "the race thing," which he sees as "ever shifting, ever changing, and becoming increasingly complex in the ways it marks intellectual and sociopolitical communities" (ix). The authors in this collection discuss the source of popular talk about race, the anti-Arab sentiment following the Oklahoma bombing in 1995, the pertinence of the Black Arts movement in the teaching of composition, the problems with multicultural pedagogies, and the mythologizing of race.

Glenn's and Gilyard's works are just two examples—important although arbitrarily chosen—of the many wonderful efforts by rhetoric and composition scholars to remap the rhetorical world, making it clear that the study of modern rhetorical theories cannot be confined within nicely drawn borders. Instead, we need to realize that the field is ever-changing, ever-expanding, unconstrained, unconfined, and largely uncharted. *Alternative Rhetorics* is intended to make sure that we continue exploring new territories, territories that were considered negligible, unimportant, or nonexistent not too long ago.

Alternative Rhetorics, then, situates itself within this new and ongoing reconceptualization of rhetoric's functions in a changing world. It grows out of our beliefs that rhetorical discourses are complex and contradictory, and that they oftentimes do not fit into easily recognizable categories or modes. *Alternative Rhetorics* challenges and puts pressure on traditional canons of rhetorical thought. Specifically, *Alternative Rhetorics* presents students, teachers, and scholars with new ways to approach the formal features of rhetorical situations such as audience, exigence, context, and constraints. Furthermore, the contributors to this collection provide new insights into rhetorics that have been marginalized in the current literature. They give voice to those whose discursive acts have gone unrecognized within Western culture. They also establish new methodologies for investigating the history of rhetorics as well as current changes to the rhetorical paradigms instigated by the use of new technologies. Furthermore, they present new insights into the rhetorics of race, ethnicity, gender, and class.

The title of our collection, *Alternative Rhetorics: Challenging the Rhetorical Tradition*, has a specific purpose. We chose the term "alternative" for a number of reasons:

1. "Alternative" proposes rhetorical approaches that draw from as well as disrupt and challenge the hierarchical nature of some traditional rhetorical studies while recognizing that such challenges are temporary and open to co-optation. This is what Donna Haraway calls "critical positioning" or the admission that "partiality and not universality is the condition of being heard" (195). In using this term, we acknowledge that no rhetoric is fully "alternative" but always both rewrites the tradition and inevitably becomes part of it. Such a term further acknowledges the significance of these emerging studies in their own right. These studies advance a critical counterpoint to the tradition, and in doing so, illuminate the tradition's form and shape as well its tendencies to construct itself as seamless despite the obvious fissures within its own narratives.

2. "Alternative" also testifies to the power relations involved in offering up these texts. These are texts which canvas rhetorics that have often been marginalized, ghettoized, neglected, or overlooked within our historical context as well as other historical contexts for particular cultural, social, and political reasons. What we aim to present is something like a Foucauldian archaeology: "a history that would not only account for the traces of the Other suppressed by conventional historiography but would also allow the Other to speak across the barrier established by the regime of reason" (Harootunian, 114). This would be an unearthing or an analysis of how neglected discourses and social practices are a critical part of the unsaid of our discipline, a tracing of what Gayatri Spivak calls "the other in the self" of our discipline (47). It entails an examination of issues of self-representation, distributions of power and knowledge, and investigations of contradictions (Hesford, xiii). By bringing these discourses to the center of inquiry within this text, by looking at their material and cultural situations, we hope to begin shifting such power relations as well as to reveal the extent of their value and importance for how we conceive of rhetoric as a scholarly as well as pedagogical enterprise.

3. "Alternative" also implies our own desires as editors and writers of texts within this book to contribute a different book, an alternative text, through which we as scholars and teachers might research and teach rhetoric. We aim to offer an alternative to what the book market now affords us in terms of text selection. With this book, we hope to furnish more diverse perspectives on the uses and applications of rhetoric, attempting to expand the territory of what constitutes students' and teachers' perceptions of rhetoric and rhetorical texts.

In addition to our choice of "alternative," we also insist on "rhetorics" to show that we do not study a single rhetoric, nor are we satisfied any longer with one rhetorical tradition. Instead, we want to emphasize multiplicity and fragmentation within and between different rhetorics and different traditions. We also know that we cannot—nor would we want to—present an encompassing view of the many rhetorics present in our lives. There are many alternative rhetorics to be considered, and we present some of them.

Furthermore, this collection intends to "challenge," not dismantle, uproot, or invalidate, the rhetorical tradition. We know that we need traditions to have a discussion about them, see beyond them, and work toward changing them if change is required. Without a solid basis, and without a solid knowledge of the foundation, we would not have the language to scrutinize the old, the used, the new, or the unexplored. Therefore, we value traditions, but we argue that we need to challenge them in order to improve our understanding of what being a rhetoric and composition scholar, teacher, or student entails.

We will meet our own challenge if we can claim success in presenting rhetorics that, in addition to providing new insights for scholars, are relevant to students' lives and that create common ground between students and the texts they read. Discourse practices, as we know, are always tied "to the production of individual and social identities" (McLaren and Giroux, 16). We want to provide alternative texts that reflect students' own experiences as individuals with diverse and interlocked identities and with alternative ways of using language to relate to their audiences. This will allow us to move toward a classroom environment that helps students understand and be proud of their own uses of language. This is especially important if we heed Gloria Anzaldúa's words that "until I can take pride in my language, I cannot take pride in myself" (59).

Alternative Rhetorics is intended for teachers who are trying to integrate diverse perspectives on rhetoric into their classrooms, for researchers who intend to explore new venues for their scholarship, and for students who are interested in different approaches to the study of rhetoric and composition. The contributions share a common desire to provide educators with the means to explore and teach the potentials of alternative rhetorics.

Organization of This Volume

The essays in this volume are organized into four parts:

- *Changing Histories, Changing Lives: Revisiting the Rhetorical Tradition*
- *Virtual Reality, Real Virtuality: Exploring the Multiple Rhetorics of Cyberspace*
- *Resisting Labels, Promoting Change: Taking a New Look at Rhetorics of Race and Ethnicity in Literature and Film*
- *Other People, Other Customs: Defying Traditional Rhetorics of Gender and Class in Asian Literatures and Cultures*

The first part, *Changing Histories, Changing Lives: Revisiting the Rhetorical Tradition*, is comprised of three essays, each of which puts pressure on the traditional histories of rhetoric we teach and use in our scholarship. The first chapter is Catherine F. Smith's "Remembering the Rhetorics of Women: The Case of Jane Lead." Smith explores Jane Lead's (1623?–1704) use of traditional religious concepts and images in a spiritual context to represent women's experience rather than men's as normative. Although Smith admits that Lead's text is traditional, she points out that the subtext of her work presents an alternative to traditional texts. Lead, according to Smith, used women's economic experience as metaphor for spiritual death and adapted traditionally feminine wisdom to refigure women's experience as spiritual life. Authorized to speak by 'inner light' theology, Smith argues, Lead devised a way of speaking publicly about private life for communal purposes by strategic adaptation of rhetorical traditions. Smith's essay in feminist rhetorical analysis explicates Lead's accomplishment as a historical woman using available rhetorical resources to put pressure on traditions manifested in religion and law.

The second chapter in this part, "Multivocal Midwife: The Writing Teacher as Rhetor," is the collaborative effort of Phyllis Mentzell Ryder, Valentina M. Abordonado, Barbara Heifferon, and Duane H. Roen to trace the figure of the midwife in various rhetorical theories. The authors examine how Plato uses the midwife metaphor to conceptualize the relationship between teacher and student, speaker and audience. Ultimately, the authors of this chapter reject the Platonic understanding of midwife rhetoric because they disagree with its contentions about the elements of the rhetorical act: "truth," language, the audience, and the rhetor. The authors also trace the midwife-rhetor in romantic-expressivist and social-epistemic/postmodern theories of rhetoric, again using the figure to identify the roles offered for teacher, student, audience, and rhetor. In the end, they argue for an alternative theory of rhetoric that bridges the gap between Plato, the expressivist view, and the social-epistemic view—a theory of midwife rhetoric that situates the student and teacher in a social context that shapes their discourse. In the authors' view, the student and the teacher, the rhetor and the audience, do not simply work together to discover a static, objective truth but co-construct dynamic, subjective truths.

The third essay in this part, Kathleen A. DeHaan's "'Wooden Shoes and Mantle Clocks': Letter Writing as a Rhetorical Forum for the Transforming Immigrant Identity," offers an examination of turn-of-the-century Dutch immigrant letters as alternative rhetorics, utilizing narrative as a theoretical screen through which to analyze, understand, and appreciate these rich and influential texts. According to the author, the exigencies of immigrant life drove many immigrants to observe, to write, and to correspond over a lifetime. As alternative rhetorics, DeHaan expostulates, letters gave voice to those who had limited access to traditional rhetorical forums. Furthermore, she sees these letters as "alternative" in their ability to bridge private and public discourse. Most significantly, DeHaan points out, these letters enabled the immigrant to be an active participant in the New World.

The second part, *Virtual Reality, Real Virtuality: Exploring the Multiple Rhetorics of Cyberspace*, examines how technology is changing the ways in which rhetoric operates. Sibylle Gruber opens this section with her essay, "The Rhetorics of Three Women Activist Groups on the Web: Building and Transforming Communities." She provides a theoretical foundation for discussing the rhetorics of online communities before analyzing the various discourse strategies used in women activists' web sites. Gruber describes how these sites have found alternatives to the rhetorics of war, aggression, and destruction to create participatory on-line communities that discuss very real problems in a virtual space. The success and continued support of these sites, she argues, is based on using rhetorics of peace, equality, cooperation, and empowerment to establish intersections between reality and virtuality, emphasize the global nature of local problems, and create a participatory focus for the sites. Gruber analyzes three sites—*Bat Shalom of the Jerusalem Link, Network of East-West Women,* and *UNIFEM: United Nations Development Fund for Women*—to show how different rhetorical strategies are used to embrace similar goals: the promotion of women's rights issues and peaceful interaction in a wide array of political, social, religious, and cultural settings.

In the second chapter, "Authority and Credibility: Classical Rhetoric, the Internet, and the Teaching of Techno-Ethos," Theresa Enos and Shane

Borrowman challenge current conceptions about ethos that dominate our rhetorical landscape. They examine the relevance of classical definitions of ethos (speaker's credibility and morality) for writing in a newly technologized environment. The authors argue that such conceptions of ethos are at the heart of contemporary concerns over authorship and the spread of knowledge on the Internet, where credibility must be formed within the cyberspeech itself and authorship is both foregrounded and relegated to anonymity.

Jacqueline J. Lambiase in "Like a Cyborg Cassandra: The Oklahoma City Bombing and the Internet's Misbegotten Rhetorical Situation" analyzes texts from a public electronic discussion about the Oklahoma City bombing, in which participants who did not conform to dominant discourse tactics were silenced. The author argues that the predicament of silenced participants in this discussion can be compared to Christa Wolf's title character in her novel *Cassandra*. By linking this ancient Cassandra's "unheard voice" with the voices of silenced participants in computer-mediated communication, this project seeks to provide a new ethos for developing more egalitarian discourse situations in cyberspace. To create a "cyborg Cassandra," the author turns to Donna Haraway's postgender cyborg writing, which offers other strategies that enable discursive agency to resist dominant discourse on-line.

The fourth essay in this section, John B. Killoran's "@ home among the .coms: Virtual Rhetoric in the Agora of the Web," draws on a study of 110 Web home page authors and their personal home pages, discussing a rhetorical strategy adopted by solo authors to claim a niche on the Web. This rhetoric, according to Killoran, consists of what social semioticians Robert Hodge and Gunther Kress characterize as low-modality messages. Without the resources to mount "real" rhetorical appeals competitive with those of institutions, Killoran argues that solo authors construct instead distorted "virtual" appeals—virtual logos, virtual ethos, and virtual pathos—derived from institutional discourses. Through Bakhtin's dialogic perspective, the author claims, these virtual appeals can be understood as parodies of authentic institutional discourses that contest the ideology, promulgated by mainstream institutions, of who one is and how one fits in within the media. Killoran argues that applied to the classroom, student-composed web parody can foster students' sense of agency and critical awareness of computer-mediated communication.

The next part, *Resisting Labels, Promoting Change: Taking a New Look at Rhetorics of Race and Ethnicity in Literature and Film,* examines texts that challenge as well as perpetuate dominant cultural rhetorics about race and ethnicity. This section begins with Laura Gray-Rosendale's essay "Geographies of Resistance: Rhetorics of Race and Mobility in Arna Bontemps' *Sad-Faced Boy* (1937)." Gray-Rosendale argues that Bontemps' 1937 *Sad-Faced*

Boy exposes and undermines economic, social, and political tactics as well as intricate operations of power relations prevalent during the period through its rhetorical choices. Initiating a complex symbolization system that is plurivocal and ambiguous resisting binary economies such as black/white, poor/wealthy, and rural/urban in favor of simultaneous differences, Gray-Rosendale postulates that the text utilizes several innovative rhetorical techniques which afford linguistic defiance of economic and cultural assimilation. The author contends that *Sad-Faced Boy* extends to its African-American child audience a highly politicized comprehension of their own situations. It offers child readers possible tentative methods by which to counteract the oppressions of their situations and strategies through which to maintain the positive aspects of their cultural lives while existing within an environment that does not value such cultural backgrounds. The geography of this mobility, according to Gray-Rosendale, necessarily enables the characters to temporarily oppose existing power relations through three tactics: performing music, riding the subway and visiting the library, and acting as viewers of and participants within a parade. The characters in this text resist urban modernism, dislocation, and confusion as they experience the problematics of technology and urban capitalism.

Anthony J. Michel in "Visual Rhetorics and Classroom Practices: Negotiating 'Contact Zones' in Julie Dash's *Daughters of the Dust*" continues the discussion about rhetorics of race and ethnicity by exploring how institutional and cultural constraints on film influence textual production. He argues for visual rhetorics as a necessary and often overlooked component of a critical pedagogy that seeks to engage students to participate effectively in democratic practices. Michel defines visual rhetoric as the exploration of film and its production practices to critique dominant assumptions about what counts as legitimate knowledge in society. An analysis of Julie Dash's *Daughter of the Dust*, a 1991 film about turn-of-the-century African Americans living on an island off the coast of South Carolina, provides a model for incorporating visual rhetorics into the classroom. Michel focuses on three "contact zones": the culture industry, technologies of historical representation, and authorial subject position. These sites of negotiation are developed in the final section of the chapter to explicate specific ways that visual rhetorics can be used to encourage students to view their own writing as embedded within processes of negotiation with historically specific institutional and cultural determinants.

The third chapter in this part, "Audience in Afrocentric Rhetoric: Promoting Human Agency and Social Change" by Daniel F. Collins, investigates the social relations generally associated with the historical development of Western rhetoric. According to Collins, agonism denotes a sort of rhetorical conflict that reflects a tendency to approach topics as polarized debates with only one right answer. He contrasts agonistic rhetoric with Afrocentric rhetoric that is informed by notions of harmony and balance. Examining Western rhetoric relative to Afrocentric rhetoric, particularly in terms of the ways audience is conceptualized in each rhetoric, Collins questions the rhetorical efficacy of agonism due to its limited ability to construct new connections across disagreements and to produce new knowledge from such connections. He offers theoretical and pedagogical strategies designed to assist students in questioning and understanding more about the kinds of social relations implied within their compositions. Collins endorses Afrocentric rhetoric because of its ability to open new rhetorical ground and expand perspectives on human knowledge.

The fourth part of the book, *Other People, Other Customs: Defying Traditional Rhetorics of Gender and Class in Asian Literatures and Cultures,* examines closely how rhetorics of gender and class operate within literature and culture. In "Rewriting the Butterfly Story: Tricksterism in Onoto Watanna's *A Japanese Nightingale* and Sui Sin Far's 'The Smuggling of Tie Co,'" Huining Ouyang examines, from a cultural studies-rhetorical perspective, the ways in which Onoto Watanna and Sui Sin Far contest or accommodate the dominant discourse in their retellings of the Butterfly story. Through her analyses of Watanna's novel *A Japanese Nightingale* (1901) and Sui Sin Far's short story "The Smuggling of Tie Co" (1900), Ouyang demonstrates how tricksterism functions rhetorically as both forms and themes that resist hegemonic relations. Ouyang argues that although they speak within the dominant language structure and thus do not ultimately transform the racial and gender status quo, both writers have reconstituted the power relations as constructed within the master plot and thereby disrupt traditional Orientalist discourses of domination.

Hui Wu continues the discussion of feminist rhetorics in "The Alternative Feminist Discourse of Post-Mao Chinese Writers: A Perspective from the Rhetorical Situation." She delineates the cultural constituents within the feminist rhetoric of post-Mao Chinese writers by expanding on the theory of rhetorical situation developed by Lloyd Bitzer. Wu examines the nonfiction of the female novelists who have gained popularity after the Cultural Revolution (1966–78). Specifically, Wu addresses the following questions: Why do post-Mao female writers reject Western feminism? What are the differences between the rhetorics of Chinese feminist writers and Western feminists? What problems may critics face when they use Western feminist theory to interpret non-Western gender politics?

In the third chapter within this section, Jeff Schonberg examines literacy as a manifestation of *kairos* that gives meaning to the Chinese government's textual methods of surmounting economic barriers and conquering inertia. In "When Worlds Collide: Rhetorics of Profit, Rhetorics of Loss in Chinese Culture," Schonberg argues that literacy can be seen as a manifestation of *kairos* that gives meaning to counterdiscourses. The author performs a close rhetorical analysis of texts. The author reveals that the government's diverse discourses and the counterdiscourses used by members of the community represent either economic or religious resistance to each other. Additionally, Schonberg contends, both sets of discourses function as a means of relieving the psychological stress created by economic stasis, a weakening cultural identity, and the inability to make corporate, religious, familial, or individual decisions.

Alternative Rhetorics presents the work of those who tackle alternative approaches to rhetorics from a variety of viewpoints. Our goal is to expand the existing canon and to include perspectives that have not yet found their way into the teaching of rhetoric. We encourage scholars, teachers, and students interested in exploring new venues for their research and teaching to use this collection as a starting point for their own investigations into the multiple methods for writing and arguing about rhetorics.

Works Cited

Anzaldúa, Gloria. *Borderlands/La Frontera: The New Mestiza*. San Francisco: Aunt Lute, 1987.

Berlin, James. "Rhetoric and Ideology in the Writing Class." *College English* 50 (September 1988): 477–94.

Blair, Kristine, & Pamela Takayoshi. *Feminist Cyberscapes: Mapping Gendered Academic Spaces*. Stanford, CT: Ablex, 1999.

Foucault, Michel. *The Archaeology of Knowledge*. Trans. A. M. Sheridan Smith. New York: Pantheon, 1972.

———. "The Subject and Power." In afterword to *Michel Foucault: Beyond Structuralism and Hermeneutics*, edited by Hubert Dreyfus and Paul Rabinow, 208–226. Chicago: Chicago University Press, 1983.

Gilyard, Keith. *Let's Flip the Script: An African-American Discourse on Language, Literature, and Learning*. Detroit: Wayne State University Press, 1996.

Giroux, Henry A. *Border Crossings: Cultural Workers and the Politics of Education*. New York: Routledge, 1992.

Glenn, Cheryl. *Rheteric Retold: Regendering the Tradition from Antiquity Through the Renaissance*. Carbondale: Southern Illinois University Press, 1997.

Haraway, Donna. *Simians, Cyborgs, and Women: The Reinvention of Nature*. New York: Routledge, 1991.

Harding, Sandra. "Introduction: Is There a Feminist Method?" In *Feminism and Methodology: Social Sciences Issues*, edited by Sandra Harding, 1–14. Bloomington: Indiana University Press, 1987.

Harootunian, H. D. "Foucault, Genealogy, History: The Pursuit of Otherness." In *After Foucault: Humanistic Knowledge, Postmodern Challenges*, 110–37. New Brunswick: Rutgers University Press, 1988.

Hawisher, Gail E., & Cynthia L. Selfe. *Global Literacies and the World-Wide Web*. New York: Routledge, 2000.

Hesford, Wendy. *Framing Identities: Autobiography and the Politics of Pedagogy*. Minneapolis: University of Minnesota Press, 1999.

hooks, bell. *Teaching to Transgress: Education as the Practice of Freedom*. New York: Routledge, 1994.

Houston, Marsha. "The Politics of Difference: Race, Class, and Women's Communication." In *Women Making Meaning: New Feminist Directions in Communication*, edited by Lana F. Rakow, 45–59. New York: Routledge, 1992.

Jarratt, Susan, and Lynn Worsham, eds. *Feminism and Composition Studies: In Other Words*. New York: MLA, 1998.

McLaren, Peter, and Henry A. Giroux. "Writing from the Margins: Geographies of Identity, Pedagogy, and Power." In *Revolutionary Multiculturalism: Pedagogies of Dissent for the New Millennium*, edited by Peter McLaren, 16–41. Boulder, Colo.: Westview Press: 1997.

McLaren, Peter, and Tomaz Tadeu da Silva. "Decentering Pedagogy: Critical Literacy, Resistance and the Politics of Memory." In *Paulo Freire: A Critical Encounter*, edited by Peter McLaren and Peter Leonard, 47–89. New York: Routledge, 1993.

Miller, Susan. *Assuming the Position: Cultural Pedagogy and the Politics of Commonplace Writing*. Pittsburgh: Pittsburgh University Press, 1998.

Olson, Gary A., and Lynn Worsham, eds. *Race, Rhetoric, and the Postcolonial*. Albany: State University of New York Press, 1999.

Roen, Duane, Stuart Brown, and Theresa Enos, eds. *Living Rhetoric and Composition: Stories of the Discipline*. Mahwah: Erlbaum, 1999.

Rosteck, Thomas. *At the Intersection: Cultural Studies and Rhetoric Studies*. New York: Guilford, 1999.

Schell, Eileen. *Gypsy Academics and Mother-Teachers: Gender, Contingent Labor, and Writing Instruction*. Portsmouth: Boynton-Cook, 1998.

Smitherman-Donaldson, Geneva. *Black Talk: Words and Phrases from the Hood to Amen Corner*. Boston: Houghton Mifflin, 1994.

Spivak, Gayatri. *The Post-Colonial Critic: Interviews, Strategies, Dialogues*. Ed. Sarah Harasym. New York: Routledge, 1990.

Villanueva, Victor. *Bootstraps: From an American Academic of Color*. Urbana: NCTE, 1993.

———, ed. *Cross-talk in Composition Theory: A Reader*. Urbana: NCTE, 1997.

Warschauer, Mark. *Electronic Literacies: Language, Culture, and Power in On-Line Education*. Mahwah: Erlbaum, 1999.

Yarbrough, Stephen. *After Rhetoric: The Study of Discourse Beyond Language and Culture*. Carbondale: Southern Illinois University Press, 1999.

PART I

Changing Histories, Changing Lives

Revisiting the Rhetorical Tradition

Historical accounts of rhetoric are never innocent, never free from rhetorical investments, and never closed to the critical eye of counter-investigations. Instead, they are stories that fulfill certain interests, be they disciplinary, institutional, or discursive. As Mark Poster reveals, when we read and write histories of our discipline, we must always ask the question: "What does the historian do to the past when he or she traces its continuity and assigns it causes?" Every history is always a reconstruction of events and interests. Therefore, history writing wields a great deal of clout since "history is a form of knowledge and a form of power at the same time; put differently, it is a means of controlling and domesticating the past in the form of knowing it" (75). History is not simply the documentation of knowledge: history *constructs* and *transforms* knowledge. Likewise, as Victor Vitanza has pointed out, without this kind of critical inquiry into the operations of history, the history of rhetoric becomes little more than a "History of Oppression," a history that "has been a representation of how rhetors have attempted to define, to obtain, and to keep *power*. And at the expense of Others" (326). In order to work against this kind of history writing, we have to recognize the complexities and implications of writing and revising the multiple histories of rhetoric.

Although we recognize that no historical account is without a complex system of motives, this part of the book is premised on the notion that history writing operates to control the past and that what has counted as worthy of historical examination in rhetoric and composition until recently may at times have been too limiting. Instead, this section seeks to explore alternative historical accounts, accounts that push against ready answers for questions such as the following: What are the historical origins of rhetoric? In

15

what ways do we need to revise the traditional, canonical views of the history of rhetoric we have received? What have been the traditional metaphoric allegiances in writing the history of rhetoric, and should they be changed? What examples of historical accounts of rhetoric should be unearthed, and how does doing so shift how we view received histories of the discipline? In effect, these essays demand that we question histories of rhetoric in the ways that Cheryl Glenn requests that we do. We need to ask questions of context, ethics, and power: In what context is this history or rhetoric produced and normalized? Whom does it benefit? To what/whom are this history's practices accountable? What/whom do they privilege? What practices might produce historical remembrances? What are the effects of such representation? As Glenn suggests, asking such questions pushes writers of rhetorical histories to make critical queries about historical evidence: "What counts? What is available? Who provided and preserved it—and why? How and to what end has it been used? And by whom? Thus, history is not frozen, not merely the past. It provides an approachable, disputable ground for engaging and transforming traditional memory or practice in the interest of both the present and the future" (389). The authors of the works that appear in this part of the book see historical inquiry as flexible, changing, and open to continual reconstruction. The alternative histories that they offer suggest new ways to view histories of rhetoric and to open inquiry into this critical terrain.

Works Cited

Glenn, Cheryl. "Truth, Lies, and Method: Revisiting Feminist Historiography." *College English* 62, no. 3 (January 2000): 387–89.

Poster, Mark. *Foucault, Marxism, and History*. Cambridge, U.K.: Polity, 1984.

Vitanza, Victor J. *Negation, Subjectivity, and the History of Rhetoric*. Albany: State University of New York Press, 1997.

Remembering the Rhetorics of Women

The Case of Jane Lead

CATHERINE F. SMITH

Introduction

Protestant visionary and prophet Jane Lead (1623?–1704) was commissioned by Christ, she said, "to declare, as I have revealed it to thee," the experience of spiritual death and rebirth "as thou has practical knowledge of it" (Epistle, *The Heavenly Cloud Now Breaking* unpaginated).

This essay focuses on Lead's remarkable rhetoric when characterizing spiritual life. I claim that in Lead's published work—fifteen tracts of spiritual guidance, a four-volume daily journal of visions, and a spiritual autobiography—is found unexpected protest against women's economic conditions as daughters, wives, and widows under contemporary law. The complaint, which I argue originated in Lead's experience, is not stated directly. Material victimization was not the exigency that motivated Lead's writing; spiritual crisis was. Nonetheless, a surprisingly accurate record of a cultural formation that ruled women's material lives, contemporary inheritance, and property law is identifiable in her account of spiritual life. More explicit is Lead's response, an alternative economy of the spirit created by reinventing ancient feminine symbolism. An example contrasting actual marriage with spiritual union, taken from Lead's journal *A Fountain of Gardens,* illustrates:

> We should serve in the Newness of Spirit; as being discharged from the Law of the first Husband, to which we were married, after the Law of a Carnal Command: Whence we are now free to be Married unto him that is raised from the Dead, and so shall become the

Lamb's Wife, jointure unto all the Lands and Possessions that he
hath. The Eternal Revenues are belonging to her, whether Invisible
or Visible: all Power in Heaven and Earth is committed her . . . from
Wisdom's breath. (*Fountain* I, 71)

The contrast of Law with Wisdom is Lead's principal device for contrasting worldly life with spiritual life. Her imagery of marriage and property is not
unique. However, Lead and the group of seventeenth-century English women
writers represented by her in this essay used such language with special effect.
By their actions and their language as preachers, prophets, and members or
leaders of communities of religious dissent, Lead and contemporary women
sectarians variously but collectively challenged contemporary English culture
in the form of state religion and its scripturally justified gendered social roles
and cultural norms. In nonconforming (outside the Church of England) congregations, they defied rules for women's behavior, including laws against
women's public speaking and doctrinal proscriptions against women's preaching. 'Inner light' sects such as the Quakers and Lead's Philadelphian Society
argued on theological grounds that male and female were alike in God, therefore women and men were spiritual equals. Those groups institutionalized
egalitarian worship practices and organizational procedures despite state prosecution for doing so (Thomas 1965). Published defenses of nonconforming
beliefs and activities provided a religious variant of the vigorous feminist pamphlet literature arguing for gender equality and against belief in women's
inherent weakness and inferiority to men (Henderson and McManus). Thus,
although social change was not their aim (spiritual community was), women
sectarian dissenters nonetheless lived, spoke, and wrote critical cultural alternatives and alternative rhetorics in their time.

Traditional Text, Nontraditional Subtext

Cultural conditions and changing conceptions of human agency are represented in texts by these early-modern sectarian women which Lead's texts
illustrate well. I focus here on her contrast of Law and Wisdom, viewing it
from a feminist perspective interested in women's ways of articulating experience relative to their historical situation.

Lead's textual mediation of her experience is not transparent to the
present-day reader. She wrote discursively within contemporary discourses
regarding the nature of spirituality. Lead practiced traditions of meditative
textual exegesis. Her adopted style copiously represented a meditation on an
authoritative text in layered interpretation, elaborated imagery, and formulaic repetition intricately varied to connect the authoritative text, weblike, to
particular life experiences.

Taking Law first, Lead's knowledgeable and targeted use of contemporary legal terminology can be reduced to the linear logic of a contract, as follows:

Christ, the bridegroom, agrees that his bride, New Spirit, is "jointured unto all the Lands and Possessions that he hath" in accord with her commitment of "such a plenty of dowry Riches and Honours, that cannot be degraded, nor plucked away," as is suitable to "qualify for such a high Marriage-Union, with the First Begotten-Son and Heir of the high God." Due to their inherent equality, she is granted "mutual interest with him in what the Father hath put into his Hand, which is all Power. . . . (H)erein for a certainty she will be put into a Joint-Possession with the Lord her Bridegroom . . . that so a Stock of Spiritual Goods being taken in may be to support and carry on the Heavenly Calling withal" (*Fountain*, I, 70; *Heavenly Cloud*, 31; *Enochian Walks*, 30; *Fountain*, I, 2; *Enochian Walks*, 30).

This reduction starkly renders Lead's metaphor as a method. The method is to mirror the laws governing ordinary domestic life in a reflection that reverses their usual meaning. Lead thus reveals another reality in ordinary existence. The method is strategic, with the aim of reminding contemporary readers of worldly experience shared by composer and audience while presenting a contrary viewpoint on experience. To help present-day readers recognize the metaphor and the strategy, explanation follows of the three legal cornerstones of women's economic position in Lead's time—primogeniture, coverture, and dower rights. Evidence of Lead's experience of these conditions based on records of her economic life as daughter, wife, and widow is included in the explanation. This rather lengthy excursion into legal history and documentation of Lead's case is necessary to my argument that her rhetorical strategy was to represent private experience publicly for communal purposes.

The social upheavals, ecclesiastical reforms, and early capitalist economy of Lead's Reformation-driven century speeded changes in marriage, inheritance, and the customary and legal practices controlling their relationships.[1] Global expansion of trade drove a search for new sources of capital for investment, and inheritance patterns changed as a result. Among landed gentry such as Jane Lead family, under increasing use of the legal doctrine of primogeniture eldest sons inherited land while daughters and younger sons received dowries, usually cash or goods, that were expected to be invested for growth. Given to daughters at marriage, the cash dowry usually was a woman's entire inheritance from the parental estate. While sons' dowries went to establish business or trade, daughters' dowries went into marriage as the sole approved vocation for women. The dowry was the basis of a woman's claim to support during marriage and widowhood.

The growth of a bride's dowry depended on good financial husbandry. Under the legal doctrine of coverture, the husband became his wife's guardian, thereby gaining use of the dowry during marriage. As insurance, settlements made at the time of marriage prescribed a future annuity, or jointure, for the wife should she outlive her husband. The jointure was usually only a percentage of the marriage's total assets, not the entire estate. As with the bridal dowry from the parental estate, the widow's jointure was her sole inheritance from the marital estate.

By Jane Lead's time, primogeniture, coverture, and dower rights defined a woman as financially dependent on father or husband and as having no rights to control assets. Public records enable us to speculate confidently about Lead's own circumstances. We know something about her dowry, for example. Among legacies to younger children in her father Hamond Ward's will, the oldest son and heir James is requested to pay "to my son-in-law William Leade of King's Lynn, merchant 110 [pounds sterling] in full recompense and discharge of his wife's portion according to certain articles between him and myself."[2] Because no copy of the marriage settlement itself survives, we cannot know if the specified amount constituted Jane Ward Lead's entire dowry agreed to at her marriage seven years before her father's death. Portions of the estate willed to younger sons are approximately the same in size as hers. Conforming to restrictions already described, the specified amount is Lead's entire inheritance. In contrast, her husband William, an only son, was left by his merchant father a house, rents, and "all the goods, chattels, plate, ships and their stocks. . . not before given."[3]

Although we do not have all the details, we know that William Lead invested their joint assets "overseas" (Lead 1978, unpaginated). We also know that nothing was recoverable at his death, and Jane Lead did not receive the jointure to which she was entitled. In this, Lead experienced what many widows in her time experienced. Two kinds of records show that widows seldom received their jointure: calendars of litigation in equity courts (Stenton, 34–5), and the case literature of wives and widows consulting astrologers to learn when or if a jointure would be awarded (Thomas 1971, 315).

These experiences arguably shape Lead's metaphoric improvements in the dowry ("cannot be degraded or plucked away"), the jointure (not a percentage but "all that he hath"), and the control of assets ("joint possession" managed according to "mutual interest").

Wisdom

Again, rather than quoting extensively, I will paraphrase Lead's idea of Wisdom, as follows:

New spirit's "Dowry so great it would . . . set . . . me free" is given not by God the Father but by Wisdom the Mother, who endows the capacity to "be brought forth after the Manner of a Spirit, conceived and born again." This capacity is Wisdom's "Command and Power . . . to create and generate spirits in her own express likeness." Outwardly, this power may be variously expressed as "Gifts of Prophecy, or of Revelation, or of Manifestation, or of Discerning of Spirits." Inwardly, it is "a Virgin's Omnipotency" "in . . . thy Centre-deep . . . thy Heavens within." Iconographically, she is the "Woman Cloathed with the Sun" of biblical *Revelation*. Simply and exuberantly in Lead's exegesis, she is "the Wonder woman" found in "one's own Native Country and original Virginity." Where is she manifest? "Know then . . . I will now help thee to it near at Hand, even in thy own enclosed Ground" (*Fountain* I, 25–27, 69–71; II, 137, 170; *Revelation*, 47).

Also called *sophia*, wisdom had a long history of development in both mainstream and occult philosophy before Lead's reuse of the concept. Lead's immediate source is her study of German idealist philosopher, Protestant mystic, and 'inner light' theologian, Jakob Boehme (1575–1625). In Boehme's cosmology, wisdom is the passive, feminine ground out of which active, masculine will-to-manifestation creates existence. In human existence, the soul retains the original, formless capacity for being, or the power to become. This capacity is symbolized as feminine, and the soul is characterized as a daughter-fragment of the original mother-ground. In existence, the soul awaits the activation of its potential. The awakener is spirit, imaged in Boehme as an androgynous Christ, with the union of soul and spirit imaged as marriage. Boehme's idea of wisdom is syncretistic, from late Hebrew theology the idea of a divine principle prior to creation, taking from Hebrew mysticism the phenomenon of irradiated consciousness, and from Christian gnosticism the image for this consciousness as an androgynous Christ. To this amalgam, Boehme added Protestant Reformation 'inner-light' theology along with aspects of magic, alchemy, and astrology (Hirst 1964).

Lead took Boehme's idea of wisdom in a practical direction. 'Marriages' of astrological signs do not require dowries and jointures; marriages of people do. Lead's "dowry so great it would set me free" speaks to this need. "Even in thy own enclosed Ground" speaks to a site of the need, women's domestic life. Lead's domestication of Wisdom recalls the earliest expressions of that traditionally feminine symbol, pre-Boehmenist idealism. In earliest Hebraic philosophy, Wisdom pragmatically addressed existential dilemmas. The scriptural Wisdom of Solomon, for example, dealt empirically and by implication with the paradoxes of lived experience, rather than abstractly and by reasoning (Von Rad 1962). Solomon's wisdom is often illustrated by the conflict of two mothers about one baby, to whom are offered the pragmatic proposal of dividing the baby in halves given to the two mothers as a way of initiating a resolution. Similarly, Lead's Wisdom addressed an everyday paradox: female people were, socially, powerless while the feminine ideal was, culturally, powerful. Lead's Wisdom does not resolve the social dilemma; rather, she refigures it on the unconventional assumption that female and male people have the same capacities for power. An implication is that a different society is possible. "And as to the outward Sex," she remarks in *Revelation of Revelations*, "there shall be no distinction, though the Typical Priesthood admitted none but Males in its day: All of that is done away. . . . Male and Female are alike here, therefore the holy Ghost doth include both" (105).

Traditional Authority, Nontraditional Authorship

In contemporary culture, Lead was not expected to speak at all. When she and other women spoke in dissenting communities, they authorized their speaking by tradition, with a difference. "God having Taught me by his Spirit . . . of Inward Redemption; I found my self Impulsed and under a Constraint to make it Publick. . . . (O)therwise . . . I should not have rendered my self publick: For every Woman praying, or prophecying with her Head uncovered, dishonoureth her Head. 1 Cor. II. 5. But Christ being my Head-covering, I have both Commission, and Munition-strength, upon which I go forward, and say something" (Lead 1694, introduction, unpaginated).

Lead can be analyzed as a transitional figure in whom premodern concepts of authority encounter early-modern concepts of authorship. Her authority, as shown in the previous quotation, is set in publicly recognizable tradition by referral to well-known scripture. The authorship is communal, co-constructed by Christ and Lead for audiences invited to find their own wisdom by means of Lead's representation of hers (Lead 1683, 8). Such authority and authorship reflect the premodern tradition of individuals composing not for personal but for communal purposes. Widely practiced in medieval culture, the tradition understood composition to be inherently rhetorical and fundamentally social (Carruthers 1996). Traced into Lead's seventeenth century, the tradition can be found variously active in both the conservative mainstream of her upbringing and the radical subcultures in which she participated as an adult.

But Lead also subverts the tradition she works within. As an early-modern Protestant breaking with institutional authority and an 'inner light' intellectual speaking on the authority of personal experience, Lead asserts individual agency. That's why Jane Lead is an interesting case for historians of women's rhetoric. She presents several problems for interpretation. One issue is theoretical: the relations of tradition and the individual talent. Another issue is theoretical and methodological: whether to attribute rhetorical features of text to a historical writer's identity and practice or to conditions for discourse archived in her text but exceeding the individual author and artifact (Biesecker 1992).

Who Was Jane Lead? A Biography

To consider rhetoric historically, it is necessary to consider both text and context. But for Lead and other noncanonical writers there are practical problems of access and availability. Lead's texts are available as full texts in historical archives (e.g., Quaker, Shaker, and other nonconformist collections in England and the United States) or as selections in recent scholarly histories of women's writing (Gilbert and Gubar 1985).

Reliable information about Lead's context is harder to come by, however. Eighteenth-century histories of religion dismissed her and other women prophets with hostility, as female fanatics (Chambers 1781). The nineteenth-century *Dictionary of National Biography* (U.K.) included a respectful, although inaccurate, life sketch. Twentieth-century scholars advanced research on Lead specifically (Bailey 1914; Thune 1948; Hirst 1964) and enriched perspective on women prophets generally (Woolf 1938). To correct the record, and to encourage continued research from the perspective of rhetoric, the remainder of this essay presents a biography of Lead. Any biography is necessarily interpretive, and the following reflects my analysis, from a feminist perspective, of circumstances shaping Lead's rhetorical choices and strategies.[4]

Home Cultures: East Anglian Domestic, Monastic, Capitalist

Born in 1623 or 1624, Jane Lead (*nee* Ward) was one of twelve children. Descended through her parents Hamond and Mary Calthorpe Ward from landed gentry in northeast England, Jane grew up during the prelude to civil war in the manor house of a Norfolk farm situated among the flat, misty fens of England's northeast coast, or East Anglia. Her home region was marked by tensions of religious tradition and reform, political conservatism and Puritan radicalism, agrarian society and commercial economy. Monastic houses could still be found in the region; earlier, the mystic nun Julian of Norwich was one of many learned women and men who had cloistered there. Because East Anglia had the coast nearest Europe with two of England's best ports, during Lead's childhood religious refugees from England, Europe, and the American colonies flowed through them. Colonists departed regularly from the region's ports to new homes and markets in North America.

Lead's family remained Anglican in a Puritan stronghold and agrarian in an economy rapidly shifting to commerce and trade. While her father Hamond Ward continued to farm the manor fields around her Norfolk village of Leatheringsett, her brother Hamond, the second son, left to become a London merchant. Records of trade in the Canary Islands suggest that he was a member of the East India Trading Company. Jane stayed home to observe monastic ways and a land-based economy give way to Puritan reform and a money-based economy. Tensions of separatism and involvement, evident in her adult ethos, might have thus begun in her earliest experience of region and family.

Education: Memory Training

About her early education, Lead says only that her father "had me taught the social graces with dignity, according to his social standing" (Lead 1978, unpaginated).

Lead does not say how she learned to read and write. Therefore, we can only speculate based on assumptions that earlier forms of instruction might have continued in the conservative culture of her upbringing (Abbott 1990; Woods 1990). On such assumptions, Lead's primary textbook might have been a bible, possibly the King James Version authorized in 1611. Her mother was perhaps her only teacher, joined occasionally by itinerant tutors. In her autobiography, Lead refers to a visiting "preacher, who was chaplain to a certain knight who at that time took his meals at my father's" whom she had questioned (Lead 1978, unpaginated).

She might have learned by methods similar to those used in Anglican petty (elementary) and grammar schools that her brothers could have attended (Abbott 1990; Woods 1990). However, because girls did not attend school, she learned at home. Thus, Lead might have learned to read and write, by memorizing scriptural passages, orally reciting them to her mother, and copying them in a copybook. By this method, she not only learned to read and write but she also stocked her mind with scripture. Beyond its pedagogical use, a memory so-trained and stocked, along with a copybook of passages, could have prepared Lead to participate in private home worship, where anyone could speak. By contrast, when Lead attended Church of England worship, males only read scripture aloud, and females did not speak at all. Thus, her childhood home was Lead's earliest situation of textual activity, and experiences there might have shaped her later motivation to write, composing methods, and the type of text she produced. Specifically, her imagery of Wisdom might reflect teaching as done by her mother.

Experience: Spirituality, Marriage, Widowhood

By her own account, the most significant event of Jane's young life occurred when she was sixteen and dancing in Christmas festivities in the manor hall. Suddenly, she recorded in her later autobiography, she was overcome by a "warm, sensitive sadness . . . and softly I perceived the words: Withdraw from all this; I know of another dance I shall lead you to, for this is vanity" (Lead 1978, unpaginated). She despaired, afflicted by deep sense of sinfulness, for three years following this event. During an extended visit to her merchant brother's home in London, Jane Ward scoured public and private religious meetings for resolution to her crisis. It came, she said, when she heard a sermon by Dr. Tobias Crisp, the famed antinomian preacher. Antinomianism was a belief in literal redemption, holding that sin was an unrepayable debt to God but, also, that Christ had already paid the debt for everyone by his death. Absolution was already given to Christ's elect, or those who freely accepted the idea that they were without sin (Hunt 1870, 249).

Jane Ward accepted, and her spiritual crisis eased. She refused to marry partners her parents selected for her because, she said, she found earthly marriage repulsive and wished to remain a virgin in Christ. Nevertheless, in 1644, at twenty-one, Ward married a cousin, William Lead, a London merchant who may have shared her antinomian beliefs. Little is known about the London household where Jane and William raised four daughters under conditions of civil war, restoration of monarchy, ongoing political instability and religious repression, a plague (two Lead daughters died), and the fire in 1666 that destroyed much of the city. It is known, however, that Jane's spiritual progress continued. In 1663, she joined a congregation led by Dr. John Pordage, a nonconforming preacher who had been tried and convicted by state authorities for holding independent religious gatherings where Quaker-like dances and trances were reported to occur. When she joined the Pordage congregation, Lead was recognized for her "Gift of Revelation [to which] y [the] Dr gave great regard to and attended upon" (Hirst 1964, 107–8).

In 1670, William Lead died, leaving no will. As the widow and executor, Jane Lead administered the settlement of his estate, but her legal power was meaningless because there was no estate. As Jane Lead recalled in an autobiography written nearly thirty years later, "because he had entrusted most of his worldly possessions to a factor overseas, and they were received by the same, the widow and orphans were stripped of their rights. He [the factor] did not relinquish anything. Due to these circumstances, I was left to dire and extreme want, which forced me even more to place my assets in Heaven. I determined to remain a Widow in God" (Lead 1978, unpaginated). This direct exposure to the economics of widowhood and to the legal constraints on domestic life, arguably, structured metaphors that Lead later composed.

Discourses: Traditions of Spirituality

At the age of forty-seven, in 1670, Lead re-formed her life. She describes a deciding moment in the journal she began in that year. While walking in a country place in April, two months after her husband died, she envisioned "an overshadowing bright Cloud and in the midst of it the Figure of a Woman." Three days later a luminous reappearance gently commanded, "Behold me as thy Mother." Six days later, in London, came the promise, "I shall now cease to appear in a Visible Figure to thee, but I will not fail to transfigure my self in thy mind; and there open the Spring of Wisdom and Understanding" (*Fountain*, I, 27). In a radical refocusing, Lead determined to know this inner Wisdom and to live by its spirit.

In 1674, she moved into John Pordage's household, where he, his wife, and sympathizers explored radical theology and practiced charismatic religion. Pordage also studied magic, astrology, and possibly alchemy. Lead became the practical leader of his private nonconforming congregation. Lead and Pordage jointly studied spiritual traditions. Particularly, they studied the transcendental theology of the German Protestant "inner light" mystic Jacob Boehme (1575–1625). Boehme's little-known work had recently become available in English translation. Lead and Pordage both read Boehme, meditated together, experienced visions (sometimes in common), and wrote separate commentaries explicating Boehme's symbolic system, especially his concept of Wisdom or the feminine aspect of deity.

In Pordage's household, Lead also might have encountered the study of magic and astrology. As intellectual practices, both depended on memory, especially the manipulation of stored information by mnemonic techniques involving imagery. Astrology, magic, and alchemy bridged uses of memory in occult tradition with seventeenth-century science and religion (Hirst 1964; Yates 1966). In this way, ancient intellectual practices came in contact with emerging modern practices. In both science and religion, to explain phenomena, reasoning from evidence through experimentation was replacing reasoning by analogy through the application of systems of correspondences. In her communities of occult learning and religious practice of the 1670s, Lead might have continued memory training through occult study at the same time that she was systematically documenting her personal experience of revelation by recording her visions in a daily journal. Both streams of influence, arguably, entered Lead's own figuration of Wisdom.

Publication: Private Experience in the Public Domain

In 1681, Pordage died. In that year, Lead published her first commentary on spiritual life, *The Heavenly Cloud Now Breaking*. She followed it in 1683 with scriptural exegesis, the *Revelation of Revelations*, in which Lead interpreted Wisdom. In the same year Lead published Pordage's commentary on Boehme, including his different interpretation of Wisdom, *Theologica Mystica*, for which she provided the introduction. By these publications and with help from the Pordage congregation, Lead was probably able to support herself and her widowed daughter. After Pordage's death, Lead sustained the congregation, then numbering about a hundred, despite continuing suppression of nonconforming groups generally and persecution of women preachers particularly. A major difficulty was finding a safe place to meet. Lead's *Revelation of Revelations* had brought her to the attention of a wealthy widow, who, saying she was deeply affected by Lead's writing, made her home available as a meeting place. After this widow's death and several dislocations of the dwindling congregation, in 1692 Lead withdrew from public life to live in a private charity home for poor women (Thune 1948, 80–81).

European distribution of Lead's publications (without her knowledge) soon attracted another benefactor who paid a living stipend for Lead herself as well as the costs of translating her work into German and Dutch (Thune 1948, 81). In 1694, Lead assembled another London congregation. In 1695, congregation members organized a new international spiritual community, the Philadelphian Society, based on Lead's principles. By this time, Lead was seventy-two and partially blind. One of the Philadelphian Society organizers, the physician and biblical scholar Francis Lee, became her son-in-law, amanuensis, editor, and publisher. In 1696–1701, Lee published Lead's journal with the title *A Fountain of Gardens,* in four volumes that went into four printings (Thune 1948, 85). Her commentaries and tracts continued to be published and distributed in England and Europe. Émigrés such as the founding Shakers in Massachusetts took Lead's tracts with them to the American colonies. In 1704, Lead, who never left England, died in London "in the 81st year of her age, and in the 65th year of her vocation to the inward and divine life" (Lee 1704, unpaginated).

Altogether, fifteen tracts (pamphlet-length books) of spiritual guidance or scriptural exegesis, one 2,000-page journal of revelations, and one spiritual autobiography were issued in Jane Lead's name, published either by her or by Francis Lee. Most probably Lead wrote and self-published the work before 1694. Between 1694 and her death in 1704, as Lead became increasingly blind, she dictated to Francis Lee. Lee also edited and published the journal Lead had kept since 1670 in "loose Shreds of Paper, for the sake of her own Memory, and for Monitions and Encouragements to some few Particular Friends" (Lee 1696, unpaginated). These circumstances of composition—the multiple functions and inherent risks of publishing, the involvement of others in constructing her public statements—are material backgrounds of Lead's authorship.

Conclusion: Cultural Rhetoric

In a study of memory's cultural significance relevant to Jane Lead, historian Mary Carruthers paraphrases anthropologist Clifford Geertz to say that "cultures can be understood as 'symbol-systems'," and that "culture is a public and social phenomenon, neither a private neurosis nor a transcendental norm" (Carruthers 1996, 259–60). Culture is public and social because it operates by symbolic exchanges, with symbols "referring to matters of relationships which must in some way be publicly recognized and remembered—they are not absolutes, but function entirely within social life" (260). Another term for culture-as-symbol-system might be culture-as-rhetoric. Cultures operate by rhetorics that activate the meanings of symbols through modes of language activity in situations of dynamic use.

Revelation is the mode of language activity that Jane Lead practiced along with others, many who were women, many anonymously, in all classes of English society in late-seventeenth-century England. The mode of revelation authorized certain social behaviors (e.g., public speaking, preaching, leadership of groups) and privileged some behaviors over others (e.g., attending to inner belief rather than outer rule). Revelation authorized a 'woman's voice,' or rhetorical practices by women reflecting women's experience. Revelation was the means by which Lead and other women spoke *as women* relative to specific conditions, continuities, and changes in their time.

What does Lead's text mean? Textual implication is both simpler and more complex than the author's identity. Simpler, in that Lead's emancipatory language is clearer than her action of remaining in the Anglican Church even as she led several independent congregations, or her reported assertion that outer separatism is not necessary for inner community. Perhaps her action and reported position were due to risk of prosecution for publishing.

More complex, in that textual indeterminacy outlives experience. Three centuries after Lead wrote, I and other readers find in her presentation a feminism, "an ethical stance that foregrounds sexual and gender concerns as a particularly productive means of demystifying and critiquing the cultural matrix" (Ratcliffe 1996, 7) that the historical Lead might not recognize (Smith 1979a, 1979b, 1984, 1987; Gilbert and Gubar 1979; Moore 1983).

Therefore, to address the questions that motivate this collection of essays: Did Lead and her contemporaries challenge rhetorical tradition? Yes, certainly. Did their rhetoric constitute an alternative to tradition? Yes, if we recognize revisionist alternatives. Fuller answers to those questions await more readings by more historians and critics of noncanonical women rhetors such as Lead, who challenge us to recognize rhetoric on their terms as well as ours.

Notes

1.   Discussion of changing patterns in dowry and jointure is based on Goody et al.; Stone; Thompson; Mingay; Carroll; Bridenthal and Koonz; and Riemer.

2. Norwich Consistory Court 81 Battelle; made February 26, 1650–51; proved March 28, 1651, by Mary his relict, at Norwich.

3. Prerogative Court of Canterbury 71 Harvey; made November 1, 1638; proved May 18, 1639, by William Lead, in London.

4. Sources for this account of Lead's life are principally published and unpublished materials found in the Dr. Williams's Library of Religious Nonconformity, London; the British Library, London; The Public Records Office, London; The Bodleian Library, Oxford; and the Norfolk County Historical Association, Norwich. These materials as well as secondary sources regarding Lead are referenced in the text of the essay as they are used. Special acknowledgments: Anneliese Gray, Bucknell University, located the sole extant copy of Lead's autobiography in the former People's Republic of East Germany and translated the text from Old High German to English. Noel Currer-Briggs located Hamond Ward's and William Lead's fathers' wills in The Public Records Office, London, as well as records of trade and investment by Ward and Calthorpe heirs in Ports Books of the Exchequer, the *Calendar of State Papers* (Domestic), and Abstracts of Virginia Patents and Land Grants.

Uncertainties in Lead's biography include the year of her birth and the spelling and pronunciation of her married name.

Works Cited

Abbott, Don Paul. "Rhetoric and Writing in Renaissance Europe and England." In *A Short History of Writing Instruction from Ancient Greece to Twentieth-Century America*, edited by James J. Murphy, 95–120. Davis, Calif.: Hermagoras, 1990.

Bailey, Margaret Lewis. *Milton and Jakob Boehme: A Study of German Mysticism in Seventeenth-Century England*. London: Oxford University Press, 1914.

Biesecker, Barbara. "Coming to Terms with Recent Attempts to Write Women into the History of Rhetoric." *Philosophy and Rhetoric* 25, no. 2 (1992): 140–61.

Bridenthal, Renata, and Claudia Koonz, editors. *Becoming Visible*. Boston: Houghton Mifflin, 1997.

Carroll, Berenice, editor. *Liberating Women's History*. Urbana: University of Illinois Press, 1976.

Carruthers, Mary. *The Book of Memory: A Study of Memory in Medieval Culture*. Cambridge: Cambridge University Press, 1996.

Chambers *Cyclopedia*. 1781. Quoted in personal letter to the author by Desiree Hirst, 1981.

Delaney, Paul. *British Autobiography in the Seventeenth Century*. London: Routledge and Kegan Paul, 1969.

Gilbert, Sandra M., and Susan Gubar, editors. *The Norton Anthology of Literature by Women: The Tradition in English.* New York: Norton, 1985.

————. *The Madwoman in the Attic: The Woman Writer and the Nineteenth-Century Imagination.* New Haven: Yale University Press, 1979.

Goody, Jack, Joan Thirsk, and E. P. Thompson, editors. *Family and Inheritance: Rural Society in Western Europe 1200–1800.* Cambridge: Cambridge University Press, 1976.

Henderson, Katherine U., and Barbara F. McManus. *Half Humankind: Contexts and Texts of the Controversy about Women in England, 1540–1640.* Urbana: University of Illinois Press, 1985.

Hirst, Desiree. *Hidden Riches: Traditional Symbolism from the Renaissance to Blake.* New York: Barnes and Noble, 1964.

Hunt, John. *Religious Thought in England from the Reformation to the Last Century: A Contribution to the History of Theology.* London: Strahan, 1870.

Lead, Jane. *The Heavenly Cloud Now Breaking. The Lord Christ's Ascension-Ladder Sent Down. . . .* London: A. Sowle, 1681.

————. *The Revelation of Revelations Particularly as an Essay Towards the Unsealing, Opening, and Discovering the Seven Seals, the Seven Thunders, and the New Jerusalem State. . . .* London: A. Sowle, 1683.

————. *The Enochian Walks with God, Found out by a Spiritual Traveller. . . .* London: Printed for the author, 1694.

————. *A Fountain of Gardens Watered by the Rivers of Divine Pleasure, and Springing up in all the Variety of Spiritual Plants. . . .* London: Printed for the author, 1696–1704.

————. *Life of the Author.* Trans. Anneliese Gray. Unpublished. Originally published 1694–96 attached to the German edition of six tracts by Jane Lead, *Sechs Unschatzbare durch Gottliche Offenbarung and Befehl ans Licht gerachte mystische Tracteien.* Coburg 1711: Herzogliche Bibliothek zu Gotha A297 and 229. Facsimila collecta opera Ernesti Salamonis Cypriani, 1978.

Lee, Francis. *The Last Hours of Jane Lead by an Eye and Ear-Witness.* Trans. Samuel Jackson. London: Dr. Williams's Library MS. Walton 186.18 c. 5.30, 1704.

————. Advertisement. In Jane Lead, *A Fountain of Gardens . . . I, Unpaginated,* 1696.

Mingay, G. L. *English Landed Society in the Eighteenth Century.* London: Routledge and Kegan Paul, 1963.

Moore, Madeline. *The Short Season between Two Silences: The Mystical and the Political in Virginia Woolf.* Boston: George Allen and Unwin, 1983.

Nelson, Beth. "Without Honor: Seventeenth Century Women Prophets and the Emergence of the Woman Writer." Unpublished. Presented at the Modern Language Association annual meeting, 1978.

Pordage, Samuel. Quoted in Carl G. Jung. 1970. *Collected Works*, 16:297. Trans. R. F. C. Hull. Princeton: Princeton University Press, N.d.

Ratcliffe, Krista. *Anglo-American Feminist Challenges to the Rhetorical Traditions: Virginia Woolf, Mary Daly, Adrienne Rich.* Carbondale: Southern Illinois University Press, 1996.

Riemer, Eleanor S. *Women and Capital Investment: The Economic Decline of Sienese Women at the Dawn of the Renaissance.* Unpublished. Presented at the Fifth Berkshire Conference of Women Historians, 1981.

Smith, Catherine F. "Virginia Woolf's prophecy." In *Virginia Woolf and Bloomsbury*, edited by Jane Marcus, 224–41. London: Macmillan, 1987.

———. "Jane Lead's wisdom: Women and Prophecy in Seventeenth-Century England." In *Poetic prophecy in Western Literature*, edited by Jan Wojcik and Raymond Frontain, 55–63. London: Associated University Presses, 1984.

———. "Jane Lead: Mysticism and the Woman Cloathed with the sun." In *Shakespeare's Sisters*, edited by Sandra Gilbert and Susan Gubar, 3–18. Bloomington: Indiana University Press, 1979a.

———. "Jane Lead: The Feminist Mind and Art of a Seventeenth-Century Protestant Mystic." In *Women of Spirit,* edited by Rosemary Ruether and Eleanor McLaughlin, 183–204. New York: Simon and Schuster, 1979b.

Stenton, Doris Mary. *The English Woman in History.* London: Publisher unknown, 1957.

Stone, Lawrence. *The Crisis of the Aristocracy 1558–1641.* Oxford: Oxford University Press, 1965.

Thomas, Keith. *Religion and the Decline of Magic.* New York: Basic, 1971.

———. Women and the Civil War Sects. In *Crisis in Europe 1560–1660*, edited by T. Aston, 317–40. New York: Basic Books, 1965.

Thompson, Roger. *Women in Stuart England and America.* London: Routledge and Kegan Paul, 1974.

Thune, Nils. *The Beheminists and the Philadelphians: A Contribution to the Study of English Mysticism in the Seventeenth and Eighteenth Centuries.* Uppsala: Almqvist and Wiksells, 1948.

Von Rad, Gerhard. *Old Testament Theology,* 1. Trans. D. Stalker, 418–53. Edinburgh: Oliver and Boyd, 1962.

Webber, Joan. *The Eloquent 'I': Style and Self in Seventeenth-Century Prose.* Madison: University of Wisconsin Press, 1968.

Woods, M. "The Teaching of Writing in Medieval Europe." In *A Short History of Writing Instruction from Ancient Greece to Twentieth-Century*

America, edited by J. Murphy, 77–94. Davis, Calif.: Hermagoras, 1990.

Woolf, Virginia. *Three Guineas.* New York: Harcourt, Brace, 1938.

Yates, Frances A. *The Art of Memory.* Chicago: University of Chicago Press, 1966.

2

Multivocal Midwife

The Writing Teacher as Rhetor

PHYLLIS MENTZELL RYDER, VALENTINA M. ABORDONADO,
BARBARA HEIFFERON, AND DUANE H. ROEN

We began this project to celebrate the metaphor of the midwife as writing teacher. We wanted to contemplate why this metaphor feels powerful to us, how it helps us understand our role as teachers, our relationships to our students, and the powerful forces of language that awe us. But, as writing projects (especially collaborative ones) tend to do, this one led us to new places. We discovered, as Sheri Laska has in her review of feminist pedagogies, that the figure of the midwife offers not only a complicated perspective on the role of a writing teacher, but also an alternative model for rhetoric itself. Examining the figure of the midwife helps us articulate and critique a nurturing role for writing teachers, and, on a broader scale, conceptualize an alternative rhetoric that breaks through some dichotomies that have troubled us. Embracing the midwife-rhetor, we argue for a rhetorical theory that refuses to split composition from rhetoric but instead pushes us to see composition as a crucial site for developing rhetorical theory. Embracing the midwife-rhetor, we resist separating the personal from the professional, believing that what has long been delegated to the "private" has a profound impact on the "public" world. Ultimately, we embrace the midwife rhetor because we see here a way to blend social-epistemic and expressivist rhetorical theories that have been set at odds by scholars in contemporary debates.

Our first project here is to trace the figure of the midwife in various rhetorical theories. We examine how Plato uses the midwife metaphor to conceptualize the relationship between teacher and student, speaker and audience. Ultimately, we reject the Platonic understanding of midwife rhetoric because we disagree with its contentions about the elements of the rhetorical act: "truth," language, the audience, and the rhetor. Then, we trace the midwife-rhetor in romantic-expressivist and social-epistemic/postmodern theories of rhetoric, again using the figure to identify the roles offered for teacher, student, audience, and rhetor. In the end, we argue for an alternative theory of rhetoric that bridges the gap among Plato, the expressivist view, and the social-epistemic view—a theory of midwife rhetoric that situates the student and teacher in a social context that shapes their discourse. In our view, the student and the teacher, the rhetor and the audience, do not simply work together to discover a static, objective truth but co-construct dynamic, subjective truths.

Our second project is born out of our awareness of the professional experiences of midwives in a culture that values technologically advanced, Western-style medicine. While we are drawn, at times, to the romanticized image of the midwife as nurturer, and while we wish, at times, that our relationships with our students could fit that model, we also recognize how such depictions of midwife-teachers deny the concrete constraints of the institutional contexts in which we work—especially the entrepreneurial contexts that Jeffrey Williams describes so vividly in his recent text, "Brave New University." When an individual or a couple hires a midwife, they signal their desire for a more "natural" health care; theoretically, everyone involved shares this value. However, as writing teachers we are only indirectly hired by our students, who may not readily accept our rhetorical or pedagogical views about the ideal environment or method for a writing classroom. Furthermore, because midwives reject the assumptions about "expertise" and "risk" that are foundational to Western medicine, the medical establishment continues to ostracize and marginalize them. Similarly, by embracing the midwife metaphor, compositionists complicate—even undermine—their attempts to be recognized as intellectual contributors in an English department. What might we learn from midwife rhetoric that can help us better position ourselves as providing valuable "expertise" in the academic context, even as we insist that our knowledge about writing and teaching is the result of our collaboration with our students?

Midwives and the Birth of Knowledge:
Implications for Rhetorical Theory

As Patricia Harkin points out in "The Postdisciplinary Politics of Lore" (1991), teaching is rarely seen as a site where teachers produce knowledge; rather, it is dismissed as a place where teachers cobble together things that work, and where teachers pick and choose willy-nilly what they will do each day in class, despite contradictions in the theoretical foundation of those activities. Because the practice appears not to be derived in a coherent manner from theory, it is seen as less valuable; the kind of inquiry it engages ("What will work with my students today?") is seen as lacking rigor. In contrast, the university culture and our society as a whole uphold scientific inquiry as a model of knowledge production. A productive professor is a prolific scholar, one whose work in the laboratory is well received by peers. In our discipline, the distinction might be made this way: composition focuses on practical questions of what to do in the classroom, while rhetoric develops theories about the relationship of language, reality, writers, and readers. Composition is about what we—writing teachers—might "do" with our students; rhetoric takes on the more global concern about what we—writers, orators, citizens—"do" with language. This second category is what counts as the "knowledge" of the field. Those who are hired to produce it—tenure-track professors—are rewarded with more time to construct this knowledge; they are "released" from the expectation that they teach composition courses. According to Harkin, the discipline of rhetoric and composition has accepted this dichotomy because it seeks recognition as a real discipline, and to do so it must conform to the standards set by the sciences.

We must question this dichotomy, Harkin urges. We need to look at what happens in the writing classroom as a kind of knowledge-making and understand why apparent contradictions seem to work. While other disciplines do not have the opportunity to see their classrooms as research sites, we do, and we should. Harkin recommends that we begin by examining what teachers do, how they envision themselves, and use that to interrogate our theories.

Finding Harkins's argument compelling, we are struck by a parallel between the compositionist/rhetorician and the midwife/medical doctor hierarchies. Just as compositionists are seen as "merely" teaching skills and performing "untrained" work, so midwives are often dismissed as lacking in expertise. By turning to the rhetoric of midwifery, then, we can find yet another argument for using marginalized fields to develop a deeper, more complex understanding of dominant ones.

In her account of women's working lives in the seventeenth century, Alice Clark notes that "women of a high level of intelligence and possessing considerable skill belonged to the profession" (1992, 268) of midwifery. Further, during the first five decades of that century, "they were considered in no way inferior to doctors" (268). Because training for midwives was available, for the most part, through apprenticeships, they were able to learn well the practical skills of the profession. However, since women were excluded from the "speculative" medical training available to men, their knowledge, it was assumed, remained at the level of craft, whereas the doctor's knowledge—because it was supposedly acquired through more scientific methods—was upheld as more thorough. By the end of the century, male physicians had ascended to a status superior to that of midwives, but not because of better practical skill in delivering babies. Clark quips, "Their prestige rested partly on an ability to use long words which convinced patients of their superior wisdom" (283). Clark further notes that this prestige was increased by both a professional unity among male physicians and the erosion of the status of women in general.

This hierarchy continues today. Obstetricians claim that they are the most appropriate people to manage pregnancies because of their extensive medical training. Yet, midwives dispute this assertion, not because midwives believe they are equally prepared to intervene in high-risk births, but because they distrust how obstetricians' training may lead them to pathologize "normal" births. In the 1985 edition of *Williams' Obstetrics*, a widely used textbook in the field, only twenty of the eleven hundred pages discuss normal labor and delivery; the rest focus on complications. Furthermore, even in hospitals set up with birthing rooms, residents and interns are assigned to work with high-risk patients. This is understandable: because the medical staff members must be prepared for all contingencies, they must have extensive experience with a wide variety of difficult births. As a result, medical staff members become experts at managing the more dangerous cases, but this expertise creates a problem for midwives when they turn over normal births to "expert" obstetricians. As midwives see it, when doctors trained to handle high-risk pregnancies look at normal pregnancies, they carry with them so much knowledge about labors gone wrong that they cannot see the labor in front of them for what it is. As one midwife explained to Sullivan and Weitz, "The midwife sees the passage of the baby through the birth canal as a healthy, positive experience that is good for both the mother and the baby. . . . The physician sees . . . a dangerous passage . . . full of pitfalls" (1998, 70). Midwives argue that doctors are more ready to interpret changes in a woman's condition as symptoms of larger problems and are too ready to intervene. Like the physician interviewed by Sullivan and Weitz, some proclaim that "there is no low-risk delivery" (138) because one only knows that a delivery was low-risk after the fact.

Midwives critique the relationship that results when one party claims expertise. They argue that by viewing themselves as the experts in the labor process, doctors enforce a hierarchy that deprives a laboring woman of her own confidence in her power to deliver. While midwives see themselves as deferring to birth, they see doctors as attempting to dominate it: as "experts." Doctors feel comfortable manipulating the birth through drugs or technology to fit with their expectations of how labor should proceed.

Drawing parallels between midwifery and the field of composition and rhetoric, we see value in questioning whether the "expertise" that comes from immersing oneself solely in rhetorical theory is the best preparation for teaching or even for developing a functional theory of rhetoric. Like the mid-wives, we are concerned that much of the "theory" is derived from examining situations different from the ones we experience daily in our classrooms. At the same time, we ask what we can learn by examining "what works." If what happens in writing classrooms is a combination of different theories and assumptions about rhetoric, and if these combinations help students write well, what new theories can we develop? We argue that rhetoricians can learn a great deal about rhetoric by examining what happens in a composition classroom: how students and teachers position themselves and their relationship to the multiple elements of rhetorical situations such as knowledge, reality, audience, context, culture, and so on. Thus, as we use the mid-wife metaphor to interrogate rhetorical theories, we look at how it operates on two levels: we examine not only how this metaphor positions the writing teacher and the student but also how it positions the rhetor and the audience. We want to study not only what these scholars say about rhetoric, but also how they use it in what we consider to be a profound site for rhetoric: the classroom.

Midwife-Rhetor/Midwife-Teacher and the Feminization of Composition

While we have taken seriously Patricia Harkins's call to value the work of composition teachers as a site of knowledge-making in composition, we cannot begin our argument for a classroom-based rhetorical theory without considering the larger implications our rhetorical/pedagogical theories might have for compositionists within the academy. If, as James Slevin's (1991) analysis of job advertisements in the field reveals, English departments as a whole have relatively little respect for the work in composition studies, does our attempt to link rhetoric so closely with composition serve to lower the status of both rhetoric and composition even farther? Is such a risk worth taking? How do we weigh the benefits of such a rhetoric against the potential damage it might do to the real people who would teach it?

Eileen Schell and Susan Miller argue that the feminization of composition has brought both good and bad news. The good news is that feminist values and practices have become more prevalent in composition studies. The bad news is that women occupy much of the bottom of the hierarchy in composition studies specifically and English studies more generally. Miller cites statistics to illustrate that many women work in the field but that they occupy a disproportionate number of part-time, temporary, or untenured positions (1991, 41). For many, their status is that of academic "nurse" (46) or "maid" (47), attending to texts perceived to be low-status (52). At Arizona State University in the fall of 1998, for example, 60.3 percent (48/81) of the

TAs teaching composition were women; 72.2 percent of the faculty associates were women; 71.4 percent (15/21) of the instructors were women; 81.8 percent (9/11) of the lecturers were women. Three of the six professors in rhetoric and composition were women, but two of them were assistant professors. Overall, 64.2 percent of the people teaching composition courses in the fall of 1998 were women. Further, the person with the highest rank in the program and with the title of director of composition was a man.

Sue Ellen Holbrook paints an even more graphic and depressing portrait of the feminization of composition. She carefully documents that women, disproportionately represented on college and university faculties in general, outnumber men in composition programs. However, within composition studies, women write less frequently for publication, publish less frequently, and hold fewer administrative positions. They are well represented, though, in work "categories associated with the nurturant, service-oriented character of practitioners" (1991, 210). Holbrook concludes with a sobering characterization of the field: "Saturated by women practitioners, focused on pedagogy, allied with education departments and school teaching, conceived as having a 'service' and elementary place in the curriculum, and pervaded by paraprofessionalism, composition has become women's work" (211).

We cannot ignore the possibility that one consequence of developing a rhetoric from the marginalized figure of the midwife is that, in an academic context that values the scientific paradigm underlying Western medicine, we, too, relegate ourselves to the margins. And, given that the practitioners in the field are primarily women, this means that, by adopting such a rhetoric, women teachers could be even further devalued in the university culture as well as the public one beyond it. Nevertheless, we still advocate such an alternative rhetoric, precisely because we believe, as does Judith Fetterly, that it is only by turning to the margins that we can see the damaging ideologies of the dominant paradigms. As we theorize and analyze the complexities of the work in composition classrooms, seeing it as a site of rhetoric, we can undermine the ideologies, such as those that George Will (1999) recently espoused, which dismiss such work as the "mere" teaching of "elementary writing courses."

In sharp contrast to George Will, James Berlin, in "Rhetoric and Ideology in the Writing Class" (1988), argues that rhetorics define different relationships between language and reality: some theories see reality—what exists, what is true—as a separate entity, which is then "captured" in language; others believe that language shapes the reality/truth that we can see. Where does the metaphor of the midwife-teacher fit in? At first glance, the metaphor seems to suggest that the "ideas" students have are theirs alone: the essays they produce are their babies, their thoughts, and our job as teachers is to both teach them how to nurture their babies and how to attend to themselves so that they produce the healthiest babies possible. But the epistemological assumptions proposed here are not straightforward. Does the midwife metaphor suggest that students can "capture" truth/reality and represent it to us? Is the "reality" changed by the experience of "gestating" in the student? What is a "healthy" idea/essay? To get at the implications of midwife rhetoric, we begin by looking at how Plato uses the midwife-teacher metaphor in his definition of rhetoric.

Plato: TEACHER, *Deliver the "Truth"*

The metaphor of the teacher as midwife is not new; it appears in the earliest conceptions of rhetorical theory. As far as we know, Plato was the first to write about the midwife-teacher. In his dialogue *Theaetetus*, Socrates invokes the midwife metaphor to persuade Theaetetus to engage in a philosophical inquiry about the nature of knowledge (Hansen 1988, 217). Socrates tells Theaetetus, "I am the son of a midwife, brave and burly, whose name was Phaenarete" and "I myself practice midwifery" (Plato 1871, 201). Socrates describes his own work as a midwife, not like a person who helps give birth to children, but rather one who helps give birth to ideas. He explains: "I look after their souls when they are in labour . . . and the triumph of my art is in thoroughly examining whether the thought which the mind of the young man brings forth is a false idol or a noble and true birth" (203).

In the Platonic scheme, then, the midwife-teacher does not transmit truth; rather, she only assists the student in discovering the truth for herself or himself by facilitating the student's thinking. As James Berlin points out, "truth is not based on sensory experience since the material world is always in flux and always unreliable. Truth is instead discovered through internal apprehension" (1982, 771). Nevertheless, Berlin notes, "preparing the soul to discover truth is often painful" (771).

Similarly, Plato's contemporary Isocrates—claimed by some to be one of Socrates' students—also approaches his work with the belief that the teacher can do no more than evoke and nurture the character and aptitude already within the student. In both *Antidosis* (1968) and "Against the Sophists" (1968), Isocrates rails against those teachers of philosophy and rhetoric who claim to be able to deliver more than what is already within the learner. A teacher can help develop a learner/rhetor's existing proficiencies, but a teacher cannot create those proficiencies.

Thus, the apprehension of truth, in this view, is the process by which the student remembers or recalls what he or she already knows. The student looks inward to find the "ideal forms" that constitute truth "through remembrance of them as they appeared to the soul before birth" (Winterowd 1994, 3).

However, Ross Winterowd calls attention to the epistemological trap the Platonic view sets:

> If "truth" comes about through divine inspiration or remembrance of prenatal visions, then either you have it or you don't. There is no way that, for instance, a teacher, godly and god-like though that pedagogue might be, could either instruct or inspire. . . . [T]ruth (knowledge) is absolute, and though you cannot discover it in the senate, the agora, the academy or your own parlor, a philosopher, one who knows the truth, can lead you to it. (3)

The role of the ideal teacher in these dialogues also indicates the role of an ideal rhetor—the role the student should take on at the end of her or his studies (for in ancient Greece, only men were enrolled in school). For Plato, a rhetor "convey[s] truth already in the rhetor's possession to an ignorant audience by any effective means, so long as the virtuous rhetor keeps the audience's best interests at heart" (Bizzell and Herzberg 1990, 28). In his work, *Symposium*, Plato characterizes the rhetor as one who finds a "soul which is pregnant . . . a fair and noble and well-nurtured soul . . . and tries to educate" that soul (1956, 376). This metaphor, as David Hansen observes, "offers an appealing portrait of teaching. It conjures up a vision of a wise, nurturing figure who can guide the inexperienced into knowledge" (1988, 213). However, Plato's view that the speaker unerringly knows the Truth, suggests the traditional banking model of teaching that Paulo Freire writes against. The facilitator of learning, both the teacher and the rhetor, not only assists in the delivery of a student/listener's ideas but also evaluates the soundness of these ideas. He or she practices the "art of midwifery," to help the student/listener distinguish between ideas that are worthy "offspring" and those that are unproductive "false phantoms" that should be abandoned (Hansen 1988, 213). In this view, however, because the teacher/rhetor knows what is best for the student/listener, the teacher/rhetor has the upper hand and dissuades the student from engaging in true dialogue.

In *Phaedrus* (1956), Plato illustrates what looks at first like a more collaborative rhetoric. In lengthy passages involving Socrates, an older man, and Phaedrus, a young man, Socrates does not simply use rhetoric to convey a preconceived truth to Phaedrus. Rather, he helps Phaedrus modify his conceptions about the truth by engaging him in dialectic, a rigorous interaction between two interlocutors who hope to glimpse the eternal truths of ideal forms. As Bizzell and Herzberg suggest, Socrates is "clearing away the conventional underbrush so that the truth can be seen" (1990, 28).

Ultimately, however, Plato "attempts to deny literacy its generative power" (Winterowd 1994, 7). Drawing on the work of Jasper Neel, Winterowd argues that in the *Phaedrus*, as with *Gorgias* earlier, Plato makes sure only those who know truth are considered real rhetors, and that dialogue is not a place of creation, but one of deliverance: Socrates must tear away the ill-conceived, false impositions to reveal an already existing truth. Once again, only some children are "worthy," and the midwife-teacher must assist to "abort" those deemed unworthy.

We reject the Platonic understanding of midwife rhetoric because we disagree with its contentions about reality, language, the reader, and the rhetor. As James Berlin observes, the Platonic view suggests that reality is unknowable, inexpressible, but attainable (only in part) through internal apprehension. The writer is "isolated, cut off from the community, and left to the lonely business of discovering truth alone" (Berlin 1982, 776). Because this truth exists prior to language, the purpose of language is only to communicate or "deliver" that knowledge. Thus, the role of the reader/teacher is limited to detecting and correcting errors.

We do not see the rhetor, or the teacher, or the student, as acting in isolation. Rather, we want a vision of midwife rhetoric that examines how the student and the teacher, rhetor, and audience are situated in a social context and are shaped by cultural discourse. Furthermore, we do not see the midwife-teacher as one who stands back to direct and correct. Rather, the midwife-teacher coaches, guides, questions, and works with the student to co-construct dynamic, subjective truths. Thus, Plato's vision fails for us because it does not account for the interaction we see as integral to meaning-making. We look, therefore, to the romantic-expressivist interpretation of rhetoric as a possible alternative.

Romantic-Expressivist Rhetoric: Student, Deliver Yourself

In many ways, the romantic-expressivist theory of rhetoric provides a useful framework for understanding the midwife-rhetor and midwife-teacher, as many of the assumptions about the power of birthing (both of children and of ideas) seem to flow from this tradition. Looking at the midwife-rhetor from this perspective, therefore, helps us to articulate the powerful attraction of the metaphor. At the same time, our concerns about the romantic-expressivist tradition, and how it can be used to essentialize and constrain different groups in society, make us reluctant to embrace this position fully. First, we consider some parallels that might be drawn between a midwife and a writing teacher; then we examine what these images might suggest in terms of rhetorical theory.

Peggy Armstrong and Sheryl Feldman, in describing the role of the midwife, emphasize women's "natural" abilities to deliver in birth. In a birth center where Phyllis gave birth to her son, a cross-stitched sign boasts that "midwife" means "with woman."

The saying is more than a slogan. Nurse-midwife Peggy Armstrong suggests that the best way to gather knowledge about women is to listen carefully, to trust them, and to trust the instinctual power of birth. Birth is explicitly and repeatedly defined as natural, normal, and healthy. Her rhetoric resonates with poetic allusions to the natural power of birth. Valuing women, in this case, means also valuing their natural abilities to deliver. Armstrong wishes to give women the power to control their own labor.

In this view, the midwife does not take on the role of the sole "expert"; she collaborates with the pregnant woman and the power of nature. She decries any imposition of social conditions or expectations. As Armstrong and coauthor Feldman put it, those people who believe in the "efficacy of birth" "do not *manage* a birth so much as they *nourish* it. They feed it. Being organic, it becomes more vital" (1990, 54).

Throughout the labor and delivery process, Armstrong insists, the midwife remains in awe of the power of creation. Birth is a process that can be monitored and guided, but the power is inherent in the mother; the mother has the strength and the knowledge that she needs to give birth. Listening to her body, she chooses the position she wishes to take during labor. Listening to her body, she knows when to push. Armstrong and Feldman describe birth as organized, natural, beautiful:

> Out of instinct and desire, we make children. Dependent on the genius of our bodies, we grow them in our wombs. If and when we defer to that same genius during birth, if and when we invite and cultivate that power, we find that women can give birth 85–90% of the time without complication or unreasonable bravery. (24)

Thus, midwives adapt their own roles in the delivery process. In surveying fifty nurse-midwives, Sullivan and Weitz (1988) found that the lay-midwives never referred to the women they attended as "patients." And they never "delivered babies"; rather, they spoke of "catching" a baby that the *woman* had "delivered." They did not speak of controlling the birth; rather, they saw themselves as "facilitating" it.

In composition classrooms (learner-centered/learning-centered classrooms), the midwife metaphor positions teachers as facilitators. Just as the experienced midwife knows which stages in the birth process are the most difficult, during which stages the woman will need the most help, and when not to interfere, similarly, the writing teacher knows when to intervene and when such intervention will hinder the student's composing process. The midwife-teacher works with each student from the moment of an idea's conception, guiding the student through the act of composing. The teacher explains the mental operations of the labor of writing, helping students recognize what we know about writing—that it is messy, recursive, cyclical, and often painfully difficult.

To extend the parallel, the midwife-teacher trusts the workings of the student's mind in the same way that the medical midwife trusts that the laboring woman's body knows just what to do. The midwife-teacher's role is to assist students in becoming empowered by "highlighting and nurturing the strengths students already have" (Mittan 1989, 207). She facilitates the birth of a student's ideas by voicing confidence and belief in that learner's ability to succeed. As John Mayher, Nancy Lester, and Gordon Pradl suggest, the midwife-teacher trusts that "the student has within her everything she needs to write powerfully" (1983, 126). Furthermore, as Carolyn Ericksen Hill explains in her analysis of how Peter Elbow, Ken McCrorie, John Shutlz, and William Coles Jr. might be categorized as midwife-teachers, such teachers are willing to take risks to bring into this work that which has been ignored or lost (1990, 104–5).

But what does the metaphor suggest about how knowledge is "conceived"? What are its rhetorical implications? Consider how labor and delivery is described as an entirely natural process. In terms of rhetorical theory, this awe at the natural power of birth parallels the romantic-expressivist view of writing. This view, according to James Berlin, is rooted in the rhetoric of Emerson and the Transcendentalists, with its ultimate source found in Plato (1982, 771). According to Bizzell and Herzberg, Emerson "advocates a rhetoric of personal expression that will stir the audience to their own efforts at creative perception" (1990, 666). The fundamental question for Emerson is how to "represent one's experience in language" in a way that the reader will be able to duplicate or regenerate (666). In sum, in the romantic-expressivist tradition, the aim of writing is spontaneous, original self-expression for the purpose of re-creating an experience in the mind of the writer. Indeed, Carolyn Ericksen Hill describes the expressivist theorists as "midwives" because of their explicit efforts to give birth to the "experiential selves" of writers (1990, 104–5). The goal of the midwife-teacher, then, is to help the student find the kernels of ideas inside and to help these kernels grow organically into whatever form they might naturally take.

Taken to its extreme, such a view suggests that it may be impossible to teach writing at all; a student either does or does not have the natural ability to write. The role of the teacher, in such an extreme view, is simply to illustrate to the student whether or not the "natural ability" is apparent. However, a more moderate interpretation of this view would suggest that the midwife-teacher provides an environment in which students can have the time, safety, and comfort to look inward and see what they might produce. This perspective helps us understand Lester Faigley's description of the romantic-expressivist tradition as one in which the student's writing develops by gradually unifying its outwardly disparate parts through the process of revision (1986, 530). In a classroom drawing on this rhetorical theory, the student is the rhetor; the teacher is the listener. The student is the creator/constructor; the teacher is the receiver. While the teacher might offer guidance and may, to some degree, direct the writing, the student-writer is the one who controls the creative act. The midwife sees herself as a facilitator, one who trusts that the mother can know what is right.

While the rhetoric of nature as well as the sense of awe and wonder associated with midwifery might suggest that the midwife-teacher is best located within the romantic tradition, we believe that this rhetoric fails to adequately describe the interactions between the midwife writing teacher and the student as co-creators of knowledge. We are concerned that it provides only one model for teachers, an essentialist vision of the nurturing maternal figure. We are conscious, as well, that such views ignore the darker side of mothering. As Elizabeth Daumer and Sandra Runzo remind us, "there is another side of maternal teaching that most of us remember, where mothers silence their daughters in the name of society" (1987, 50). Susan Jarratt suggests that the notion of "teacher as mother naively ignores the deep ambivalence toward and repression of the mother in our culture" ("Feminism," 1991, 113). We also risk reifying a "humanistic model of the autonomous self" that, as recent work in feminist and identity theory points out, would serve to cover over the shifting subject positions we all embody (Ritchie and Boardman 1999, 594). Ending with an image of the purely "nurturing" mother, it seems, accurately captures neither the complexity of mothering nor the demands of teaching.

In our view, effective teaching goes beyond nurturing. As Jarratt argues, we sometimes need to put a student's thinking in opposition to other ideas— a Hegelian dialectical journey from thesis and antithesis to synthesis—to help give voice to those ideas (*Rereading*, 1991, 112–16). Similarly, in *Talking Back* (1989), bell hooks reflects on her own coming to voice through oppositional thinking. In her more recent *Teaching to Transgress*, hooks makes it clear that teachers who best help students come to voice are those who are "on a mission" to engage intellect through a Freireian liberatory pedagogy (1994, 2). For this to work, participants in the classroom must have "interest in one another, in hearing one another's voices, in recognizing one another's presence" (8). In other words, we must demand a whole relationship, not one based on a vision of easy harmony that ignores conflict. We cannot subordinate our own concerns, always putting the student first; nor should we expect students to only nurture each other. Such pedagogy must be marked by honest responses to students, not the kind of false optimism that the biblical midwife uttered to Rachel—"Fear not; thou shalt have this son also"—just before Rachel died in labor (Gen. 35:17). That is, such pedagogy is more learning-centered than it is learner-centered.

We take to heart the caution that, by encouraging an image of the composition teacher as a "nurturing" figure, we might reinscribe a dangerous ideology for the women teaching such courses: we would put them into the often essentialized role of woman as caretaker. (We note only briefly how such a position is differently constructed for male teachers, a point Susan Jarratt elaborates. See "Feminism and Composition.") We seek to retain the term "midwife-teacher" without reducing the teacher to only the caretaking role; we see her as facilitator and equal. We wish to transform the romanticized, "nurturing" image of the midwife-teacher into one that recognizes that the relationship in the birthing room is one of equals—the midwife, who has experience with labor, and the mother, who knows herself and her own needs. The baby, in this model, is born through the cooperation of both parties. In the same way, the midwife-teacher and the student engage in an alternative rhetoric, one in which knowledge is co-created, in a dialogue that acts as a bridge between the expressivist view of rhetoric and the social-epistemic view. We retain an image of the midwife-teacher as nurturing, as attentive to the mother-student, as a guide, but we do not keep only to that image. We build on it.

Rhetoric as Dialogic: Teacher-Student Constructors

An alternative rhetoric of the midwife-teacher, then, might be one in which the student constructs knowledge in a dialogic relationship with the teacher and with other students—or one in which knowledge is constructed by the rhetor in a dialogic relationship with her audience. Friedrich Nietzsche extols true dialectic: "One seeks a midwife for his thoughts, another someone to whom he can be a midwife: thus originates a good conversation" (1966, 88). Janice Hays echoes this sentiment: "[W]e need the presence of facilitating others who guide and support us and who can also grow and change with us" (1995, 160). Kay Halasek describes the interaction as dialogic: "a maieutic pedagogy is dialogic, for it encourages the search for knowledge, not the passive acceptance of authority" (1999, 182).

When we refer to midwife-teachers, we often think of them as working together with students to construct knowledge: we, like John Dewey in *Democracy and Education*, prefer to think of student-teacher relationships as collaborative (1966, 160). Thus, we focus on the coaching aspect of teaching rather than the evaluative one. In this ideal setting, the midwife-coach guides the student to think deeply and diligently, and pushes the student to revise an essay for a third audience. Both the teacher and student are invested in constructing the most rhetorically effective text for the third audience. Imagine, for example, working with a student to produce an argument exposing the sexism in her university. The teacher here acts as a mentor, an educated peer, offering knowledge about audience, writing strategies, and discourse conventions to help the student produce a text suitable to the purpose.

Within this model, the midwife-teacher works with a student dialogically rather than hierarchically so that the two may develop a synergy. Together, these collaborators harness what Kenneth Bruffee calls the "powerful educative force of peer influence" (1984, 638); together they transform their social context into a "community of status equals" (642). This dialogic process is also what Paulo Freire invokes when he uses the midwife metaphor to illuminate the student's role. He suggests that students "contribute to the midwifery of their liberating pedagogy" by their "authentic struggle to transform the situation" (1970, 32–33). Freire further understands that, like childbirth, this liberation is "a painful one" (33). For a student to take responsibility for her own writing and her own education always requires more pain and labor than putting herself in the hands of someone else and making that person responsible for her education.

In terms of rhetorical theory, this view of the relationship between teacher and student implies a parallel relationship between rhetor and audience. Just as the teacher is no longer the source of knowledge, the one passing down the "truth," so the rhetor is no longer the arbiter of what is "right" and "wrong." Rather, the rhetor draws on the perspectives of the audience to rethink his or her own experiences, and together they build knowledge.

Rhetoric as Multivocal: Teacher, Student, and Culture

But even this vision of teacher and student, rhetor and audience, as co-creators does not go far enough in examining the influence of culture on writing. Within postmodern thought, in particular, the idea of "creation"—even if it is "co-creation" involving two collaborators—is problematic because no writers are isolated from cultural, familial, institutional, or other surroundings. Midwives are tenaciously aware of how the image of birth is constructed and projected by our culture—usually in melodramatic narratives of sirens blazing to the safety of sterile operating rooms. A midwife teaches a couple to analyze and critique the dominant view of childbirth as pathological; she devotes time in check-ups and birthing classes to reveal how mothers can be constructed as victims, helpless and docile, by the rhetoric of western medicine. Similarly, midwife writing teachers must examine the multiple codes that are activated by the "mere" act of putting pen to page or fingertips to keyboard in the particular setting of a composition classroom.

A key cultural context highlighted by the midwife metaphor is that of the institutional context. In many of our descriptions, we have depicted the work of a midwife as it might take place in a stand-alone birthing center or if the midwife were invited to a home delivery. However, our institutional context is more like that of a midwife working within a hospital setting, trying to simultaneously critique the rhetoric of obstetrics even as she is surrounded by an apparatus that reinforces that view. The midwife-teacher, then, has to do more than co-construct knowledge with students; the teacher must also work with them to analyze how various perspectives are "always already" constructed by the codes of a culture, to interrogate those perspectives, and to understand the ideology inherent in the language used to name them. Consider again the writing teacher working with a student to build an argument exposing the sexism in her university. As part of the rhetorical analysis the teacher offers about discourse conventions, including audience criticism and other components, the teacher must engage the student in an investigation into the cultural role a sexist ideology might play in the university being critiqued. The teacher works with the student to examine how men and women are constructed by the rhetoric of the institution.

Such critiques may be neither expected nor welcomed by students. While parents may choose to attend birthing centers because they agree with the philosophy of birth that midwives have, students rarely have the opportunity to choose their composition teachers. While expectant couples may have the time and resources to research the philosophies and methods of birthing, students rarely have the opportunity to consider models of composition teaching or the rhetorical implications of those models. They rarely even realize that there are multiple theories of rhetoric or of teaching. Part of our job, then, is to discuss our methods with students—frequently, openly, honestly—so that they understand why we teach the ways we do.

Indeed, the institutional context works hard to obscure these differences and to "naturalize" the traditional, "banking" concepts of education. Some messages are subtle: we arrange our classrooms so the chairs are in a circle so that we and our students can all see and speak with each other, but each time we return, the chairs are lined up in rows facing the podium. Thus, the midwife-teacher lives daily with the reminder that all actions carry in them an ideology, a prescription of what exists, what is good, and what is possible (Berlin 1996). Therefore, the midwife-teacher will have to not only lead the students through the writing-theorizing process, but may also have to persuade reluctant students that this pedagogy is in their best interest.

Thus, the figures of midwife and midwife-teacher add another layer to our analysis of the rhetor-audience relationship. While the ideal relationship between student-teacher and rhetor-audience would be one of equals, such relationships are rare—if not impossible—given the invisible, powerful ideological systems at work in cultural institutions such as schools and hospitals. A midwife rhetoric demands that we don't use our desire for equality between rhetor and audience as an excuse to forego close analysis of the ideological forces at work within and upon that relationship.

Conclusion

By advocating and re-figuring the image of the writing teacher as midwife, we seek to disrupt several narratives simultaneously. As Linda Alcoff and Laura Gray-Rosendale accomplish with survivor discourse (1996), we wish to question the categories that set composition apart from rhetoric, with one as pure practice and the other as pure theory. We wish to claim the composition classroom as an important site for inquiry into rhetorical theory, for it is a site where institutional, cultural, and individual constructs impose visibly on the writing work that goes on there. We wish to claim the midwife as a positive figure, a nurturing, confident co-creator; we seek to disrupt the way that the figure has been used to essentialize women, especially women teachers, as having primary roles as caretakers, but at the same time we wish to disrupt the patriarchal assertion that nurturing and caretaking are not appropriate stances for teachers to take. Rather than discard the midwife metaphor, we seek to reaffirm it, in all its complexity, as a way to interrogate the historical, theoretical, and disciplinary histories in rhetoric and composition.

Plato might not be able to recognize us modern-day midwives who refuse to stamp our young writers' ideas as a "noble and true birth," who recognize the value of students in the birthing of ideas, and who do not see the birth act as isolated from its cultural surroundings. If women's power was distanced from the act of birth in Plato's dialogues, we hope that we have here recovered that power—as Louise Wetherbee Phelps suggests can happen in writing programs—through our characterization and by positioning the midwife-teacher back where she belongs, as co-constructor, not invisible, nor overpowered, nor overpowering in the writing classroom.

Note

We thank Maureen Daly Goggin, John Ramage, Frank D'Angelo, Gregory Castle, Cordelia Candelaria, Judith Sensibar, Peter Mosenthal, Susan Hynds, Linda Milosky, Barbara Combs, Bonnie Hankin, Kathleen Hinchman, Jennifer Kagan , Saundra Schwartz, Houston Wood, William Potter, Catherine Sustana, Carol Perrin, Angela Morris, and Deborah Ackerman for comments on earlier versions of this essay. We especially wish to thank Laura Gray-Rosendale and Sibylle Gruber for their astute advice for revising this piece.

Works Cited

Alcoff, Linda Martin, and Laura Gray-Rosendale. "Survivor discourse: Transgression or recuperation?" In *Getting a Life: Everyday Uses of Autobiography*, edited by Sidonie Smith and Julia Watson, 198–225. Minneapolis: University of Minnesota Press, 1996.

Armstrong, Peggy, and Sheryl Feldman. *A Wise Birth: Bringing Together the Best of Natural Childbirth with Modern Medicine*. New York: William Morrow, 1990.

Berlin, James. "Contemporary Composition: The Major Pedagogical Theories." *College English* 44 (1982): 765–77.

———. "Rhetoric and Ideology in the Writing Class." *College English* 50 (1988): 477–94.

———. *Rhetorics, Poetics, and Culture: Reconfiguring College English Studies*. Urbana, Ill.: NCTE, 1996

Bizzell, Patricia. "Power, Authority, and Critical Pedagogy." *Journal of Basic Writing* 10, no. 2 (1991): 54–70.

Bizzell, Patricia, and Bruce Herzberg, eds. *The Rhetorical Tradition: Readings from Classical Times to the Present*. Boston: Bedford, 1990.

Bruffee, Kenneth A. Collaborative Learning and the "Conversation of Mankind." *College English* 46 (1984): 635–52.

Clark, Alice. *Working Life of Women in the Seventeenth Century*. 3rd ed. Ed. Amy Louise Erickson. 1919. Rpt., New York: Routledge, 1992.

Daumer, Elizabeth, and Sandra Runzu. "Transforming the Composition Classroom." In *Teaching Writing: Pedagogy, Gender and Equity*, edited by Cynthia L. Caywood and Gillian R. Overing, 45–62. Albany: State University of New York Press, 1987.

Dewey, John. *Democracy and Education: An Introduction to the Philosophy of Education*. 1916. Rpt., New York: The Free Press, 1966.

Faigley, Lester. "Competing Theories of Process: A Critique and a Proposal." *College English* 48 (1986): 527–42.

Fetterly, Judith. "Dreaming the Future of English." *College English* 61 (1999): 702–11.

Freire, Paulo. *Pedagogy of the Oppressed*. Trans. Myra Bergman Ramos. New York: Seabury, 1970.

Genesis 35:17. King James Version. Cleveland: The World Publishing Company.

Halasek, Kay. *A Pedagogy of Possibility: Bakhtinian Perspectives on Composition Studies.* Carbondale and Edwardsville: Southern Illinois University Press, 1999.

Hansen, David T. "Was Socrates a "Socratic teacher"?" *Educational Theory* 38 (1988): 213–24.

Harkin, Patricia. "The Postdisciplinary Politics of Lore." In *Contending with Words: Composition and Rhetoric in a Postmodern Age,* edited by Patricia Harkin and John Schilb, 124–38. New York: MLA, 1991.

Harkin, Patricia, and John Schilb, eds. *Contending with Words: Composition and Rhetoric in a Postmodern Age.* New York: MLA, 1991.

Hays, Janice. "Intellectual Parenting and a Developmental Feminist Pedagogy of Writing." In *Feminist Principles and Women's Experience in American Composition and Rhetoric,* edited by Louise Wetherbee Phelps and Janet Emig, 153–90. Pittsburgh: University of Pittsburgh Press, 1995.

Hill, Carolyn Eriksen. "Four midwives." In *Writing from the Margins: Power and Pedagogy for Teachers of Composition,* 101–39. New York: Oxford University Press, 1990.

Holbrook, Sue Ellen. "Women's Work: The Feminizing of Composition." *Rhetoric Review* 9 (1991): 201–29.

hooks, bell. *Talking Back: Thinking Feminist, Thinking Black.* Boston: South End, 1989.

———. *Teaching to Transgress: Education as the Practice of Freedom.* New York: Routledge, 1994.

Isocrates. *Against the Sophists.* Vol. 2 of *Isocrates.* Trans. George Norlin. Loeb Classical Library. Cambridge, Mass.: Harvard University Press, 1968.

———. From *Antidosis.* Vol. 2 of *Isocrates.* Trans. George Nolin. Loeb Classical Library. Cambridge, Mass.: Harvard University Press, 1968.

Jarratt, Susan C. "Feminism and Composition: The Case for Conflict." In *Contending with Words: Composition and Rhetoric in a Postmodern Age,* edited by Patricia Harkin and John Schilb, 105–23. New York: MLA, 1991.

———. *Rereading the Sophists: Classical Rhetoric Refigured.* Carbondale: Southern Illinois University Press, 1991.

Laska, Sheri. "Annotated Bibliography on Feminist Pedagogy in the Composition Classroom: Feminization, Maternal Paradigms, and Essentialism." [database on-line] [cited July 20, 1998]. Available from <http://www.as.wvu.edu/~lbrady/laska.html>. 1998.

Mayher, John, Nancy Lester, and Gordon Pradl. *Learning to Write/Learning to Learn.* Upper Montclair, N.J.: Boynton/Cook, 1983.

Miller, Susan. "The Feminization of Composition." In *The Politics of Writing Instruction: Postsecondary,* edited by Richard Bullock and John Trimbur, 39–53. Portsmouth, N.H.: Heinemann-Boynton/Cook, 1991.

————. *Rescuing the Subject: A Critical Introduction to Rhetoric and the Writer*. Carbondale: Southern Illinois University Press, 1989.

Mittan, Robert. "The Peer Review Process: Harnessing Students' Communicative Power." In *Richness in Writing: Empowering ESL Students*, edited by Donna M. Johnson and Duane H. Roen, 207–19. New York: Longman, 1989.

Nietzsche, Friedrich. *Beyond Good and Evil*. Trans. Walter Kaufmann. 1886. Rpt., New York: Vintage, 1966.

Phelps, Louise Wetherbee. "Becoming a Warrior: Lessons of the Feminist Workplace." In *Feminine Principles and Women's Experience in American Composition and Rhetoric*, edited by Louise Wetherbee Phelps and Janet Emig, 289–339. Pittsburgh: University of Pittsburgh Press, 1995.

Plato. *Gorgias*. Trans. W. C. Helmbold. Indianapolis: Bobbs-Merrill, 1952.

————. *Phaedrus*. Trans. W. C. Helmbold. Indianapolis: Bobbs-Merrill, 1956.

————. *Symposium*. In *The Works of Plato*. Trans. Benjamin Jowett and ed. Irwin Edman. New York: The Modern Library, 1956.

————. *Theaetetus*. In *The Dialogues of Plato*. Vol. IV. Trans. and ed. Benjamin Jowett. London: Oxford University Press, 1871.

Ritchie, Joy, and Kathleen Boardman. "Feminism in Composition: Inclusion, Metonymy, and Disruption." *College Composition and Communication* 50, no. 4 (June 1999): 585–606.

Schell, Eileen E. "The Costs of Caring: 'Feminism' and Contingent Women Workers in Composition Studies." In *Feminism and Composition Studies: In Other Words*, edited by Susan C. Jarratt and Lynn Worsham, 74–93. New York: MLA, 1998.

Slevin, James F. "The Politics of the Profession." In *An Introduction to Composition Studies*, edited by Erika Lindemann and Gary Tate, 135–59. New York: Oxford University Press, 1991.

Sullivan, Deborah, and Rose Weitz. *Labor Pains: Modern Midwives and Home Birth*. New Haven: Yale University Press, 1988.

Will, George. "A Glut of Ph.D.s." In Sacbee Voices National [database online] [cited April 25, 1999]. Available from <*http://www.sacbee.com/voices/national/will/will_19990425.html*>. 1999.

Williams, J. Whitridge, Jack A. Pritchard, Paul C. MacDonald, and Norman F. Grant. *Williams' Obstetrics*. 17th ed. Norwalk, Conn.: Appleton-Century-Crofts, 1985.

Williams, Jeffrey. "Brave New University." *College English* 61 (1999): 742–51.

Winterowd, Ross W., with Jack Blum. *A Teacher's Introduction to Composition in the Rhetorical Tradition*. Urbana, Ill.: NCTE, 1994.

3

"Wooden Shoes and Mantle Clocks"

Letter Writing as a Rhetorical Forum for the Transforming Immigrant Identity

KATHLEEN A. DEHAAN

In his landmark series about Swedish immigration, Vilhelm Moberg acknowledged the power of the written word: "And to a new generation, able to read, came the printed word with tales of a land far away, a land which emerged from the mists of the page and took on the clearing, tempting aspects of reality."[1] Typically, immigrants used the printed word to describe critical moments of their experience, such as ocean crossing and settling into a new home. "America letters," as immigrant correspondence was called, were filled with the seemingly mundane, acting as a space in which these apparent trivialities of life were recorded and shared. Facts and figures, costs and comparisons, observations about food and livestock filled the pages. This very correspondence was also nearly the only means to celebrate epideictic occasions such as births, weddings, illnesses, and deaths. And yet, immigrant letters were not simply inventories or greeting cards as Hugh Duncan helps us understand. In *Symbols in Society*, he writes, "The new audiences created by modern means of communication want their voices to be heard, and to be heard in dialogue."[2] Duncan's observation, although intended for "modern" twentieth-century communications forms, certainly helps us to understand the important impact letter writing had on diasporic development.

Letter writing itself is not a new field of study; letters have been the focus of historical, scientific, religious, political, military, and sociological investigations. *Ars dictaminis* and the "epistolary form" have been around as long as literate people have been separated by distance. However, few scholars have explored immigrant letters as alternative rhetorical forms.

Letters are especially meaningful rhetorical artifacts for several reasons. Letters are "of the moment," not retrospectives.[3] The writer's persuasive strategies, arguments, desires, and aspirations are all laid out in personal correspondence. Because the immigrant letter was a major means of communication during this era, it acquired special importance for both writer and receiver, behaving as both a relational lifeline and as a means for the development and expression of identity.

Certainly the immigrant had other "alternative" rhetorical channels available in addition to letters—diary entries, journals, news articles, historical reconstructions, immigrant reminiscences, and so on. What makes all of these significant "alternative" forms of rhetoric is that most immigrants did not have access to those public forums, such as speeches, news columns, pamphleteering, and the like, which constituted traditional rhetorical opportunities of the time. While not wholly private, like a diary, nor completely public, like a speech, the letter is an intermediary forum in which the writer can bridge the private audience of the self and the public audience of the world. For example, many letters written to friends or family were posted for all to see in the town hall. Although some immigrants were oblivious to this larger dissemination, many seem to have been fully aware that their "intimate" family letter would become part of public discussion.

Immigrant letters are alternative rhetorical forums in another sense as well: they provide access to literate and nonliterate men, women, young, and minority alike.[4] While different genders, ages, or ethnicities might have emphasized alternative issues, all had some degree of access to expression. As Trinh has said,

> You who understand the dehumanization of forced removal-relocation-reeducation-redefinition, the humiliation of having to falsify your own reality, your voice—you know. And often cannot say it. You try and keep on trying to unsay it, for if you don't, they will not fail to fill in the blanks on your behalf, and you will be said.[5]

This is clearly the case for many immigrants; the letter was their voice. Therefore I argue that the narrative of the immigrant letter enabled negotiation of the tensions present in the exigencies of the moment, while simultaneously facilitating evolution of identity within a rhetorical drama. In making this argument I utilize narrative theory as a means through which we can rhetorically evaluate these letters.[6] This chapter proceeds by first discussing narrative drama and narrative theory. Next, I introduce the Schoonbeek family letters as rhetorical narratives. Finally, I offer a discussion and pedagogical applications of letter writing in the composition classroom.

Letter Writing as Rhetorical Drama

As long as human beings are embedded in social drama, symbolic actions play an important role in carrying out human relations. What role do letters perform when the everyday is disrupted? How does the drama continue? The aesthetic qualities and performative characteristics of narration, I suggest, enter into the drama enacted by letter writing among immigrants.

These letters are wonderfully rich life stories. They are constructed social dramas. Each has a plot, a subject, a voice, and a connection between events. It is a "structure of relationships by which the events contained in the account are endowed with a meaning by being identified as parts of an integrated whole."[7]

While it may seem "just" a letter, this discourse makes rational the immigrant's world, evaluates the strange or unknown, deliberates on that which was in question, and constructs and deconstructs the immigrant's identity. In so doing the immigrant letter seeks to generate a new identity, new knowledge—*narrate, narrare, gnarus*. This knowledge is at the heart of the immigrant's social drama.

The archetype of immigrant as storyteller is consistent with recent theoretical writing on narrative. MacIntyre notes that "man is in his actions and practice, as well as in his fictions, essentially a story-telling animal."[8] Fisher extends Burke's conception of man as the symbol-using animal to man as *Homo narrans*, or as storyteller.[9] He says, "symbols are stories meant to give order to human experience and to induce others to dwell in them to establish ways of living in common, in communities in which there is sanction for the story that constitutes one's life."[10] In essence, the rhetorical strategies function to explain the immigrant story as reality.

We are all storytellers. We understand life via story. It is how we communicate our existence, our journeys, and our dramas. In the great drama of mass migration, immigrants were able to situate themselves in time and space as part of this unfolding drama. They were cast as actors amid morally ambiguous landscapes of undefined territory. Thus, storytelling through letters enabled immigrants to share fantasies and experiences so as to create a larger consciousness. They acted as communication to the transatlantic audience, yet they also furnished a reconstruction of the same story to the self.[11]

Letters, however, are constructed with an "interpretive lens." As Lucaites and Condit contend, in such a case "both content and form of the rhetorical narrative are thus subservient to demands of the relationship between the specific audience to which it is addressed, the specific context in which it appears, and the specific gain toward which it strives."[12] The immigrant message is contingent. It relies on the writer, the public/private audience(s), prior experiences, the storytelling education, context, motives and constraints.[13] The author is strategically ordering events and choosing the sequence of importance, as well as selecting what to omit. There are also elements present in immigrants' narratives about which they may not have been conscious. We must be attentive to actual content as well as to that which was left out.[14]

Rhetorical Strategy: Narrative

Narrative, long the subject of academic discussion, is utilized in this chapter as a theoretical screen through which we can understand how letters operate rhetorically. As previously noted, the Latin placement of narrative or narrate is *narrare* (to tell or relate), from *gnarus* or knowing. An age-old theoretical connection exists between telling and knowing or producing knowledge, which is worth briefly considering. White calls narrative a "metacode." It is "a human universal on the basis of which transcultural messages about the nature of a shared reality can be transmitted."[15] Waldman suggests that narrative is "knowledge of the past—pieces of information organized and integrated."[16] For Burke narrative is to be found in his "parlor" with life as the ongoing conversation into which we arrive, participate, and depart.[17] Fisher offers narrative as episodes in the larger story of life.[18] Lucaites and Condit view narrative as the "formation of political and social consciousness."[19]

Narrative as storytelling is a universal expression culturally acquired or taught via experience. For this reason, narrative is to some degree egalitarian. It speaks of similar qualities of life: taste, sound, images—that which is sensory; and of social experiences—family, religion, economics, and tradition. Thus, narrative was accessible to most immigrants, regardless of gender, age, or ethnicity. But they used it to different ends and with different results, as we will see with the following analysis of the Schoonbeek letters.

Several scholars view narrative as egalitarian and easily accessible. Ricoeur, for example, suggests that this form of narrative is not only epistemic in that the telling provides a way of knowing, but it also serves as a means of ordering life.[20] Duncan agrees with this sense of "order" and places this communication as "the constituent element in the creation of order and disorder in human relationships."[21] In this whole process, the immigrant experiences power and control over ritual changes and traditions since he or she is now in control of the symbolic environment via the letter. Perhaps Fisher's Narrative Paradigm, explained in the following section, offers one of the most focused strategies for reading letters rhetorically.

Narrative Paradigm

Walter Fisher's Narrative Paradigm defines rhetoric as an art or a means of finding and effectively presenting good reasons. From this perspective, then, narrative takes on a reasoned rhetorical strategy. We can look closer at the Narrative Paradigm by understanding its two components of narrative rationality: narrative probability and narrative fidelity. Fisher's narrative probability relies on a sense of coherence, consistency, and noncontradiction.[22] Fidelity seeks that which is reliable and truthful.[23]

As alternative rhetorics, immigrant letters are by their very nature narratives of the unfolding lives of the emigrant, immigrant, and naturalized citizen. Not all traditional views of rhetoric serve immigrant letters well, as syllogistic logic is typically absent while generally accepted premises may change. Thus, reasoning in immigrant letters is "rational" to the extent that it draws on practical wisdom to guide judgment.

Nevertheless, narrative does help us to understand immigrant letters as a means of rhetorical exploration and explanation. When we view such letters via narrative theory, we can better understand their inherent logic and their challenge—to sustain the audience by weaving a story that does not negate the old audience. Narrative also aids us in seeing how letters struggle to recall and maintain points of comparison while negotiating the shifting histories, cultures, biographies, and contingencies. In the letters, narrative also develops the self as audience since we often tell stories to help ourselves understand, justify, persuade, or simply create an audience of one. While there are some inherent problems with the Narrative Paradigm, it does offer a starting point for development of method for analyzing immigrant letters.

Fisher views the Narrative Paradigm as a philosophical statement "meant to offer an approach to interpretation and assessment of human communication—assuming that all forms of human communication can be seen fundamentally as stories, as interpretations of aspects of the world occurring in time and shaped by history, culture, and character."[24] While I would not contend that all forms of human communication are stories, I do agree with his statement that we can "learn (the) truths by listening to the narratives."[25] We can understand the immigrant reality or what the immigrant has come to know as truth by acknowledging the letters' rhetorical form. Nevertheless, we have to be careful when applying the Narrative Paradigm. There are some potential points of friction.

Narrative rationality as a combination of narrative probability (the coherence, consistency, and lack of contradictions within a story) and narrative fidelity (the truth and reliability of a story) are problematized because of the constantly shifting ground on which immigrants live. There is little if any

coherence or consistency, and contradictions abound. Old truths and reliabilities are gone. Consider the immigrant, encountering a very foreign world
replete with strange and curious traditions, culture, transportation, housing,
food, nature, money, government, politics, and more. Truths are culturally
acquired. In the immigrant narrative, what was reliable and truthful about a
former life may no longer be applicable. The past may not be a reliable lens
through which to interpret the present and future. So the letter becomes a
means of ordering new truths and reliabilities in relation to the immigrant's
nascent world.

Contrary to Lucaites and Condit's writings, that "a rhetorical narrative
must be consistent with the audience's general outlook on the world, with
both its logical and sociological expectations," the narrative of immigrant
letters can be highly inconsistent with established expectations of both the
speaker and the audience without invalidating either old or new worlds.[26]

The question remains, "How can theories of narrative and the Narrative Paradigm serve immigrant letters?" Old narratives must be understood
in combination with these new stories or narratives as a means of getting at
the social drama of immigration. For example: "We used to call ourselves X,
now we call ourselves Y. We used to do things this way. Here they do them
differently. We used to think this would generate these results. Now we
know differently." The result is that the *incoherence, inconsistencies,* and
contradictions created in the immigrant reality are also products of the
social drama and a dynamic of the diasporic experience.

Having discussed narrative theory as a means with which to evaluate
immigrant letters, let us now turn to one family's correspondence to understand the rhetorical significance of these texts.

The Schoonbeek Letters, 1873–1931

> So, now, after a very difficult trip and much inconvenience,
> we can rejoice. We don't know what the future holds but
> everyone encourages us and we can see that they are all
> getting along well as long as they are healthy. So, in short,
> I'm well impressed here.
>
> (Marten Schoonbeek, 1873)[27]

Such was the sentiment in Marten Schoonbeek's second letter to his son
as a newly arrived immigrant in 1873. As optimistic as this early correspondence was, later letters revealed a very difficult immigrant experience.
Schoonbeek, a carpenter by trade, and his wife, Frouwke Pul, left their village of Nieuwolda, Groningen, in the far northeastern corner of the Nether-

lands in May 1873. Together with five of their six children, they traveled for twenty-one days, finally settling in Grand Rapids, Michigan. Their grown daughters, Harmanna and Tryntje, lived and worked outside the home as housemaids. Jetje and Harm, a younger daughter and son, and Klaas, a "mentally handicapped" son, remained with their parents. The other child, Jacobus, the oldest son and recipient of all twenty-nine family letters, stayed in the Netherlands to pursue his career as a teacher, with the understanding that he would join the family at a later date.[28]

Having moved to the United States during the financial panic of 1873, Schoonbeek encountered a sluggish and depressed economy. His letters discuss the family's financial struggles, but also argue that the decision to emigrate was sound. Throughout 1873 and into early 1874, Marten writes of his family's health and financial situation, occasionally making reference to his own continuing illness. Suddenly, in May 1874, Marten dies, leaving behind his destitute wife and children.

At this point Frouwke, and her two older daughters, Harmanna and Tryntje, continued the family correspondence. Frouwke writes to her son about her dire circumstances and her daughters' lack of financial support. Frouwke's letters reveal that she has become dependent on local charity for fuel, food, and debt assistance. Eventually Frouwke remarries, but it is an abusive second marriage. The letters tell of theft and beatings. Most of her letters are characterized by plaintive pleadings to her son, Jacobus, not to forget her or to bring her back to the Netherlands.

However, in constructing a distinctly antithetical reality, the daughters' letters speak about how well the family is, their mother's financial security, and their own developing status. Both daughters marry and write of their own families. Their letters account for their new homes and acquisitions, their husbands' jobs, and their continued financial support of their mother. Both mother's and daughters' letters suggest that Jacobus should not believe what he might have read in the others' writings, and encourage him to react and respond in a certain way, such as with pity, anger, despair, or love—suiting the writer's reality. Making this correspondence even more fascinating and multidimensional are letters written by "advocates" on behalf of the mother, Frouwke. These letters describe her destitute state and the daughters' lack of financial support, and demand that Jacobus take action to remedy the situation. Hence the narrative of each letter writer constructs a tremendously varied account of the Schoonbeek family's life. We will see that letters are a space in which each writer negotiates both private and public audiences, editorializes about social and political issues, disputes others' claims, and attempts to make sense of the contradictions inherent in a new world. For the Schoonbeeks, narrative offers a means to construct new truths out of the confusions of their lives.

Marten writes, "The first year is always difficult for an immigrant because a great deal of money is needed to set up housekeeping. It's like young people starting out with nothing." This simile is designed to communicate that Marten and family are much like everyone else, and that their poverty is not anomalous to the immigrant experience.

The final three letters before his death are both poignant and significant in that the tensions between the optimistic immigrant and the unfortunate, ill, unemployed father and husband are candidly negotiated. "I keep busy making wooden shoes and sometimes [I go out selling them from door to door]. When I come to a door where Yankees live I often hear, 'No! No! These are hard times. I have no money.' Actually the Yankees do not want to wear wooden shoes."[29] Obviously, Schoonbeek positions himself as a hard-working man amid this drama. "Yankees," however, are the spoilers, denying him the opportunity for gain. Bear in mind that most immigrants came to the United States believing that fortune was merely a boat ride away, that streets were indeed paved with gold, and that this country was their Canaan. Thus, Schoonbeek's narrative grapples with the contradictions between an unfulfilled promise and the everyday reality he and his family encounter.

Later in this letter, Schoonbeek writes to his son about his job in what sounds like a rationalization for demeaning work. "Perhaps it does not seem proper to you—that I have to go door to door [selling wooden shoes] to make these calls. Well, it is not pleasant, I admit, but this is America, and people here respect a person who tries to help himself in an honest manner. And then a person does not have to be ashamed." Despite his words to the contrary, it appears that Schoonbeek was "ashamed" about his shoe peddling and had to defend his actions to his son.

So, there was an exigence for Schoonbeek to address and upgrade the status of this activity—both to his son as well as to himself. It is evident from this selection that he used his narrative to reposition himself in a more flattering light. "(B)ut this is America," he writes, where he can be respected and not be "ashamed" of his status. Perhaps this is what he said to himself each morning as he set out to sell. Perhaps this strategy enabled him to move beyond the stigma associated with door-to-door sales, investing it with the greater worth of self-sufficiency. Schoonbeek uses context strategically to refurbish his own identity. In constructing "America" as something of his own making, he is able to save face before his son. Regardless, Marten Schoonbeek used his letters as a forum through which he could address his public audience as well as privately reflect on his own situation while generating arguments to justify his own poverty and the inescapable "peddling" of wooden shoes.

You doubtless understand that I have no money because I earned very little during the summer. I have been ill most of the time and in addition I have built my own house. Now it is winter. . . . It is impossible to earn anything. . . . So I just make wooden shoes and go out peddling them—that's what they call it here. Actually I enjoy it rather well. I make only a little money from it, but a person can buy quite a bit with a little money.

Through this letter Schoonbeek can rationalize his poverty and work status while strategically repositioning these as being acceptable. At the same time, Schoonbeek's letters become rather long justifications for having uprooted his family, having moved to a foreign land, and having been reduced to door-to-door sales simply to survive. "You doubtless understand," he begins, suggesting that in fact, he does not expect his audience to understand his predicament. And perhaps Marten doesn't quite understand it either. "I have been ill," he notes, yet through some heroic effort he has been able to build a home. Thus, his story is still trying to weave an image of protagonist, sacrificing for his family at all costs. Marten's reference to peddling wooden shoes, followed by the qualifier, "that's what they call it here," implies that he is trying to position this practice as being acceptable and honorable in America, not disgraceful and shameful. He knows very well that it's the same activity the world over, and no amount of rhetorical positioning can change that. Yet, as his only way to cope and to accept, his letter continues to tell the audience that he "enjoy[s] it rather well." While it doesn't seem genuinely so, Marten is using his narrative to persuade himself and others that this is indeed his attitude.

Marten continues, "I make only a little money," again admitting that his circumstances are poor. But this should be acceptable he counters, as a "little" will go a long way. So, Schoonbeek is making the best of a bad situation— making the best of a situation that is out of his control. His entire narrative is created so as to demonstrate that the reasons for his despair are not of his own making. Rather, fault lies with external cultural and social sources such as sickness, familial responsibility, winter, and low earnings. His letter seems to be one of the few places in which he can control his life and his identity.

However sanguine Marten may have been about his ability to earn money, this confidence dramatically changes within the year as the new reality of economic depression sets in. He then is forced to fix different truths— to make sense of the inconsistencies between two very discrepant views of America via his letters: "I have heard little about the money crisis here lately but I experience the lack of money daily. No one tries to hide the fact that he has no money because it is a common ailment." While Marten might be poor, he is quick to paint this scene as being broad in scope, discriminating against none. "I, along with many others, still have no work. This is the result of the money crisis. Ordinary people are quickly out of money and those who still have some are afraid to spend it." So, the new norm of poverty is set and it affects even "ordinary people." Evidently the letter was an important means for Marten Schoonbeek to reconstitute his changing versions of self, life, and experience, while providing a space for editorializing about the social and political conditions around him.

As in the case of the Schoonbeeks, the letters document a faltering family economic state, which suddenly turns indigent with Marten's death. Widowed and now dependent on others for aid, Frouwke takes up the correspondence.[30] She writes to her son, Jacobus, about her financial standing.

> Tryntje and Harmanna each give me one dollar per week, but the way I figure it, Tryntje does not pay for her board. But when I ask her for more she becomes very angry. . . . And then she tells me . . . that she will get married as soon as she can. Just after Father died she told me, "We will not leave you to yourself," and then she pressed my hand.[31]

Frouwke's narrative is trying to make sense out of what seems to be inconsistent behavior. Clearly she is creating a reality or truth based on her own cultural and historical background as she positions herself as deserving victim and Tryntje and Harmanna as being disobedient. This passage seems to be a tongue-in-cheek commentary of her daughters' hypocritical actions. Trying to purge all of the emotion she is experiencing—anger, anxiety, loss, betrayal— Frouwke wants her audience to feel the same.

The rhetorical strategizing of these letters becomes even more evident as this thread is continued in Frouwke's letter: "But dear son, when you write [Tryntje] be careful not to offend her because then matters will become still worse. Tell her that she must help me until you arrive. And tell Harmanna that too. . . . But she has a boyfriend whom she thinks about all the time, and she forgets about her mother and brothers and sisters." Frouwke's narrative demonstrates the contest for audience and voice as the struggles over familial obligation and financial independence are appearing.

In contrast, Trytntje's correspondence continues to document the growth and well-being of the other siblings and urges Jacobus to "come to this very large country very soon and make plenty of money." Her letter concludes with the reassurance that their mother is better off in the United States: "If Mother were still in Humrik, she would be in want. Mother often says, 'Thank the Lord I am in America.'" Tryntje makes a grand effort to persuade her audiences, both private and public, that Frouwke is indeed happy. Why does she do this? Perhaps to assuage her own guilt or perhaps to build a straw-man against those who might criticize her. "Saturday morning a wagon load of wood was delivered to Mother from her neighbors—for her birthday. . . . A Dutch farmer would not do that—give fuel to someone."

Here the daughter's narrative positions this type of welfare as normal, and her letters suggest that her mother is well cared for. With similar pathos, Harmanna writes,

> Mother has been given another fifty cents per week from the poor relief fund. Now she receives one dollar and fifty cents from that and one dollar from Tryntje and one dollar from me. I would say that three dollars and fifty cents per week is enough. She would not be able to live on that in the old country. The poor relief fund has also agreed to supply Mother with fuel for the winter. . . . Don't worry about her. We will help as much as we can.

Harmanna uses the letter to establish several convictions. First, the poor fund will tend to all of Frouwke's needs. Second, the support she and her sister give their mother is substantial. Third, Frouwke's life is better in the United States than it would be back in the Netherlands. With a lack of adjectives but with an emphasis on numbers and facts, this passage reads as an emotionally detached transaction or ledger. It is "enough," Harmanna writes, so as to distance herself from the private and public shame of her mother's suffering. Her mother "receives" one dollar from Harmanna. Were she to have written that she "gives" her mother money, a reader might think that she should give her more. The rhetorical difference between "receives" and "gives" is a difference of obligation, and Harmanna claims to have fulfilled her responsibility. She admonishes her brother not to worry, again with a lack of emotion. "We will help as much as we can" suggests further qualified support. Thus, in this one letter, Harmanna creates a private space for her reality, editorializes about welfare and Dutch economy, and establishes new norms for the public audience about the nature of filial responsibility.

Van Aarten, a "social worker" writing on behalf of Frouwke, proposes several solutions to the predicament. First, he suggests to the brother that Frouwke should request more public aid. A second, alternative resolution is to "advertise in the paper describing the conduct of your sisters, and publicly requesting support for your mother and three needy children. This would destroy the honor of your unworthy sisters. They deserve that, however, because they have continued to live in constant contention with your mother." His final suggestion is to sell the family property and send Frouwke as well as her younger children back to the Netherlands. However, Van Aarten believes this to be "the least desirable, because what would there be for her to do in The Netherlands? To depend upon charity is like being allowed only to smell the bacon." He concludes, "having brought your mother and her pathetic circumstance to your attention, I close this letter." Van Aarten's narrative builds the argument for Frouwke's poor economic status as well as Tryntje's and Harmanna's neglected duties. Further, he offers several solutions in his own attempt to define reality and reset narrative probability and fidelity.

After a two-year gap in the letters, the writing resumes on June 18 of 1877 with letters from Frouwke and another agent writing on her behalf. By this time Frouwke has remarried, and Tryntje, Harmanna, and Jacobus have married. Both older daughters have given birth to children. In her letter Frouwke makes reference to her unhappy marriage: "that man treats me and the children in a terrible way. He says he would like to dash open our heads with an ax and he beats me too. . . . On the sixteenth he walked out and he came back on the eighteenth. Then I showed him the door." This was truly an abusive situation for the widow and her children. An illiterate man, as was noted in one letter, Frouwke's new husband also beat the "mentally handicapped" son, Klaas, resulting in a jail stay. Again she reiterates her desire to return to Holland in September. "Money is the main problem because there is no work. . . . I don't know where to find food for myself and the children." Here, Frouwke's narrative becomes an invaluable public forum through which she can safely reposition her own domestic abuse. She does not want to be perceived as a victim. Clearly her life seems to be out of her control—her husband has died, her daughters are no longer obedient nor are they fulfilling their obligations, she marries an abusive second husband, and she has become destitute and dependent. So Frouwke seems to be struggling to demonstrate via letter writing that she has some control, some agency. By "show[ing] him the door" and writing that she is still responsible for "food for myself and the children," Frouwke is grasping for some authority over her world.

Tryntje writes two letters in January 1878, six months later, "I can tell you our brothers and sisters are in good health and also Mother is about the same as usual. . . . She has no reason to complain. . . . She goes to church regularly and I often sit near her." Tryntje's private and public narrative tries to create an identity of caring daughter and social climber. Tryntje closes this letter, "Your sister, Mrs. Stormzandt." It is important to note that it was unusual for women, especially Dutch women, to use the title of Mrs. along with a husband's surname. During this era, primarily women of the "upper classes" utilized this form of address.[32] The use of Mrs. Stormzandt was a case of intentional identity shifting and grasping for status. Thus, her narrative is epistemic in that it establishes her own version of reality—a well-cared-for mother and a religious, wealthy daughter. Once again, narrative offers the letter writer the opportunity to make sense of contradictions presented not only in the journey, but also in other writers' versions of this new life.

Her second January letter notes, "As far as I know Mother, our new father, and our brothers and sister are all well. We do not get together very often. Nor do we see Harmanna very often. They live more than an hour away from us and, since it is as cold as any winter we have had here, we don't go out so much." In this letter Tryntje establishes a norm of distance as well as family disconnectedness. However, the reader will recall that six months prior Frouwke wrote about her own new marriage, its abusive nature and resultant abandonment. Thus, the eldest son, Jacobus, was faced with conflicting realities. But the letters as rhetorical mediums through which these realities are created, exhibited, then exposed, are his only means to understand truth as it is constructed by the writer. Narrative in letters, then, becomes a very powerful tool for immigrants to clarify contradictions by creating their own realities.

The daughters' letters were clearly forums through which they constructed their New World selves and abandoned the past. In this *same* January letter, Tryntje comments about the "great deal of poverty in this city [Grand Rapids]" and the great unemployment. Letters obviously offer her the opportunity to editorialize or comment on social issues. However, in this letter she also boasts of her husband's job and their latest purchase. "Last week we bought a new clock and it cost seven dollars. I don't believe a single farmer in the old country has ever seen a clock as nice as this one." Dutch historian and letter editor Herbert Brinks footnotes this passage: "Larger wall clocks were and are a major ornamental feature in the living rooms of wealthy Netherlanders."[33] By juxtaposing unemployment with their own material gain, Tryntje's narrative speaks both to herself as private audience as well as to the larger public audience—those people with whom her brother might share her letter—to ease guilt and to strategically develop an alternative and more prestigious identity. Tryntje is not terribly subtle about her changing station, and it appears that she writes her letters in order to develop the divide between her new identity and her own family, as well as to boost her own status.

Obviously, the Schoonbeek letters resonate with rhetorical strategizing; attempting to persuade the audience and the self of the writer's newly constructed reality. The letters were written to induce the audience and the self to accept and act within this reality. These letters have various tones, suggesting they were written with at least three strategies. The first would seem to be self-address, as a rationalization of the immigration decision and as a means of justifying their actions and status. A second appears in which the Schoonbeek writers could editorialize about issues in which they may not normally have engaged. The third arises as a space for disputing others' claims, and then for resolving contradictions that are born out of these antithetical realities.

The Schoonbeek letters are also remarkable examples of the use of letters to discuss how old norms are satisfied and new ones are introduced. Indeed, these family letters demonstrate how the mother and daughters employed their writings to establish their own standards of familial duty and roles. It was the cultural dislocation of immigration that necessitated this reconstitution of the realities of family, money, welfare, and work amid conflicting testimony back to a distanced son and brother. Immigration provided both an exigence and an opportunity to create new meaning and significance through personal advocacy. The Schoonbeek letters offer engaging insight into the different perspectives reaffirming and tearing apart the family.

This analysis of the Schoonbeek correspondence shows that by bridging private and public forums, letters can contribute to the development of and changes in an immigrant's identity. As forums for both private justification and public expression, correspondence enabled the elder Marten to gradually abandon the designation of "Dutchman" as well as the stigma associated with poverty. For the rest of the family, the letters offered a means to transform themselves, at least rhetorically, from poor farmer's children to affluent social climbers. In this way the letters were powerful expressions of authority over their own destinies. Not only could these immigrants live out lives of their own devising, but they could also write their new lives into letters, created for audiences afar. Furthermore, letters provided Frouwke, Tryntje, and Harmanna rhetorical forums in which they could comment on various issues, such as poverty, welfare, and familial responsibility, while weaving seemingly contradictory truths through their narratives. Having examined narrative theory and analyzed one family's letters, let us now explore some of the pedagogical opportunities presented by these rich texts.

Pedagogical Implications

Working with immigrant letters is not only an intellectual pursuit but a very personal one for me as well. I am fortunate to have letters from my Dutch great-grandfather who emigrated in 1916. Pedagogically speaking, such a connection is an extremely powerful motivation for students and researchers alike. Therefore, I will conclude this chapter with a discussion of pedagogical implications offered by immigrant letter research.

The question emerges, "How can we integrate letters into our classrooms?" My rhetorical reading of immigrant letters carries from this research into my teaching in critical ways. In my course, "Rhetoric and Identity," my students and I explore various rhetorical negotiations of identity—one of which is immigrant letters. Some of the key objectives guiding class discussions include tracing the history of rhetorical developments of selected specific identities while gaining a new perspective on the power of rhetorical devices in the construction of larger, perhaps hegemonic, identities.[34] We also seek to become more aware of how rhetoric can be used to hide difference and/or exclude/minimize identities while learning to be critical of how existing states, nations, or groups construct and maintain their identities. Finally, we hope to have an educated experience with rhetoric and identity, so we can construct our own rhetorical positions.

Taught primarily to upper-division students, the course integrates rhetorical readings of letters in several ways. We begin with the question, "Who am I?" and are often met with an exceptional series of answers, demographic to intimate. We know that this was a question with which many immigrant letter writers struggled through their letters. So, by asking this question of ourselves and of our students, we are "forced" into a similar frame of mind. Thus, I begin the semester by asking students to write a brief essay simply titled, "Who am I?" This helps to start the discussion, making research into these alternative rhetorics all the more personally accessible as we have to think about (sometimes for the first time) how we came to be who we are today. Students often end up searching for their own letters, diaries, family trees, grandparents' stories, and the like.

The next stage of the semester is to move students into theoretical readings such as Burke, Bitzer, Fisher, and Foucault as rhetorical screens for analysis.[35] Following this theoretical context, we look to primary texts such as those found in letter collections.[36] Research, essays, and group work focus on the alternative rhetorical nature of immigrant letters, raising questions about issues such as illiteracy, agency, and economics.

Once we have grounded ourselves in the personal and tangible nature of this identity struggle, we have the opportunity to explore alternative rhetorics of displacement. Letters are alternative forums for the development of identity for displaced people, not just the Dutch. So application of this research into other ethnic correspondence should focus on issues of agency and how all correspondence varies not only in its rhetorically situated thematics, but perhaps more significantly in how various cultural groups might negotiate their ethnic identities quite differently via their letters.

Rhetorical research into letters thus offers useful rhetorical tools to our students and helps them make 'everyday texts' come alive. Quite by accident and not by design, students report writing more letters. They seem to be more aware of those significant moments in history and in their own lives which they formerly overlooked. They are learning to see and embrace those 'everyday texts'—family slave quilts, spirituals, culturally significant dances, and yes, even letters from a parent—as being rhetorically critical discursive forums.

In the final analysis, then, immigrant letters are individual negotiations of the tensions inherent in the displacement of immigration. The letter becomes a significant means for writers to advocate their own causes to the larger audience while engaging in self-reflection and address. These letters are also instrumental in establishing new normative conditions and alternative realities while crafting rhetorical strategies to the writers' advantage. Finally, immigrant letters are, indeed, sites of reconstituted identity—alternative rhetorical forums in which immigrants could renovate the self according to their own relative needs.

Reading this correspondence, one is struck by how consequential each letter was in contributing to the conversation. Were Marten, Frouwke, Tryntje, or Harmanna to have been illiterate or not have access to letter writing materials, their voices would not have been heard. They would not have had a forum of their own. Their realities would have been defined by others, and they truly would have been "said."

White is quite right then, when he suggests that

> the art is the activity by which the individual makes out of common materials a new version of what he has inherited, a reconstitution of his language and culture. . . . He finds ways to give new meaning, and sometimes new form to the terms, structures, and methods of the language—reconstitutions of facts, feelings, values—into new patterns of significance, new movements of the minds.[37]

The letter was indeed an alternative rhetorical art for the immigrant, enabling her to make a passage through the "unknown world" to reconstitute identity anew.

Notes

I am indebted to Caroline C. Hunt of the College of Charleston and Laura Gray-Rosendale of Northern Arizona University for their valuable assistance and insights.

1.   Vilhelm Moberg, *The Emigrants,* trans. Gustaf Lannestock, 1951, rpt. (St. Paul: Minnesota Historical Society 1995), xxvii.

2.   Hugh Duncan, *Symbols in Society* (New York: Oxford University Press, 1968), 248.

3.   There is a parallel to the sophistic concept of *kairos,* suggesting that letters were significant rhetorical moves making best use of timing, opportunity, and decorous response.

4.   Research shows that ghost writers and preprinted forms were sometimes available to immigrants who were unable to write their own letters.

5.   Trinh T. Minh-ha, *Woman, Native, Other* (Bloomington: Indiana University Press, 1989), 80.

6.   Since this chapter is limited in length, I chose to focus only on narrative as one rhetorical strategy for reading letters. My other research, how-

ever, draws from a multilayered approach. First, I explore letters for recurring themes. Second, these themes are contextualized within the time period in which the immigrant wrote, noting parallel historical, political, and sociological issues. Third, letters are then examined for their specific use of all three rhetorical strategies—narrative, deliberative, and differentiative. Finally, letters are evaluated as negotiations of identity within an epic, comic, or tragic frame. For my full research design, see Kathleen A. DeHaan, "He Looks Like a Yankee in His New Suit" (Ph.D. diss., Northwestern University, 1998).

7. Hayden White, "The Value of Narrativity in the Representation of Reality," in *On Narrative*, ed. W. J. T. Mitchell (Chicago: University of Chicago Press, 1981), 9.

8. Alasdair MacIntyre, *After Virtue: A Study in Moral Theory* (Notre Dame: University of Notre Dame Press, 1981), 201.

9. Kenneth Burke, *A Rhetoric of Motives* (Berkeley: University of California Press, 1969), 192.

10. Walter Fisher, "Narration as a Human Communication Paradigm: The Case of Public Moral Argument," *Communication Monographs* 51 (1984): 6.

11. Roy Schafer, "Narration in the Psychoanalytic Dialogue," in *On Narrative*, ed. W. J. T. Mitchell (Chicago: University of Chicago Press, 1981), 31.

12. John Louis Lucaites and Celeste Michelle Condit, "Re-constructing Narrative Theory: A Functional Perspective," *Journal of Communication* (Autumn 1985): 94.

13. Barbara Herrnstein Smith, "Narrative Versions, Narrative Theories," in *On Narrative*, ed. W. J. T. Mitchell (Chicago: University of Chicago Press, 1981), 213–22.

14. Besides sounding the alarm for the contingent quality of narrative, we must also acknowledge that not all rhetoric or rhetorical forms are narrative in nature. Rowland holds that all symbolic action cannot be narrative, and that we should "limit the scope of the paradigm and treat narrative as one among many modes of discourse and epistemic instruments." One can acknowledge Rowland's criticism and still find that narrative offers strong perspective to illuminate and evaluate immigrant letters, and in so doing helps us to uncover the rich and varied rhetorical strategies the letters possess. Robert Rowland, "On Limiting the Narrative Paradigm," in *On Narrative*, ed. W. J. T. Mitchell (Chicago: University of Chicago Press, 1981), 53.

15. White, "Value of Narrativity," 2.

16. Marilyn Robinson Waldman, "'The Otherwise Unnoteworthy Year 711,' A Reply to Hayden White," in *On Narrative*, ed. W. J. T. Mitchell (Chicago: University of Chicago Press, 1981), 247.

17. Kenneth Burke, *The Philosophy of Literary Form* (Berkeley: University of California Press, 1973), 94.

18.   Walter Fisher, "Clarifying the Narrative Paradigm," *Communication Monographs* 56 (1989): 87.
19.   Lucaites and Condit, "Re-constructing Narrative Theory," 90.
20.   Paul Ricoeur, "Narrative Time," in *On Narrative*, ed. W. J. T. Mitchell (Chicago: University of Chicago Press, 1981), 165–86.
21.   Duncan, *Symbols in Society*, 33.
22.   Schutz uses the terms "coherence," "clarity," and "consistency." Alfred Schutz, *Collected Papers II: Studies in Social Theory* (The Hague: Martinus Nijhoff, 1964), 91–119. Schafer also utilizes similar language: coherence, consistency, comprehensiveness, and common sense (Schafer, "Narration in the Psychoanalytic Dialogue," 25–50).
23.   Similar themes are discussed by Schafer: reliability and intelligibility (Schafer, "Narration in the Psychoanalytic Dialogue," 46, 47).
24.   Fisher, "Clarifying the Narrative Paradigm," 57.
25.   Fisher, "Narration as a Human Communication Paradigm," 14–150.
26.   Lucaites and Condit, "Re-constructing Narrative Theory," 96.
27.   Schoonbeek family background and letters from Brinks, *Dutch American Voices*, 252–55), and the Calvin College immigrant letter collection. The bulk of my research draws primarily from Dutch immigrant letter archives, of which there are approximately four thousand at Calvin College, Michigan, and two thousand at Hope College, Michigan. More information on immigrant letters and the Schoonbeek family can also be found in DeHaan, "He Looks Like a Yankee in His New Suit."
28.   This concept of a "family correspondence" is rather unique in that it offers the audience multiple perspectives into how these related immigrants utilize their letters as a forum for developing a familial reality and identity.
29.   Interestingly enough, Vanderstel documents quite a profitable wooden shoe industry in Grand Rapids, especially the business owned by John Ter Braak. Emigrating from the Netherlands in 1873, Ter Braak opened his own wooden shoe business. By 1888 he was producing nearly 12,000 wooden shoes for farmers and factory workers. His business, The Grand Rapids Wooden Shoe Factory, eventually spread into seventeen states, earning him great fame and fortune. David G. Vanderstel, "Dutch Immigrant Neighborhood Development in Grand Rapids, 1850–1900," in *The Dutch in America: Immigration, Settlement, and Cultural Change*, ed. Robert P. Swierenga (New Brunswick: Rutgers University Press, 1985), 367.
30.   Frouwke was not very different from many other poor women during this time. Patterson found that 30 percent of poor households in this era were headed by widows. James T. Patterson, *America's Struggle Against Poverty, 1900–1980* (Cambridge, Mass.: Harvard University Press, 1981), 8.
31.   Dutch children, male and female, were often expected to turn all of their incomes over to the head of the household. Suzanne Sinke, "Home is

Where You Build It" (Ph.D. diss., University of Minnesota, 1993), 205. In fact, during this period in the Netherlands, according to the law, a young woman's wages were not her own until she reached the age of twenty-five. (ibid., 236). "The family was the most important institution in turn-of-the-century Dutch America, even more important than the church," Sinke writes (78). Often, Dutch immigrants would wait until they had "several teenage children before setting off for America, improving chances for success, assuring chances for wage earners" (116).

32.   Ibid., 105.

33.   Brinks, *Dutch American Voices*, 278.

34.   I say "hegemonic" here to alert students to the very real differences in discursive power and control. They read Foucault as one theoretical screen through which to understand hegemony.

35.   Obviously we should not limit ourselves to Burke, Bitzer, Foucault, and Fisher.

36.   See, for example, H. Arnold Barton, "As They Tell It Themselves: The Testimony of Immigrant Letters," in *Nordics in America: The Future of Their Past*, ed. Odd S. Lovoll (Northfield: Norwegian-American Historical Association, 1993, 138–45; *Letters from the Promised Land: Swedes in America, 1840–1914* (Minneapolis: University of Minnesota Press, 1975); Brian W. Beltman, *Dutch Farmer in the Missouri Valley: The Life and Letters of Ulbe Eringa, 1866–1950* (Chicago: University of Illinois Press, 1996); John W. Blassingame, ed., *Slave Testimony: Two Centuries of Letters, Speeches, Interviews and Autobiographies* (Baton Rouge: Louisiana State Press, 1977); Theodore C. Blegen, ed., *Land of Their Choice: The Immigrants Write Home* (St. Paul: University of Minnesota Press, 1955); Mireille Bossis, "Methodological Journeys Through Correspondences," *Yale French Studies* 71 (1986): 63–75; Herbert Brinks, *Dutch American Voices: Letters from the United States, 1850–1930* (Ithaca: Cornell University Press, 1995); idem, *Write Back Soon: Letters from Immigrants in America* (Grand Rapids: CRC, 1986); Charlotte Erickson, *Invisible Immigrants: The Adaptation of English and Scottish Immigrants in Nineteenth-Century America* (Coral Gables: University of Miami Press, 1972); Lloyd Hustvedt, "Immigrant Letters and Diaries," in *The Prairie Frontier*, ed. Sandra Looney et al. (Sioux Falls: Nordland Heritage Foundation, 1984); Henry S. Lucas, *Dutch Immigrant Memoirs and Related Writings*, rev. ed. (Grand Rapids: William B. Eerdmans, 1997); William I. Thomas, and Florian Znaniecki, *The Polish Peasant in Europe and America* (Chicago: University of Chicago Press, 1918); Jacob Van Hinte, *Netherlanders in America* (Grand Rapids: Baker, 1985).

37.   James Boyd White, *When Words Lose Their Meaning* (Chicago: University of Chicago Press, 1984), 283.

Works Cited

Brinks, Herbert. *Dutch American Voices: Letters from the United States, 1850–1930.* Ithaca: Cornell University Press, 1995.

Burke, Kenneth. *A Rhetoric of Motives.* Berkeley: University of California Press, 1969.

———. *The Philosophy of Literary Form.* Berkeley: University of California Press, 1973.

DeHaan, Kathleen A. "He Looks Like a Yankee in His New Suit." Ph.D. diss. Northwestern University, 1998.

Duncan, Hugh. *Symbols in Society.* New York: Oxford University Press, 1968.

Fisher, Walter. "Clarifying the Narrative Paradigm." *Communication Monographs* 56 (1989): 55–58.

———. "Narration as a Human Communication Paradigm: The Case of Public Moral Argument." *Communication Monographs* 51 (1984): 1–21.

———. "The Narrative Paradigm: In the Beginning." *Journal of Communication* (Autumn 1985): 74–89.

Lucaites, John Louis, and Celeste Michelle Condit. "Re-constructing Narrative Theory: A Functional Perspective." *Journal of Communication* (Autumn 1985): 90–108.

MacIntyre, Alasdair. *After Virtue: A Study in Moral Theory.* Notre Dame: University of Notre Dame Press, 1981.

Mitchell, W. J. T. "Foreword." In *On Narrative*, edited by W. J. T. Mitchell, vii–x. Chicago: University of Chicago Press, 1981.

Moberg, Vilhelm. *The Emigrants.* 1949; trans. 1951 Gustaf Lannestock; rpt. St. Paul: Minnesota Historical Society, 1995.

Patterson, James T. *America's Struggle Against Poverty, 1900-1980.* Cambridge, Mass.: Harvard University Press, 1981.

Ricoeur, Paul. "Narrative Time." In *On Narrative*, edited by W. J. T. Mitchell, 165–86. Chicago: University of Chicago Press, 1981.

Rowland, Robert. "On Limiting the Narrative Paradigm: Three Case Studies." *Communication Monographs* 56 (1989): 39–54.

Schafer, Roy. "Narration in the Psychoanalytic Dialogue." In *On Narrative*, edited by W. J. T. Mitchell, 25–50. Chicago: University of Chicago Press, 1981.

Schutz, Alfred. *Collected Papers II: Studies in Social Theory.* The Hague: Martinus Nijhoff, 1964.

Sinke, Suzanne Marie. "Home Is Where You Build It: Dutch Immigrant Women in the United States, 1880–1920." Ph.D. diss. University of Minnesota, 1993.

Smith, Barbara Harrnstein. "Narrative Versions, Narrative Theories." In *On Narrative*, edited by W. J. T. Mitchell, 209–32. Chicago: University of Chicago Press, 1981.

Trinh, Minh-ha T. *Woman, Native, Other*. Bloomington: Indiana University Press, 1989.

Vanderstel, David G. "The Dutch of Grand Rapids MI., 1848–1900: Immigrant Neighborhood and Community Development in a Nineteenth Century City." Ph.D. diss. Kent State, 1983.

Waldman, Marilyn Robinson. "'The Otherwise Unnoteworthy Year 711': A Reply to Hayden White." In *On Narrative*, edited by W. J. T. Mitchell, 240–48. Chicago: University of Chicago Press, 1981.

White, Hayden. "The Value of Narrativity in the Representation of Reality." In *On Narrative* edited by W. J. T. Mitchell, 1–24. Chicago: University of Chicago Press, 1981.

White, James Boyd. *When Words Lose Their Meaning*. Chicago: University of Chicago Press, 1984.

PART II

Virtual Reality, Real Virtuality

Exploring the Multiple Rhetorics of Cyberspace

Similar to historical accounts of rhetoric, accounts of technologies and technological literacies are never without bias. We hear much about the technological world and its benefits to the individual user of the Internet and the World Wide Web; we also know that technologies are used for political purposes; and, as Philip Elmer-DeWitt has pointed out, corporations and businesses "are scrambling to stake out their own claims in cyberspace" (5). Similarly, many educational institutions are promoting new technologies as a way to increase access to learning, create new ways of approaching knowledge, and enhance students' opportunities in their future careers. However, the widespread focus on technology as the creator of opportunities and change ignores an important aspect of the technological revolution: it is not the machine that creates change but the *user* of the machine who is responsible for how computers and computer software are applied at home or at work. We therefore need to recognize that technological literacy is our responsibility.

This means that we must undertake additional examinations of the ideological systems and cultural formations currently informing the literacy-technology link, and, as Cynthia Selfe argues, we need to make connections to historical patterns established by other literacy technologies. For example, it is important to explore the wide range of technological literacy goals for different populations as well as access issues concerning women of color, poor populations, populations in countries often referred to as "third world." According to Selfe, "the poorer you are and the less educated you are in this country—both of which conditions are correlated with race—the less likely you are to have access to computers and to high-paying, high-tech jobs in the American workplace" (421). As a result, the voices of these populations are often ignored or not represented when writing and arguing about the uses and abuses of new technologies.

To make sure that the needs of these populations are heard, it is important to find out how individuals' perceptions about cyberspace and social, cultural, and political contexts affect the communication that occurs with the help of computer technologies. This part seeks answers to such questions as: How do people from different cultures use the World Wide Web to promote their ideas about politics? How do they call for active participation in volunteer organizations? How do women and minority groups gain access to information technologies? How do they use these technologies to make their voices heard? How can language and alternative uses of language affect the ways in which individuals and groups use the Internet? How can we teach students to be critical of the information presented on the Web? What strategies can help them become aware that the Web, similar to other information sources, needs to be evaluated carefully? The authors of the chapters in the following part attempt to provide a number of perspectives on the effects of new information technologies on our personal and public lives. They examine the uses of technologies in a variety of settings to show the need for an extensive remapping of traditionally conceived cyberspaces.

Works Cited

Elmer-DeWitt, Philip. "Welcome to Cyberspace." *Time,* Spring 1995, 4–11.

Hawisher, Gail E., and Cynthia Selfe. *Global Literacies and the World-Wide Web*. New York: Routledge, 2000.

Selfe, Cynthia L. "Technology and Literacy: A Story About the Perils of Not Paying Attention." *College Composition and Communication* 50, no. 3 (February 1999): 411–37.

4

The Rhetorics of Three Women Activist Groups on the Web

Building and Transforming Communities

SIBYLLE GRUBER

> In order to bring about participatory development communication is imperative.
>
> Oomen, 198

Women activist groups have been at the forefront of political, social, and religious movements for decades. They have used a wide range of rhetorics—some radical and incendiary, others patient and tolerant—to instigate change in their communities. In Argentina, for example, the Mothers of the Plaza de Maya marched for years armed with photographs of missing children and lists of names of those who had disappeared. They used a rhetoric of silent outrage combined with the visual rhetoric of their children's pictures to protest against state-initiated repression. Arab women have started to organize support groups in which they write about their position in a world that prohibits them to speak. Before and during the war in Yugoslavia, "Women in Black" protested against violence in this religiously, ethnically, and culturally diverse country. They have used rhetorics of peace, freedom, and democracy to establish their position against the cruelties of war. Furthermore, women activists in South Africa have used rhetorics of inclusion to fight against apartheid and to gain acceptance in the newly formed government.[1] What these groups have in common is their use of various rhetorical strategies to fight for their rights and to move against passive positions of silence and unquestioning acceptance of discrimination, war, and cruelties to humanity. They have established a communication system that allows them to build a network for themselves and others and to demand attention for their causes. And although they live in different worlds and maintain a "culturally different orientation" (Ross, xvi) toward women's roles in their communities, their efforts to improve women's positions unite otherwise diverse activist groups.

To foreground the struggles of women against patrifocal societies in diverse political and social settings, and to encourage women's communication and communities across cultural, economic, and continental divides, women activists have moved beyond locally organized groups and have started to explore the potentials of the World Wide Web for promoting women's rights issues. Although scholars in Rhetoric and Composition Studies refer to women activist sites from time to time (see Hawisher, Gerrard), they have not yet provided close analyses of the sites themselves. This chapter, then, is a starting point for such explorations. In the following pages, I provide a theoretical foundation for discussing the rhetorics of on-line communities before analyzing the various discourse strategies used in women activists' web sites. I describe how these sites have found alternatives to the rhetorics of war, aggression, and destruction used by the heads of many governments to create participatory on-line communities that discuss very real problems in a virtual space. The success and continued support of these sites, I argue, is based on using rhetorics of peace, equality, cooperation, and empowerment to establish intersections between reality and virtuality, emphasize the global nature of local problems, and create a participatory focus of the sites. I analyze three sites—*Bat Shalom of the Jerusalem Link, Network of East-West Women*, and *UNIFEM: United Nations Development Fund for Women*[2]— to show how different rhetorical strategies are used to embrace similar goals: the promotion of women's rights issues and peaceful interaction in a wide array of political, social, religious, and cultural settings.

The Rhetorics of On-line Communities

"As a woman I have no country. As a woman my country
is the whole world.

—Virginia Woolf

Community, according to Iris Marion Young, "is an understandable dream expressing a desire for selves that are transparent to one another, relationships of mutual identification, social closeness and comfort" (300). This desire for unity and wholeness and the desire to "reconcile the differences of subjects" (308) creates an environment in which behavior can be predicted, belief systems are similar, and knowledge is shared. However, this definition of community as adhering to similar values inevitably creates dichotomies and borders that isolate one community from the other and that exclude those who are unwilling to conform to a group's ideological and political worldviews and who object to or do not understand the rules that govern communication and interaction.

Supporters of virtual communities have argued that cyberspace moves beyond the restrictions of face-to-face communities and creates opportunities for communication that do not exist in "real" space. According to Derek Foster, for example, on-line communities are held together by "the subjective criterion of togetherness, a feeling of connectedness that confers a sense of belonging" (29). Thus, the Web can become an arbiter in recasting "established definitions of national and economic identity and relation" because of its "heterogenous and often contradictory material" (Harpold; see also Kolko, Rheingold).

These positive perspectives about on-line communities, however, are counteracted by those who are skeptical about the Web's function as an arbiter for positive change. Thus, Andrew Shapiro argues that "online associations tend to splinter into narrower and narrower factions" (12), partly because interests change and users can leave one community behind and join another one instead, or because they feel little responsibility for maintaining on-line relationships. The ease with which users can move from one on-line community to the next is not only a positive improvement to the restrictions of local communities; it is at the same time a problem for building strong and lasting communities on-line. In other words, critics warn that the ability to communicate on a more global level does not result in global communities. Furthermore, they claim that the ability to interact on-line rarely results in positive action in "real" communities (Lockard, Healy) and rarely leads to a change in already accepted value systems that divide groups according to culture, religion, politics, class, gender, or ethnicity.

Despite the justified concerns voiced by critics of largely utopian on-line communities, various women activist groups have started to "recast" their positions within larger social movements and are now promoting their issues and goals on-line. In doing so, they do not intend to create a virtual image remote from real causes; instead, they desire to increase their visibility and broaden their appeal to those who would otherwise be restricted by localized borders, barbed wire, and religious or political persecution, while at the same time keeping their local concerns in mind. The *Israel Women's Network*, for example, has created a nonpartisan organization for women who, "while representing a wide range of political opinions and religious outlooks, are nonetheless united in our desire to improve the status of women in Israel" (*IWN*). *The Feminist Majority Foundation Online*, another group that advocates nonviolence and the elimination of social and economic injustice, views feminism as a global movement. They seek "to eliminate discrimination of all kinds—sex, race, sexual orientation, age, religion, national origin, disability, and marital status" (*The Feminist Majority*). Other women organize around their quilting projects and create peace/friendship quilts for people of rival nations to affirm "common humanity" and to take a "tangible step toward understanding and cooperation" (*Boise Peace Quilt Project*). And the on-line group *Frauen (nicht nur) in Oesterreich* provides its readers with information about women's situation in Austria, discusses media representations of women, and provides links to multiple and diverse feminist web sites addressing local and global women's issues (*Frauen*).

These groups, like many other women's activist groups, have established an on-line presence to be heard beyond currently existing borders. Their sense of community arises from their belief in the rights of women, and although they acknowledge widely diverse value systems, their rhetorical choices (unite, improve, eliminate discrimination, common humanity) also emphasize the possibility of maintaining communities that require sensitivity toward and awareness of differences among members. The close analysis of three such groups shows how rhetoric becomes an integral part in providing readers with a sense of community that transcends differences and moves beyond the virtual world to encourage readers to become participants in improving women's positions locally and globally.

Bat Shalom: A Rhetoric of Real and Just Peace

Similar to an informational flyer handed out during a meeting, or a mail package sent out by various organizations, the web spaces created by women activists try to capture their readers' interest by establishing connections between the issues at hand and the audience. For this purpose, many web sites create a visually and aesthetically pleasing layout while at the same time providing information about themselves and the services they offer. Following these principles, *Bat Shalom*'s home page includes a well-organized layout with an introduction to the site and the group's mission statement:

> Bat Shalom is a feminist peace organization of Israeli women. We work toward a just peace between Israel and its Arab neighbors that includes recognition of a Palestinian state side-by-side with Israel and Jerusalem as the capitol of both. . . . As Israeli and Palestinian women of The Jerusalem Link, we work together toward real peace—not merely a treaty of mutual deterrence, but a culture of peace and cooperation between our peoples.[3]

Clearly, members of *Bat Shalom* consider peace between Israelis and Palestinians their primary mission. Interestingly, they reinforce their call for peace by using adjectives such as "just" and "real," implicitly stating that the peace negotiations so far—undertaken by male politicians—have not achieved the desired results. Thus, although efforts have been made to end the war, and peace talks have led to intermittent promises of non-violent coexistence in the region, the rhetorical choices used in *Bat Shalom*'s site show an awareness of different levels of "peace" often absent in current discussions of conflict resolutions. The creators of the site apparently distinguish between "peace" for political and economic gains and "real peace" based in mutual respect, acknowledgment of differences, and human compassion. Furthermore, unlike current rhetoric used by Palestinians, Israelis, and outside forces involved in the negotiations—a rhetoric of largely unyielding authority, power, and domination, as well as a rhetoric that emphasizes winners and losers—*Bat Shalom* articulates an alternative rhetoric of peace through cooperation and mutual recognition of both states.

Implied in the mission statement, then, is the notion that real and just peace can only be achieved if the people living in these regions agree to move beyond notions of mere coexistence or "mutual deterrence": *Bat Shalom* wants to establish a social and political situation where people with different religious and political convictions can cooperate and work with each other. Thus, in addition to a revised rhetoric of peace, *Bat Shalom* also deploys a rhetoric of active political and social change that would profit both Israelis and Palestinians. Unlike those officially involved in the negotiations, *Bat Shalom* moves beyond a politics that only asks citizens to resist violent actions without resisting covert animosities against the Other (implied in "mutual deterrence") who is only tolerated but not accepted. Instead, the group asks for a political agenda that acknowledges the problems but works actively to create an environment where opposing sides can communicate with each other and form alliances based on mutual interests and concerns about similar issues.

Bat Shalom's home page generates a feeling of urgency, partly through the choice of graphics and partly through the choice of words used by the web creators. The picture included on the first page shows women marching in the streets, holding signs that ask for international peace agreements and that promote continued efforts to arrive at a peaceful solution to the current conflict. Implicitly, the picture encourages readers to get involved as well and to help those who struggle for peace and equality. For one, readers of the web page can see that the women involved in the protest move beyond their confined roles as passive onlookers and try to make a difference with their peaceful but dynamic protest. Furthermore, the spirit of community action and mutual support conveyed in the picture provides a strong incentive to join a group that promotes the end of violence and conflict—a goal shared by many women opposed to the slaughtering of their sons, daughters, and husbands.

In addition to the visual implications, *Bat Shalom* uses action words such as "immediate," "join," "help," and "call on women" to expose the need for further action in the peace efforts. Thus, the site encourages readers to help against the demolition of Palestinian homes by writing a letter to government officials. Additionally, a bright yellow background in a flashing text box alerts readers to Barak's election victory and also includes a detailed analysis of women representatives in the Knesset. Its audience, "women and men in the region and elsewhere," is encouraged to move from passive browsing to active participation in the struggle for "real peace." An outside link connects readers with Bat Shalom's coordinating body, *The Jerusalem Link*, which promotes "women's political, social, and cultural activities and leadership in the service of women's rights and the realization of peace on the basis of justice and equality." The rhetoric of peace, justice, and action is thus not only confined to the mission statement but continues into linked pages as well.

To reinforce the importance of personal involvement, the site also includes recent e-mail messages from women concerned with the political situation in Israel, the destruction of homes, the continued murder of Palestinians and Israelis, and economic and psychological warfare. One of the writers points out that it is time to "call upon those who are not army trained—women, children, conscientious objectors, and the elderly who have forgotten their marching orders—to join the negotiating teams" of the new Barak government. In another message, the writer vents her frustrations about the current political situation: "In another life, the three of us [an Israeli woman, a Palestinian woman, and a woman from Geneva] would have been exchanging books and recipes. In this life, we are talking about the imminence of an attack against the beautiful home in whose garden we were sipping coffee." All messages start with the address "Friends," resisting the more traditional rhetorics of authority and hatred so often adopted by Israeli and Palestinian political leaders. Instead, the writers employ rhetorics that emphasize the importance of a supportive community that opposes war, murder, human rights abuses, and political unrest.

The rhetorical strategies used in these messages show that women's issues across different factions are closely related and impossible to separate from larger political and economic issues. Thus, Israeli and Palestinian women have to be concerned about being evicted; they have to worry about losing family and friends in the continued conflict; and they have to fight for economic survival and political representation in the new government. Furthermore, although the situation is serious, the writers suggest alternatives to the current situation—whether it be a new negotiating team or a new attitude toward former "enemies"—to promote peace and friendship in a region that has been at war for decades.

NEWW: A Rhetoric of Sharing and Networking

Cooperation and networking, not political power games, are also the goals of the *Network of East-West Women (NEWW)*. The group's home page provides information on the organization, includes news flashes, and lists grant and job opportunities as well as conferences for the viewers. On the top of the page, *NEWW* offers buttons that link to on-line services, information about and projects by *NEWW*, membership information, publications, and external links. The mission statement is preceded by a graphic that shows two women reaching out toward each other, thus encouraging and promoting peaceful interaction. In addition to the implied message of the image—to communicate and interact with each other—used on the page, the group's web site explicitly encourages women to participate fully in "all aspects of public life." More specifically, they point out in their on-line description of their goals:

> The Network of East-West Women links women across national and regional boundaries to share resources, knowledge, and skills. *NEWW*'s mission is to empower women and girls throughout the East (Central and Eastern Europe, and NIS and the Russian Federation) and the West by dialogue, networking, campaigns, and educational and informational exchanges. *NEWW* supports action and joint projects inspired by feminist principles.

Similar to the women of *Bat Shalom*, the women of *NEWW* promote peaceful interactions that move beyond regional boundaries. Instead of using rhetoric to encourage the launching (or threat thereof) of missiles, the site uses rhetoric to argue for empowerment through dialogue. The group advocates a network that crosses traditional boundaries imposed by different ideological alignments, thus reaching out to people who in the past were unable to communicate with each other. The absence of a rhetoric of aggression and oppression so often found in East-West interactions and the alternative rhetoric of women's empowerment used in this site assumes—and rightly so—that cross-border communication is no longer impossible or prohibited. Instead of focusing on a rhetoric of inequality, which would be quite understandable considering the economic problems in some countries, they use rhetoric to establish an equal relationship in which "sharing" and "exchanging" knowledge, resources, and information is at the forefront. *NEWW*'s approach, then, indicates that economic questions, although they might be important later on, are less pressing than establishing basic relationships of trust and cooperation on which to build future interactions.

In addition to advocating cooperation that is not bound by borders, a quote by Slavenka Drakulic—"democracy without women is no democracy"—

broadens the site's appeal to include politics in their mission. Drakulic's quote establishes a belief in the equality of women and the necessity of including women in political changes and discussions. Once again, women are seen as an integral part of the political, economic, and social well-being of the country. Such rhetorics of democratic politics have only recently been introduced to former communist countries, where much of the traditional rhetoric is still mired in firmly established power games. Similarly, Western countries play political games based in authoritarian and patriarchal discourse by deciding which of the former East bloc countries is politically and economically worthy of acceptance into the European Community. *NEWW*'s on-line site, on the other hand, advocates "tolerance, democracy, non-violence, health and respect for the institutions of a civil society." Like *Bat Shalom*, *NEWW* moves away from a rhetoric of violence and aggression and instead supports an alternative rhetoric of cooperation and tolerance.

Moving to *NEWW*'s Information and Projects link, the web designers reiterate the mission statement and also include a detailed outline of principles. For example, they include women's rights to "equal participation in the creation of a just and inclusive civil society" as well as their right to "be free of violence in the private and public sphere" and to "be free of racial and ethnic hatred." Furthermore, they point out that "while *NEWW* primarily supports women's projects and activism, its long-range interest is in changing what gender means and how it functions in society." The focus here is not on women's issues as abstract concepts but on how women and gender issues can be addressed in a larger context. With this, *NEWW* is in accord with scholars who question the concept of gender as an essentialist trait and are interested in the intersections of gender, race, class, and politics (see, e.g., Flax, Hourigan, Houston, hooks, Anzaldúa). In addition, by contextualizing gender issues and focusing on how gender "functions in society," *NEWW* emphasizes its primary concern with the real, everyday lives of women. Similar to *Bat Shalom*, the virtual space in which the web site presides is only a means to promote very real issues and goals to a larger number of women. As the rhetorical choices suggest, *NEWW* is concerned with creating virtual and real environments in which women can meet, cooperate, and build a democratic society.

In addition to addressing more general concerns faced by women in different European countries, *NEWW* specifically addresses how the war in Kosova influences women and children in this region. To bring home the immediacy of the problem, the web site includes a link to pictures of protesters, victims, survivors, and displaced people. For example, one picture shows women protesters outside a small village facing an expressionless police/military force in the streets. Others show women and children in refugee camps and hospitals, their faces and bodies marked by wounds inflicted by guns and snipers. Pictures also include destroyed homes and villages with live-stock dead on the ground, and people living in tents after their homes were demolished. These pictures reiterate the cruelty of the war and the senseless devastation and destruction of people's lives.

In addition to the pictures, *NEWW* also includes a link to commentary about the war in Kosova "as reported by women in the region." The stories included come from Prishtina, Kosova, from Belgrade, Serbia, and from Zagreb, Croatia. Independent women journalists write about the missiles in Kosova, they report on a fifteen-year-old girl who is beaten and raped, women and children in hiding, and massacres taking place in the area. The horrors of war and the violence done to all segments of the population are part of each entry. One journalist reports on the murder of a six-year-old girl who "was sitting in her room when the bullet killed her. She was killed because of being someone's daughter, because of being part of a certain back-ground, in conflict with Serbs." Another one writes about the women who are trying to help the refugees: "They are working under incredible condi-tions, . . . living with pain of being expelled by force, pain of humiliation, individual and collective, and with fantastic energy and hope for the future."

The nonpartisan approach to reporting on this web site—stories included are from Kosova, Serbia, and Croatia—encourages women from a war-torn country to look beyond easy religious, political, and cultural distinctions. The similarities in the stories and the focus on unnecessary suffering of civil-ians, women, and children create a new perspective on the futility of war. In addition, the personal narratives and the emotional involvement of the women journalists provide an account of the war that is largely missing from mainstream media. We no longer hear only a rhetoric of victory or loss based on political considerations; instead, the cruelty and inhumanity of war are apparent in the pictures of the war-torn country and the reporters' com-ments, creating an even greater aversion to the horrors of war. However, the rhetoric of despair is interlaced with a rhetoric of hope that acknowledges women's strength, their cooperation, and their willingness to help despite the dangerous circumstances under which they work.

UNIFEM: A Rhetoric of Global Change and Empowerment

The third web site, *UNIFEM: United Nations Development Fund for Women,* asserts its legitimacy and its potential authority by placing itself within the larger framework of the United Nations. It continues the call for women's participation in economic and political arenas addressed by *Bat Shalom* and *NEWW*:

UNIFEM promotes women's empowerment and gender equality. It works to ensure the participation of women in all levels of development planning and practice, and acts as a catalyst within the UN system, supporting efforts that link the needs and concerns of women to all critical issues on the national, regional and global agendas.

According to the mission statement, *UNIFEM* is concerned with the welfare of all women. Unlike *Bat Shalom* and *NEWW*, who focus on local concerns by addressing a local as well as a global audience, *UNIFEM* appeals to a global audience by foregrounding global concerns. Although its emphasis is on larger issues such as a "Global Campaign to End Violence against Women," it also points out that this campaign grew out of regional efforts, thus providing a specific context for activist campaigns. As a result, *UNIFEM* alerts readers that it is specifically interested in encouraging women to participate in local *and* global decision-making processes. Even more forcefully, it considers itself a "catalyst" within an established system that has not always taken women's issues seriously in the past. Furthermore, the group makes it clear that women's concerns cannot be isolated but need to be seen in relation to "all critical issues," again emphasizing the connections between "women's issues" and largely "human issues" that influence the position of women in all areas of life. The rhetoric of inclusiveness used by *UNIFEM* establishes the group's concerns with the underlying economic, political, cultural, or religious reasons for women's unequal position in regional and global settings. Furthermore, *UNIFEM*'s stance expresses the need to uproot "dualistic thinking" and to "heal the split" that keeps women's issues separate from other issues (Anzaldúa 80). *UNIFEM's* rhetoric, similar to the rhetoric used by Gloria Anzaldúa, emphasizes connections and crossroads instead of unnecessary borders and divisions.

UNIFEM's home page presents a mixture of asking viewers for active participation and of providing information about a variety of issues. The title of the page includes a picture of a white dove. This is followed by links to "new features" and "news events." Similar to *NEWW*'s top bar, *UNIFEM*'s sidebar provides links to more information about the organization and about women's rights issues. Graphics in the center of the page are complemented by short descriptions of newsworthy items such as the Hague Appeal for Peace 1999 and women's efforts to increase economic empowerment. The links, short summaries of current events, and graphics promote further browsing. Viewers are also encouraged to participate and "join" a virtual working group promoting the end of violence against women. In addition, they can link to information about three global campaign efforts against violence launched by *UNIFEM*.

Viewers' attention to *UNIFEM* is not only captured through the printed word, but also through the visual representations embedded in the page.

One of the graphics, for example, portrays two women under the inscription "A life free of violence: It's our right." Here, women are implicitly urged to protest against and eliminate violence in their own lives. Furthermore, using "our" instead of "everybody's" reinforces the personal involvement and the potential for violence not just in other women's lives but in *each* woman's life. *UNIFEM*'s rhetorical choice additionally affirms "our rights," thus indicating that previous rhetoric of a woman's *privilege* to live in a nonviolent situation is outdated and needs to be reconsidered not only in private situations but also in the public sphere.

UNIFEM's linked pages provide a wide variety of information on violence against women, women's equal rights, and women's equal representation in local and global politics. Their page "About *UNIFEM*" includes a paragraph written by Noeleen Heyzer, director of *UNIFEM*: "It is not acceptable for Women to constitute 70 percent of the world's 1.3 billion absolute poor. Nor is it acceptable for women to work two-thirds of the world's working hours, but earn only one tenth of the world's income and own less than one-tenth of the world's property. Many fundamental changes must be made." Although Heyzer does not use the first person in this paragraph, the emotional appeal to her audience is clearly in the forefront. In addition to the depressing statistical evidence cited in this paragraph, Heyzer's final comment—"many fundamental changes must be made"—establishes the urgency of the appeal for equal rights of women. And although she doesn't address a specific political or economic body responsible for women's disproportionate poverty, readers can assume that those changes need to be made at all levels, be they governmental, political, economic, or cultural. Furthermore, Heyzer's affirmative tone expressed in words such as "must" and phrases such as "it is not acceptable" does not leave room for what has traditionally been termed "women's rhetoric" of hedges, conditionals, and tentativeness (see Fishman, Henley, Kraemerae and Treichler). As an alternative, Heyzer uses discourse strategies that have largely been attributed to men—assertive, authoritative, precise, and to the point—to firmly point out the need for change and action to improve women's economic situation.

UNIFEM's effectiveness in promoting women's issues is the rhetoric of active involvement in local and global issues, the rhetoric of empowerment that encourages women to take on unjust situations at home and on a broader scale, and the rhetoric of openness that allows interested women to participate in a virtual working group. In this group, women can voice their concerns and opinions about violence based on religious extremism, crisis centers for women, or the rape of Chinese women in Indonesia. Again, similar to the mailing lists used by *Bat Shalom* and *NEWW*, *UNIFEM*'s list asks women to speak up, voice their concerns, and promote change in local and global arenas. Rhetoric once again becomes a means to break silence and promote women's issues in a virtual world inhabited by real people with real concerns.

Silent No More

At the end of the twentieth century and the beginning of the twenty-first century, women's groups have broadened their readership and their support through providing information about women's issues on the Web and enlisting support from a constituency that is no longer restricted by artificial borders. Despite concerns about virtual communities raised by Healy, Lockard, and Shapiro, many women activist groups explore the World Wide Web as a venue for distributing information, asking for on-line and off-line participation, and promoting local and global involvement with women's issues.

Through their web sites, *Bat Shalom, NEWW,* and *UNIFEM* encourage women to become visible and to give voice to their concerns. They apprise readers of current events, ask for participation, and offer help on a wide range of issues. For example, *UNIFEM* informs its readers of violations against women's rights and asks for help in eradicating violence against women. Furthermore, by presenting information about the situation of women in Israel, Palestine, Kosovo, Croatia, Indonesia, and other countries, these groups raise awareness about women's political, religious, and cultural oppression that might otherwise be ignored.

In addition to providing important information, all three sites encourage women to participate in improving the situation of women at home and around the world. They provide opportunities for local members to contact their organizations, participate in marches, or write letters to officials. They also encourage virtual participation on discussion lists that bring together women from diverse backgrounds and diverse geographic locations. The high amount of participation in the on-line discussions shows a definite need for on-line communities that value the experiences and voices of women in many different locations. Furthermore, the sites offer help to those who need further information on other organizations, who need to locate resources, and who need funding for individual or group projects. And readers are encouraged to help by participating in local events or by donating money, clothing, or food to those in need of help.

In all areas, the rhetorical strategies used reflect the longing for peaceful interactions on all political, economic, and social levels. *Bat Shalom, NEWW,* and *UNIFEM* use alternative rhetorics of peace, cooperation, equality, and empowerment to help women and to encourage them to participate in their own local causes; they also use rhetoric considered traditional and largely male-dominated—assertive, authoritative, precise—to achieve alternative goals such as women's equal presentation in local and global economic and political endeavors.

The success of these on-line sites can be attributed to a number of factors. First, the virtual spaces created by the activist groups studied in this essay and the virtual audience and participants in the on-line exchanges are not separate from the issues and concerns addressed by off-line communities. Their on-line presence is only an extension of already existing off-line communities, thus creating a partnership between off-line and on-line worlds. Second, although the groups appeal to a global audience, many of the issues they address are anchored in local politics and local economic situations. And although *UNIFEM* focuses on global issues, it too stresses the importance of looking at the context in which women's oppression takes place. All three sites encourage readers to participate in specific goals set by each group—to lobby for peaceful interactions between Israelis and Palestinians, to strengthen the connections between East and West women in Europe, and to promote women's equality in political and economic situations on a local and global level. Third, the issues addressed are not part of a virtual world but they are "real" issues that influence women's everyday lives, such as violence, poverty, and other forms of oppression. Fourth, all three sites encourage participation online through discussion groups, and offline through getting involved with specific women's issues. Again, the combination of online interactions and offline activities promotes the connections between virtual worlds and real lives. Finally, the sites create a sense of community through their rhetorical strategies, many of which can be considered an alternative to current rhetorics of domination and authoritarianism. And even if the rhetoric used is "traditional" in its tone, it is used for alternative reasons—to create a world that defies war, oppression, and hate.

Notes

1.   For a detailed analysis of these groups of women, see Anderson 1993; Cooke 1993; Hughes 1999; and Seidman 1999.

2.   The sites discussed in this chapter were accessed in July 1999. Changes made to the sites since then are not part of the discussion in this chapter.

3.   All excerpts, if not otherwise stated, refer to the web site discussed in the particular section.

Works Cited

Anderson, Teresa. "The Whirlwind and the Spiral: State-Sponsored Terror and Psychic Resistance in Marta Traba's *Mothers and Shadows*." In *To Speak or Be Silent: The Paradox of Disobedience in the Lives of Women*, edited by Lena B. Ross, 120–29. Wilmette, Ill.: Chiron, 1993.

Anzaldúa, Gloria. *Borderlands/La Frontera: The New Mestiza.* San Francisco: Aunt Lute, 1987.

Bat Shalom of the Jerusalem Link. <http://www.batshalom.org> [July 1999].

Boise Peace Quilt Project. <http://www.peacequilt.org> [July 1999].

Bunch, Charlotte. *Through Women's Eyes: Global Forces Facing Women in the 21st Century.* <http://www.feminist.com/center.htm>. [June 1999], 1995.

Cooke, Miriam. "Apple, Nabila, and Ramza: Arab Women's Narratives of Resistance." In *To Speak or Be Silent: The Paradox of Disobedience in the Lives of Women*, edited by Lena B. Ross, 85–96. Wilmette, Ill.: Chiron, 1993.

Fishman, Pamela M. "Interaction: The Work Women Do." In *Language, Gender, and Society*, edited by Barrie Thorne, Cheris Kramarae, and Nancy Henley, 89–102. Rowley, MA: Newbury House Publishers, 1983.

Flax, Jane. "Postmodernism and Gender Relations in Feminist Theory." In *Feminism/Postmodernism*, edited by Linda J. Nicholson, 39–62. New York: Routledge, 1990.

Foster, Derek. "Community and Identity in the Electronic Village." In *Internet Culture*, edited by David Porter, 23–37. New York: Routledge, 1997.

Frauen (nicht nur) in Oesterreich. <http://www.tirol.com/women/women.html> [July 1999].

Gerrard, Lisa. "Gender, Culture, and the Internet." Paper presented at the Conference on College Composition and Communication. Phoenix, Ariz., 1997.

Harpold, Terry. "Dark Continents: A Critique of Internet Metageographies." *Postmodern Culture* 9, no. 2. <http://www.iath.virginia.edu/pmc/text-only/issue.199/9.2harpold.txt>. [June 1999).

Hawisher, Gail E. "Feminist Transgressions on the World Wide Web: International Connections." Paper presented at the Conference of Rhetoric and Composition: Multiple Literacies for the 21st Century, October 1998, University of Louisville, Louisville, KY.

Healy, Dave. "Cyberspace and Place: The Internet as Middle Landscape on the Electronic Frontier." In *Internet Culture*, edited by David Porter, 55–68. New York: Routledge, 1996.

Henley, Nancy. "Power, Sex, and Nonverbal Communication." In *Language and Sex: Difference and Dominance*, edited by Barrie Thorne and Nancy Henley, 185–203. Rowley, Mass.: Newbury, 1975.

Hourigan, Maureen M. *Literacy as Social Exchange: Intersections of Class, Gender, and Culture.* Albany, NY: State University of New York Press, 1994.

Houston, Marsha. "The Politics of Difference: Race, Class, and Women's Communication." In *Women Making Meaning: New Feminist Direc-*

tions in Communication, edited by Lana F. Rakow, 45–59. New York: Routledge, 1992.

Hughes, Donna. "Women in Black Against the War in Yugoslavia." *Feminista* 3, no. 1. <http://www.feminist.com/v3n1/hughes.htm> [June 1999]

Israel Women's Network. <http://www.iwn.org/index.html> [July 1999].

Kramarae, Cheris, and Paula Treichler. "Power Relations in the Classroom." In *Gender in the Classroom: Power and Pedagogy,* edited by Susan L. Gabriel and Isaiah Smithson, 41–59. Urbana: University of Illinois Press, 1990.

Kolko, Beth E. "We Are Not Just (Electronic) Words: Learning the Literacies of Culture, Body and Politics." In *Literacy Theory in the Age of the Internet,* edited by Todd Taylor and Irene Ward, 61–78. New York: Columbia University Press, 1998.

Lockard, Joseph. "Progressive Politics, Electronic Individualism and the Myth of Virtual Community." In *Internet Culture,* edited by David Porter, 219–31. New York: Routledge, 1996.

Lorde, Audre. "Age, Race, Class, and Sex: Women Redefining Difference." In *Out There: Marginalization and Contemporary Cultures,* edited by Russell Ferguson, Martha Gever, Trinh T. Minh-ha, and Cornel West, 281–87. Cambridge, Mass.: MIT Press, 1990.

Mohanty, Chandra Talpade. "Under Western Eyes: Feminist Scholarship and Colonial Discourses." In *Third World Women & the Politics of Feminism,* edited by Chandra Talpade Mohanty, Ann Russo, and Lourdes Torres, 51–80. Bloomington: Indiana Univeristy Press, 1991.

Network of East-West Women. <http://www.neww.org./> [July 1999].

Rheingold, Howard. *The Virtual Community: Homesteading on the Electronic Frontier.* Reading, MA: Addison-Wesley, 1993.

Ross, Lena B. "Introduction." In *To Speak or Be Silent: The Paradox of Disobedience in the Lives of Women,* edited by Lena B. Ross, xi–xxiv. Wilmette, Ill: Chiron, 1993.

Roy, Manisha. "Women Who Disobey: Examples from India." In *To Speak or Be Silent: The Paradox of Disobedience in the Lives of Women,* edited by Lena B. Ross, 111–19. Wilmette, Ill.: Chiron, 1993.

Seidman, Gay W. "Gendered Citizenship: South Africa's Democratic Transition and the Construction of a Gendered State." *Gender and Society* 13 (1999): 287–307.

Shapiro, Andrew L. "Street Corners in Cyberspace." *The Nation* (July 3, 1995): 10–14.

The Feminist Majority Foundation Online. <http://www.feminist.org>. [July 1999].

Unifem: United Nations Development Fund for Women. <http://www.unifem.undp.org/index.htm> [July 1999].

Gruber

Walker, Alice. *In Search of Our Mothers' Gardens.* New York: Harcourt, 1983.
Young, Iris Marion. "The Ideal of Community and the Politics of Difference." In *Feminism/Postmodernism,* edited by Linda J. Nicholson, 300–23. New York: Routledge, 1990.

5

Authority and Credibility

Classical Rhetoric, the Internet, and the Teaching of Techno-Ethos

THERESA ENOS AND SHANE BORROWMAN

Introduction: The Internet, Credibility, and Authority

When teachers of rhetoric and composition discuss the use of on-line sources in undergraduate writing, the moment is always over-determined. Sides are taken. Extreme statements are often made: "My students all use the Internet in their research" versus "I ban the use of on-line sources in my classes." As with the debates over the value of television and its place in American culture that raged during the 1950s, the debates over the Internet can be plotted along a continuum of good versus bad. In this chapter we explore a third "point" on this continuum, one outside the reductive binary that begins with bad and works toward good.

Concern over questions of authorship and authority on the Internet develops out of a key concept in the traditionally defined history of rhetoric: ethos. Because the Internet is a virtual agora in which any rhetor with a small amount of technological know-how and in possession of minimal hardware can make her or his voice heard, our preoccupation with this new technology turns, very naturally, to questions of credibility and authority—to classical notions of ethos.

To elaborate on ethos as a "third alternative" in the debates over virtual credibility and authority, we have divided this work into three main areas. In the introduction we paint, in broad strokes, the current professional concern many of us in rhetoric and composition have over the use of information resources that reside in cyberspace. In our second section, we briefly elaborate on the definition of ethos with which we are working. In our third section, we turn to examples; specifically, we focus our analysis on an extreme case to illustrate contemporary fears over credibility and the Internet: Holocaust denial. To conclude, we turn to pedagogy and personal experience. Before we discuss ethos and hate speech on the Internet, however, we consider the *MLA Handbook* and a recent study on student use of on-line materials.

In 1995 the *MLA Handbook* first acknowledged the use of on-line sources such as e-mail in research papers. Students were given advice about joining moderated discussions and searching various databases such as ERIC. While the electronic texts were being described, however, a brief word of caution was offered: "[R]emember that not all texts are equally reliable or authoritative" (166). This statement was never elaborated, and students looking for more information were simply referred to sections on "scholarly editions." Four years later, the *Handbook* devotes considerably larger space to its discussion of on-line materials.

In the fifth edition of the *MLA Handbook*, the section on on-line sources opens with the statement that "researchers regularly use facts and ideas from Internet sources to complement those derived from traditional sources" (20). The infinitive around which this sentence revolves is indicative of the growing concern over credibility on-line: researchers do *real* research to advance their arguments and only use on-line sources *to complement* those other, more traditional, sources. Later in the *Handbook*, students are warned to be wary of Internet sources if they are browsing "without professional guidance" and cautioned that "few [instructors] consider a search of the World Wide Web alone adequate research for a paper" (21, 22). Some on-line sources, such as e-mail from listservs, simply "are not deemed acceptable resources for research papers" (22). The point of this entire section is clear: nonprint sources are suspect, and students use them at their own risk.

As teachers, we understand the concerns over credibility and authority that form the foundation for these pronouncements by the MLA. Our students, however, may not. For many of them, the Internet truly is the global source of information, and teachers' concerns are based on outdated respect for the world-of-the-book and fears of the new medium. Many students surf the Internet for sources, paying little attention to matters of credibility and authority, and it is often difficult for them to realize that in cyberspace not all sources are created equal. To mediate between our concerns over on-line sources and our students' affinity for such sources, we have found an analysis of the creation of techno-ethos particularly effective. As one student said during a conference in the spring of 1997, "Techno-ethos means looking at the Web to see if you're dealing with Grandma or the Wolf." But this savvy awareness of the creation of on-line credibility is the exception rather than the norm, as a recent study by Mary Ann Gillette and Carol Videon shows.

In their study dealing with student use of on-line sources, entitled "Seeking Quality on the Internet," Gillette and Videon touch on a series of issues that are at the heart of contemporary concerns over the use of the Internet, particularly when reliable information (that "god" term of the twentieth century) is sought. Gillette and Videon identify two key problems that exist on the Internet and not in the traditional textual world: (1) sources on the Internet appear and disappear at a webmaster's whim; (2) and sources on the Internet are either without apparent authors—they are simply lone voices speaking in the electronic wilderness—or the author who is identified has few (if any) verifiable cues to associate him or her with the topic in which expertise is being professed (or conferred by an unwitting audience).

The first of these concerns focuses on the nature of this new medium, for cyberspace is far more transitory in nature than is the printed world of the popular press and professional book/article. The second concern we have identified in Gillette and Videon's study, that of authorship, is far more problematic than the first. The Internet does not have the controls placed on it that traditional media, such as television and print, do. In such an open forum, traditional notions of authorship and ethos are challenged. And when there is a challenge, the temptation is to retreat into tradition, into the comfortable world of the known-and-familiar. As Cynthia Selfe writes, "We are much more used to dealing with older technologies like print, a technology conventional enough so that we don't have to think so much about it" (413). This echoes the statement from the *MLA Handbook* with which we began and is well illustrated by the example of student research: when students do research that involves books and articles, the rules are understood; if something comes into print from a university press or other respectable publisher, it can be afforded a certain amount of credibility.

On the Internet this is simply not the case. Anyone can be a published writer, and ethos can be constructed in any number of ways. Writing about *actio* in relation to the field of composition, Robert Connors comments that "by presenting the reader with a legible, neat, pleasing manuscript, the writer is creating an image of herself for that reader, an image that can support or sabotage her message" (64–65). Connors analyzes the ethos construction that takes place *on* the typed page, as font and margin sizes are manipulated by the writer. On the Internet, even more manipulation is possible. Credibility that has not been earned in the traditional senses of education, publication, or experience can be created from nothing—constructed through a few keystrokes in a setting wherein the checking of credentials is difficult at best. In fact, as we argue later, in an updated and expanded echo of Connors's work, credibility can be created quite handily through the manipulation of graphics, colors, and other on-line cues.

To discuss these issues of authority and credibility with our students, we have found it useful to begin with a brief discussion of Aristotle, Cicero, and

Quintilian and their notions of ethos. With this beginning, it becomes easier to move students into a critical awareness of the importance of ethos in cyberspace and in their own writing—a critical awareness that goes beyond the shallow and reductive binary of Internet Good versus Internet Bad.

Classical Definitions of Ethos Meet the Internet

The struggle over the concept of ethos, as we have identified it, has two components: credibility and character. For Aristotle credibility represents that conception of a speaker that a rhetor crafts during the speech act itself; it is a belief in the wisdom of the rhetor that is encouraged in the audience by the rhetor. Credibility, then, is a construct wherein a rhetor's authority to speak on various matters rests. In classical rhetoric, however, it was a given that a rhetor with no credibility would ultimately reveal himself or herself. Quintilian, echoing Aristotle's ideas about credibility and ethos, writes, "for however we strive to conceal it, insincerity will always betray itself" (cited in Corder, 3). The evil person, even if he or she is speaking well, will supposedly always be revealed and discredited in the rhetorical systems represented here, rhetorical systems aimed at producing, according to Quintilian, "the perfect orator, who cannot exist unless he is above all a good man" (6). Thus credibility is inextricably bound to good character—not merely to the *appearance* of goodness.

On the Internet credibility can be falsified easily—and only discredited occasionally. As Gillette and Videon found in their study, the students whose on-line sources were examined often cited other students as authorities. Like the gentle padding that sometimes fills out a hollow vita, credentials, publications, volunteer work, and so on, can all be falsified or exaggerated. Research into claims made by writers on-line is simply not always possible, especially for students who may be working under the exigency of a rapidly approaching deadline. The night before an assignment is due, claims to credibility by on-line writers are likely to go unexamined—despite the warnings of instructors, librarians, and handbooks.

The second component of this struggle for meaning within the term "ethos" is character. Concerns about character are not foregrounded in Aristotle's *Rhetoric* (although, as Eugene Garver argues in *Aristotle's Rhetoric: An Art of Character*, the *Rhetoric* is, in fact, a philosophical work whose central concern is the creation and maintenance of a virtuous character). In the *Nicomachean Ethics*, Aristotle makes the link between virtue and ethos much more explicit: "Virtue of character [i.e., of ethos] results from habit . . . hence its name 'ethical'" (2.2.1). In Aristotle's system the speaker attains ethos through ethical habits, through being the type of good person by whom an audience can be persuaded. But the speaker can effectively use ethos only by practicing the virtuous habits that lead one to develop good character: "Virtue comes about, not by a process of nature, but by habituation" (2.2.1). Thus ethos, although it is crafted and conveyed through the speech act, must also reflect the good character of the speaker. Character, then, is more than a construct; it is a reflection of a rhetor's virtue that can only be built through good habits. But, as Cicero points out, character, like credibility, can be falsified (although it is easier to exaggerate than to simply fabricate positive character attributes): "Now feelings are won over by a man's merit, achievements or reputable life, qualifications easier to embellish, if only they are real, than to fabricate where nonexistent" (182). Again, these classical notions about the innate persuasion of strong ethical character are challenged on the Internet.

On-line, credibility can be constructed in numerous ways, and web surfers are left on their own to decide if information is being presented by someone who is of good character. To illustrate the struggle over these conflicting views of ethos, we turn to cyberspace. Specifically, we have drawn our examples of ethos construction on the Internet from the camp of Holocaust deniers. We have found Holocaust denial a useful example for two reasons. (1) Students are fascinated by this credible-looking genre of hate speech. It is the intellectual equivalent of a terrible car accident, and students are compelled to give it their attention. (2) At the same time that students are drawn to Holocaust denial, however, they intuitively understand its illegitimacy. They understand that it is scholarship driven by bigotry and are thus able to examine it from a more objective distance than other issues (such as gun control, abortion, or euthanasia—the trinity of first-year composition—issues about which nearly every student has an unwavering, unshakable opinion).

Holocaust Denial: Traditional Ethos, Techno-Ethos

Before we bring our examples into the foreground, a few comments about the phenomenon of Holocaust denial are in order. First, Holocaust denial is a blanket term that refers to a wide range of beliefs. At one end of the spectrum are groups/individuals who argue that the entire Holocaust (the systematic extermination of millions of European Jews, homosexuals, gypsies, Communists, etc.) is a lie, a story told to, among other things, justify American support for Israel. Moving back from this extreme are groups that question the received history of the Holocaust. They argue such positions as "four million Jews were killed rather than six million" and "Hitler himself had little or no knowledge of the Final Solution." For our purposes here, all such groups fall under the umbrella of Holocaust denial, although none of the individuals/groups we examine here choose to label themselves in this way.

The first Holocaust denier on whom we have chosen to focus is Arthur Butz, probably the most famous denier in America. Before we examine his ethos construction on the Internet, however, we consider the way in which he constructs himself in the print medium, for he relies heavily on traditional means of ethos construction in American popular culture and academia when he enters cyberspace.

In the introduction to his book *The Hoax of the Twentieth Century: The Case against the Presumed Extermination of European Jewry*, Butz takes careful steps to construct his credibility and hint at his virtuous character. Justifying his exploration of Holocaust history, for example, and specifically dealing with the charge that he is an electrical engineer and not a historian, Butz writes,

> There will be those who will say that I am not qualified to undertake such a work [of historical revisionism] and there will even be those who will say that I have no right to publish such things. So be it. If a scholar, regardless of his specialty, perceives that scholarship is acquiescing, from whatever motivation, in a monstrous lie, then it is his duty to expose the lie, whatever his qualifications. (8)

In this passage Butz makes two very important rhetorical moves: he builds his character by constructing himself as a martyr, a man persecuted for his unorthodox beliefs, and he establishes his credibility as an academic, a "scholar" engaged in a Platonic search for the Truth about the Holocaust *lie*. Butz portrays himself as a good man, one facing an uphill battle against the prejudices and ignorance of others but determined to succeed regardless. It is traditional, classical ethos construction. On the Internet, Butz relies on the same tactic.

Butz's web site is, at the time of this writing (1999), three years old (see figure 1). In the three years that we have observed it, little has changed. Butz begins by stating his credentials and naming his place of employment. He notes that the site is copyrighted. He then states, "I am the author of the book *The Hoax of the Twentieth Century* (1976), a work of 'Holocaust revisionism.'" The ethos construction is clear and unambiguous. Butz wants his audience to know that he is an associate professor at a major institution and the author of a monograph on the Holocaust. He also writes that "the initial aim of this site . . . is to present my article *A short introduction to the study of Holocaust revisionism*, published in 1991 in the *Daily Northwestern*, with supplementing commentary and documentation." Again, Butz identifies himself as a published author, which generally establishes him as a

Figure 1

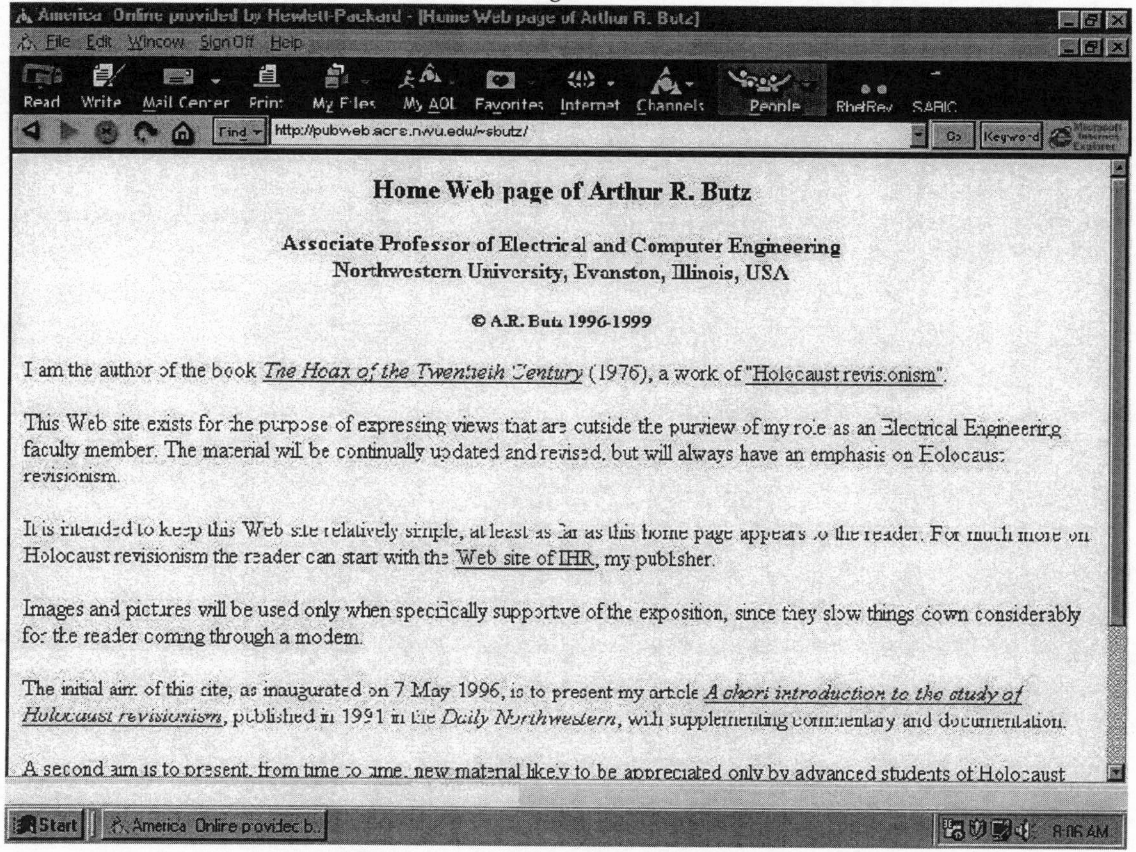
America Online provided by Hewlett-Packard - [Home Web page of Arthur R. Butz]
File Edit Window Sign Off Help
Read Write Mail Center Print My Files My AOL Favorites Internet Channels People RhetRev SABIC
Find
http://pubweb.acns.nwu.edu/~abutz/
Go Keyword
Home Web page of Arthur R. Butz
Associate Professor of Electrical and Computer Engineering
Northwestern University, Evanston, Illinois, USA
© A.R. Butz 1996-1999
I am the author of the book The Hoax of the Twentieth Century (1976), a work of "Holocaust revisionism".
This Web site exists for the purpose of expressing views that are outside the purview of my role as an Electrical Engineering faculty member. The material will be continually updated and revised, but will always have an emphasis on Holocaust revisionism.
It is intended to keep this Web site relatively simple, at least as far as this home page appears to the reader. For much more on Holocaust revisionism the reader can start with the Web site of IHR, my publisher.
Images and pictures will be used only when specifically supportive of the exposition, since they slow things down considerably for the reader coming through a modem.
The initial aim of this site, as inaugurated on 7 May 1996, is to present my article A short introduction to the study of Holocaust revisionism, published in 1991 in the Daily Northwestern, with supplementing commentary and documentation.
A second aim is to present, from time to time, new material likely to be appreciated only by advanced students of Holocaust
Start
America Online provided b...
8:06 AM

credible source in the eyes of students. Through such means he hopes to persuade his audience that he is a man to whom people should listen—and in whom they can believe.

Elaborating on the creation and maintenance of Butz's ethos, Deborah Lipstadt writes, "Butz's position as a professor at one of the more prestigious universities in the country enhanced the sense of controversy [that his book generated]. It was hard for the public to reconcile Holocaust denial with the pursuit of truth to which universities and their faculty are supposedly dedicated" (123). Butz—in his book and on his web site—possesses the outward markers of credibility; his posture as a martyred academic hints at his virtuous character. Thus his ethos is constructed in traditional ways. The fact that his argument is hollow at its core does not even enter the discussion at this point, for Butz appears, to most audiences, to possess and deploy an effective ethos both on and off the Internet.

The Institute for Historical Review (IHR) is a group of deniers with which Butz is loosely connected; the IHR is, in fact, the publisher of his book. Like Butz, the IHR constructs its ethos in traditional ways. Beneath the title of its web site (see figure 2), the IHR displays its motto: "Bringing history into accord with the facts." Like Butz's statements about scholars exposing lies, this line hints that the IHR is a group concerned with truth. Thus their scholarly credibility is established.

After a quick list of topics on which members of the IHR have written, many dealing with Holocaust denial in one form or another, the IHR bluntly states that "the Institute for Historical Review is non-ideological, non-religious, and non-political." In this list of negatives, the IHR attempts to establish its unbiased character. The group is, it seems, above the petty squabbles of the material world—squabbles over political, moral, and social beliefs. Like Butz, the Institute is concerned only with the "facts" that fail to support the commonly taught history of the Holocaust.

Butz's web site is rather simple and unadorned; it contains a main page and several related pages. The IHR's site, on the other hand, is much more extravagant, but it is equally inelegant. Screen after screen of text is present. The only variation that breaks the monotony (at the time of this writing) is the size of the text, along with the use of boldface, italics, and underlining. Both sites are, then, simply conceived of as extensions of print-based ethos construction. Butz relies on his credentials, his twenty-three-year-old book, and his eight-year-old article. The IHR relies on its extensive collection of articles, pamphlets, and other scholarly looking works of Holocaust denial. Aside from the use of hyperlinks, neither site takes advantage of the technology available on the Internet. Other deniers do use the Internet to its fullest capabilities while constructing their ethos, though, and it is to one of these groups that we now turn.

Figure 2

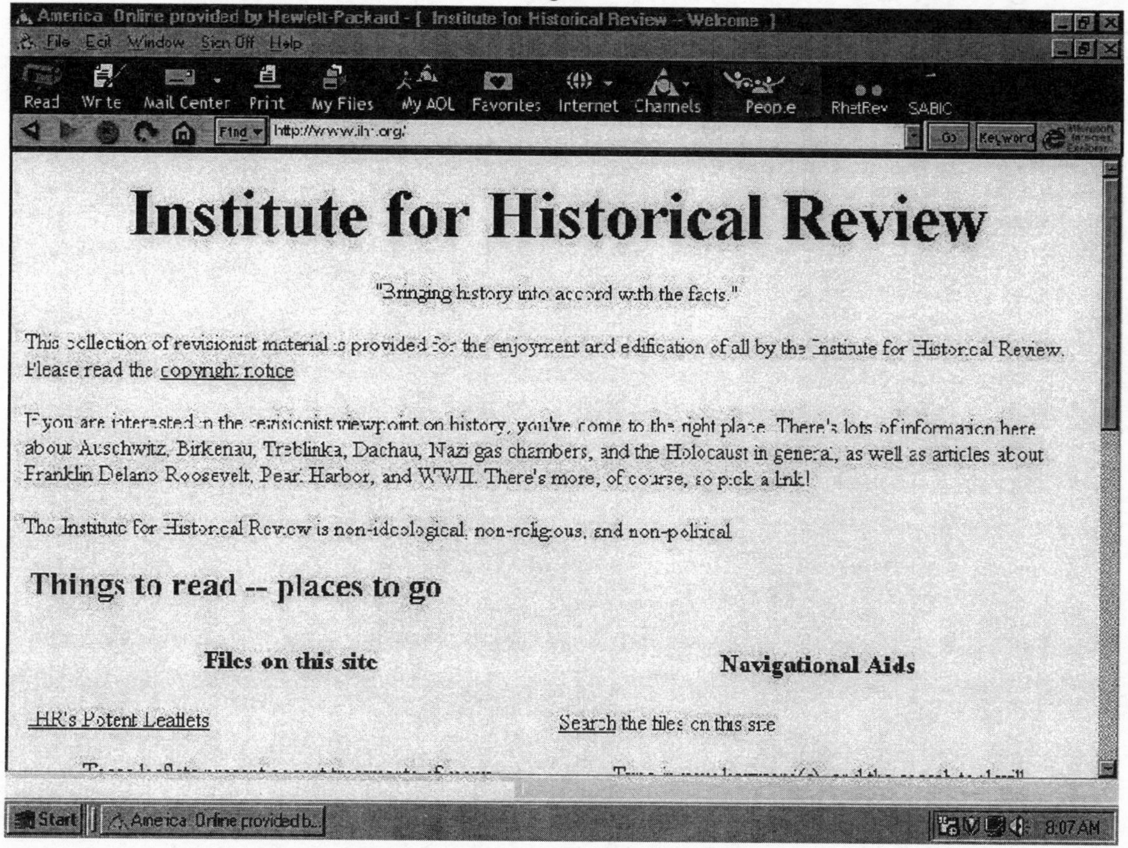

America Online provided by Hewlett-Packard - [Institute for Historical Review - Welcome]

File Edit Window Sign Off Help

Read Write Mail Center Print My Files My AOL Favorites Internet Channels People RhetRev SABIC

http://www.ihr.org/

Institute for Historical Review

"Bringing history into accord with the facts."

This collection of revisionist material is provided for the enjoyment and edification of all by the Institute for Historical Review. Please read the copyright notice.

If you are interested in the revisionist viewpoint on history, you've come to the right place. There's lots of information here about Auschwitz, Birkenau, Treblinka, Dachau, Nazi gas chambers, and the Holocaust in general, as well as articles about Franklin Delano Roosevelt, Pearl Harbor, and WWII. There's more, of course, so pick a link!

The Institute for Historical Review is non-ideological, non-religious, and non-political.

Things to read -- places to go

Files on this site

Navigational Aids

HR's Potent Leaflets

Search the files on this site

Start   America Online provided b...   8:07 AM

Like Butz, the Committee for Open Debate on the Holocaust has had a web site for approximately three years. Unlike Butz's site, CODOH's web site has undergone radical change during this time. These changes reflect the group's awareness of the ethos construction that new technology makes possible. First, though, we consider the traditional ways in which the group constructs its credibility and exposes its virtuous character.

On the CODOH home page, Bradley R. Smith, the founder of the group, explains that

> The aim of this site is to promote intellectual freedom with regard to this one historical event, which in turn will promote intellectual freedom toward all historical events (thus all other issues). We have chosen to concentrate on the gas chamber stories and war crimes trials because they are emblematic of the allegedly unique monstrosity of the Germans before and during World War II. We believe it profoundly vulgar, and emasculating, to spend half a century condemning others for their violence and brutality when we have not yet learned to condemn our own, or even recognize it. We want to help civilize Americans. We're not Germans and we're not Jews (well, some of us are) and we are not focused on how naughty they were or were not. We're focused on American culture, on the American ideal that liberty has the power to wash a people clean and that there is no liberty without intellectual freedom.

The credibility and virtuous character that are constructed in this passage are impressive due, in part, to the fact that denial of the Holocaust is never mentioned, although the group's preoccupation with the Holocaust is explained away in the name of intellectual freedom. Like Butz and the IHR, CODOH presents itself as a group engaged in the search for truth, a truth buried beneath the crushing weight of fifty years of "vulgar" and "emasculating" condemnation.

In this extended statement of purpose, CODOH makes its virtuous character evident through disclosure. The audience is told the purpose of this site—and of the focus solely on the Holocaust. The audience is told that some of CODOH's members are Germans and Jews. The audience is told that this is a group with an absolute commitment to intellectual freedom. Honesty and virtue seem to suffuse this passage. CODOH builds its ethos, then, in traditional ways from the very beginning, starting with the first page that a web surfer encounters. At the same time, though, CODOH begins to construct its ethos in ways made possible by the technology of the Web, and it is with an analysis of this techno-ethos that we end this section.

Although the CODOH home page's menu appears to be purely textual, it is, in fact, a collection of "buttons" that link to other pages (see figure 3).

Figure 3

A America Online provided by Hewlett-Packard - [Bradley R. Smith/CODOH Home Page]

File   Edit   Window   Sign Off   Help

Read   Write   Mail Center   Print   My Files   My AOL   Favorites   Internet   Channels   People   PfletRev   SABO

Find ▾   http://www.codoh.com/   Go   Keyword

Committee for Open Debate on the Holocaust

CODOH
HOME PAGE

Site Contents

- MAIN SITE INDEX
- TEXT ONLY INDEX
- FRAMES
- Bradley R. Smith
- Intellectual Freedom
- Revisionism
- Smith's $250,000 Offer - Campus Project Update
- CODOH's BBS - World Wide Web Message Board

- Guest Book 1
- Guest Book 2
- Campus Guest Book
- HotLinks
- CODOH International
- Zionism: Tangled Web

- What's New
- NewsDesk
- Author Index
- Title Index
- Site Map
- Search, Site or Web
- Intro to Revisionism
- AnswerMan!

THE AIM OF THIS SITE is to promote intellectual freedom with regard to this one historical event, which in turn will promote intellectual freedom toward all historical events (thus all other issues). We have chosen to concentrate on the gas chamber

Start   America Online provided b...   8:03 AM

As the buttons suggest, browsers can choose from several parallel sites: text only, with frames, and so on. Other small pictures dot the home page as well. Several pull-down menus (not visible in the figure) are also present, as is a counter. According to the counter, CODOH's home page had been accessed 64,504 times in the month prior to our visit. CODOH's techno-ethos is thus built on a firm foundation of technological know-how. The site is not plain, as are the sites of Butz and the IHR. There are graphics. There are multiple colors. A counter hints that thousands of people have used the site. Like the textual features of ethos construction discussed earlier, these bits of techno-ethos construction are simultaneously seen and left unseen. The CODOH site is well organized and thus easy for a reader to browse through. No links lead to dead-ends, and no graphics are so large that they take a great deal of time to load. Even web surfers with slow Internet connections are not put off by the CODOH site's use of technology.

CODOH's construction of its techno-ethos continues as a browser moves deeper into its site, especially when frames are employed (see figure 4). In the main frame, CODOH lists a series of topics, each a hyperlink to more information. The list is extremely long and varied, containing, at the time of this writing, 263 separate items on the Holocaust. Again a counter tells the web surfer how many visitors have entered the site prior to her or his arrival. The smaller rectangular frame on the left side of the screen contains, among other things, a series of international flags. Clicking on a flag will take a web surfer to a parallel version of the CODOH site that is written in the primary language of the country represented by the flag. More than a dozen countries are represented.

On pages such as the one described above, techno-ethos is truly built. CODOH can demonstrate its technological proficiency—the use of frames, graphics, and the pleasing/accessible arrangement of text on the screen. Such clear mastery of the medium lends the group credibility. But the multilingual feature of the web site is an excellent way of demonstrating the group's all-inclusive approach to their topic. This site is not for one group of people; it is for all people. Like the statement by Smith concerning the multiethnic makeup of CODOH, the flags represent inclusion rather than exclusion.

Even when it is presenting information that is purely textual—on-line versions of pamphlets that the group distributes, for example—CODOH utilizes the Web's technology to good effect. Their pamphlet, "An Introduction to Holocaust Revisionism," is a prime example of this (see figure 5). When a browser "opens" the pamphlet, he or she is immediately confronted by two things: a table of contents and a navigation bar. By clicking on the appropriate arrow on the bar, a browser can move back and forth in the text, reading it, essentially, in the same way that a normal book or pamphlet is read. The navigation bar remains constant on the screen, so browsers can

Figure 4

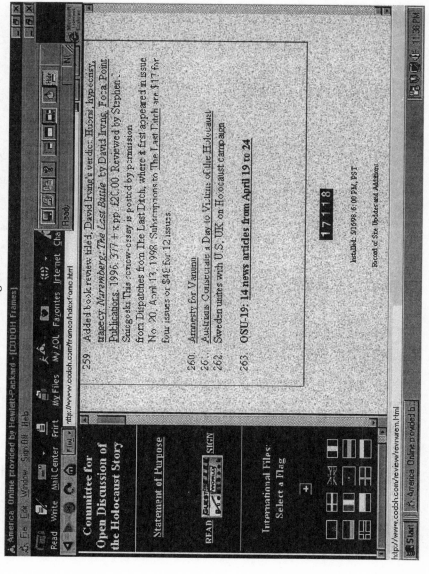

**Committee for
Open Discussion of
the Holocaust Story**

Statement of Purpose

READ [logo] SIGN

International Files:
Select a Flag

Ready

259   Added book review titled, David Irving's verdict: Huons, hypocrisy, hypocrisy: *Nuremberg: The Last Battle* by David Irving, Focal Point Publications, 1996; 377 + x pp. £20.00 Reviewed by Stephen Smugoski This :cview-cssay is posted by permission from Dispatches from The Last Ditch, where it first appeared in issue No. 20, April 13, 1998. Subscriptions to The Last Ditch are $17 for four issues or $48 for 12 issues.

260   Amnesty for Vanunu

261   Austrians Consecrate a Day to Victims of the Holocaust

262   Sweden unites with U.S., UK on Holocaust campaign

263   OSU-19: 14 news articles from April 19 to 24

17·1·18

Installed: 5/1698 6:00 PM, PST

Record of Site Updates and Additions

Figure 5

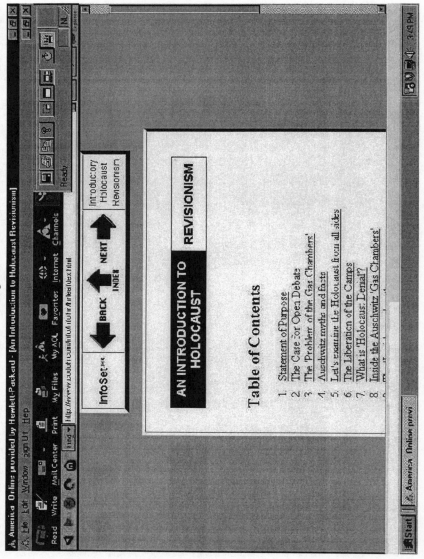

easily move about. The table of contents is, of course, hypertextual. Browsers can pick and choose from the topics covered. The text appears dark against a light backdrop, and a different colored background sets the block of text off from the rest of the screen and the navigation bar. The ultimate effect is an easily readable text that is easily navigable as well.

CODOH, the IHR, and Butz all construct an effective ethos on the Web. For Butz and the IHR, the Web is simply an extension of the print medium, another way to convey the same message in the same familiar way. CODOH takes an entirely different approach, one that utilizes the graphical features that are readily available on the Web to good use. They construct their ethos in the traditional print-based ways, but they move beyond that construction as well. They demonstrate credibility through their scrupulously maintained site, a site that is easy to navigate and easy on the computer-tired eye. They demonstrate character through their inclusiveness, and through their clear desire to transcend political and linguistic barriers. All three deniers take arguments that are potentially offensive and unethical and present them in a pleasing, for lack of a better term, and authoritative manner—through the construction and maintenance of traditional ethos for Butz and the IHR and through the manipulation of techno-ethos on the CODOH site.

Techno-Ethos and Composition Pedagogy

Some of our students profess either fear or ignorance of the Internet, but they are a shrinking minority. Most students embrace on-line resources with an exuberance that library books rarely see. On-line texts are generally short, readily understandable, and accessible in full-text format. As one composition student at the University of Arizona wrote several years ago, in an essay comparing college life in the 1990s with college life in the 1960s, "Research is easier now. There's no reason to even leave your dorm room." For teachers, such a statement may cause a shudder, sigh, or gag. Students, often pressed for time, react differently. They react differently, that is, until they can be shown that concepts like character and credibility are of ultimate importance on-line.

Dealing with print-based sources, students often intuitively work through issues of credibility. They know, for example, that *Time* is a better source than *The Daily Wildcat*, our campus newspaper. They know that neither is as good as an article from a scholarly journal or new anthology published by a university press. They know that quoting from the *National Enquirer* is more likely to raise eyebrows than to change opinions. The critical eye these students have for printed materials is rarely turned up for on-line sources, though.

Checklists for students to use when evaluating on-line sources are common; most university libraries provide them, in fact, and they are easily located on the Web. Gillette and Videon, in the study cited earlier, call for the use of such a tool. The *MLA Handbook* makes gestures in this direction as well, directing students to look for an on-line "author's credentials," "a statement of mission or purpose" about a group, and "information about the organization" represented in cyberspace (27). All of this is good advice, of course, but the Holocaust denial sites we discussed earlier effectively do each of these things. Butz lists his credentials, the IHR provides a mission statement, and CODOH gives plenty of information about the group.

As composition instructors, we have walked our students through the library—literally, in many cases—and discussed the critical evaluation of sources with them. In recent years, we have shared various on-line source evaluation checklists with students, and now we read through the *MLA Handbook*'s expanded section on the Internet with them. To our discussions of ethos construction, we have added lengthy discussions of techno-ethos. When students see the trappings of authority being perverted for anti-Semitic ends, however, the message that credibility of on-line sources must be questioned goes home. More important, the message goes back to the dorm room.

While students are exploring these issues of credibility and authority, while they are mulling over the perversity and bigotry of Holocaust denial, they always ask one question about the deniers eventually: "How can they argue that?" This seemingly simple question is worth unpacking with students when it arises, for it has three interpretations that bear heavily on the topics we have discussed here.

"How can they argue that?" is a rhetorical question in that it is a question about rhetoric. By exploring the ways in which bigotry can be covered with a patina of scholarship (and pseudo-legitimacy), students gain a heightened awareness of the conventions of academic discourse and the construction of credibility. They begin to understand not only *how* scholarship is constructed in the modern academy but *why* it is constructed in such ways as well.

"How can they argue that?" is an ethical question. Often students know of Holocaust denial, but rarely have they actually read any of the works produced by these self-proclaimed revisionists. When students examine Holocaust denial texts, many of them are shocked and dismayed that such hurtful arguments are being made—and that they are being made in such powerful ways in a public forum. The pain of Holocaust survivors is effaced and erased by deniers, and students find the ethical dimensions of this area fascinating—and the lessons memorable.

In recent years "How can they argue that?" has become a technological question as well. Before the rise of the Internet, the public exposure deniers sought was limited. Their access to mainstream publishing was small at best;

their access to television was limited to television talk shows, for the most part. While both media allowed the deniers to spread their message, both media were outside the deniers' control. The Internet is not.

On the Internet Holocaust deniers are able to publish widely. They are able to construct their arguments in a scholarly guise, and their web sites employ the new medium far more effectively than many legitimate sites. By examining these web sites and discussing the construction of ethos, students become more aware of the misinformation that exists on-line. This awareness is, ultimately, far more important and memorable than a checklist which deals with source credibility or a cautionary statement from the *MLA Handbook*.

Works Cited

Aristotle. *Nicomachean Ethics*. Trans. Terence Irwin. Indianapolis: Hackett, 1985.

———. *On Rhetoric*. Trans. George A. Kennedy. New York: Oxford University Press, 1991.

Butz, Arthur R. "Home Web page of Arthur R. Butz." April 16, 1999. http://pubweb.acns.nwu.edu/~abutz/

Cicero. *De Oratore*. Trans. E. W. Sutton. Cambridge, Mass.: Harvard University Press, 1942.

Committee for Open Debate on the Holocaust. "CODOH Home Page." April 16, 1999. http://www.codoh.com/

Connors, Robert J. "*Actio*: A Rhetoric of Manuscripts." *Rhetoric Review* 2 (Fall 1983): 64–73.

Corder, Jim. "Varieties of Ethical Argument, With Some Account of the Significance of *Ethos* in the Teaching of Composition." *Freshman English News* (Winter 1978): 1–23.

Garver, Eugene. *Aristotle's* Rhetoric: *An Art of Character*. Chicago: University of Chicago Press, 1994.

Gillette, Mary Ann, and Carol Videon. "Seeking Quality on the Internet: A Case Study of Composition Students' Works Cited." *Teaching English in the Two-Year College* 26 (December 1998): 189–94.

Institute for Historical Review. April 16, 1999. http://www.ihr.org/

Lipstadt, Deborah. *Denying the Holocaust: The Growing Assault on Truth and Memory*. New York: Plume, 1994.

Modern Language Association. *MLA Handbook for Writers of Research Papers*. 4th ed. New York: MLA, 1995.

———. *MLA Handbook for Writers of Research Papers*. 5th ed. New York: MLA, 1999.

Quintilian. *On the Teaching of Speaking and Writing: Translations from Books One, Two, and Ten of the Institutio oratoria.* Trans. John Selby Watson (and rev. James J. Murphy). Carbondale: Southern Illinois University Press, 1987.

Selfe, Cynthia L. "Technology and Literacy: A Story about the Perils of Not Paying Attention." *College Composition and Communication* 50 (February 1999): 411–36.

6

Like a Cyborg Cassandra

The Oklahoma City Bombing and the Internet's Misbegotten Rhetorical Situation

JACQUELINE J. LAMBIASE

The mythical figure of Cassandra possesses "illegitimate knowledges" (Foucault's term), and in narratives about the Trojan War, she is disqualified from affecting the unitary discourse and actions of her warring brothers and father, Priam. In ancient and contemporary narratives about this war, Cassandra's prophetic warnings about the dangers of the Trojan horse are received but ignored. Since she is a woman, Cassandra's tentative place in the rhetorical situation of contest and survival gives her no traction for her prophecies, which as a result slip into nothingness. German feminist Christa Wolf, in an essay following her novel *Cassandra* (1984), observes that "[f]or women there have been three thousand years of muteness or, at best, sporadic speech." She deconstructs the sacred text about the Trojan War (and the male midrash of centuries) to expose gaps and to revive Cassandra's voice. Since Cassandra's time, Wolf asserts, women compulsively still feel the need "to adapt" to the patriarchal discourse "or disappear" (299–300), even in the twenty-first century. Their expressions are limited by the powerful framework of Aristotle's rhetorical situation, centuries after he articulated it in *The Rhetoric*.

Not only does Aristotle deny women any place within the rhetorical situation, he also denies them passive roles as listeners who might affect a male speaker's message. Trapped within his scientific delusions of woman as a "misbegotten man," Aristotle forgets that female bodies have ears.[1] It is a convenient and political oversight, for if women are not listeners, neither can they be speakers. Constructed as those who are deaf, women also are made mute. Cassandra, from this perspective, does not have a voice because she lacks the audience that would listen to her.

A twentieth-century example of women's continued muteness can be found in an on-line discussion of the Oklahoma City bombing. In these texts, some male-presenting participants—most importantly, the listowner—construct a rhetorical situation that excludes others, particularly female-presenting participants who requested that guidelines for the public forum be enforced and who sought changes in the tone of political discussion. This project uses the image of Cassandra as described in Wolf's novel to displace the notion of an idealized or most appropriate speaker in a polis—in Aristotle's time and through the millennia, this has usually been a male—and to suggest tactics that would enlarge the rhetorical situations of electronic discourse. Because this traditional exclusion or limiting of women occurs during computer-mediated communication, it is important to consider tactics that female speakers have utilized in the past and may use in the present to counter the gendered discourse on the Internet, and indeed, about the Internet. For not only have male voices almost exclusively created the framework of language that gives meaning to information technology, but these same voices also have claimed a disproportionate textual presence through this technology.

In this case study, I analyzed more than three hundred messages over nine days of this asynchronous public discussion, which was handled in a mailing list format and was named OKLABOMB.[2] Between three hundred and five hundred people (including the author, who did not participate) subscribed to the mailing list during the week following the bombing of a federal building in Oklahoma City on April 19, 1995. The discussion was established on the day after the bombing occurred. My rhetorical and ethnographic analyses of electronic texts demonstrate that dominance of the discussion was gained by posting inflammatory messages, by "misunderstanding" previous discussions in order to appropriate them for one's own agenda, and by overloading the group with multiple postings on one topic. In other words, dominance was established by those who engaged in a kind of verbal warfare.

Cassandra as a Signifier for the "Unheard Voice"

In Christa Wolf's novel *Cassandra*, the title character serves as a sign of the "unheard voice," since she tries to find a place for speaking about her country's war and leadership, but cannot. Throughout this narrative, Cassandra moves among her options of speaking but not being heard, of withdrawing from discourse altogether, or of adopting the patriarchal discourse in order to participate. In much the same way some OKLABOMB subscribers tried to be heard or to participate without being domineering themselves. The most "successful" participants of OKLABOMB maintained their dominance through a sheer volume of words; men posted almost double the messages of women (206 compared to 112). The four men and four women who participated most contributed more than one-third of the total messages. Beyond the sheer volume of words, group leaders dominated in other ways, mainly through selective rule enforcement. When two female members express disgust with a message written by someone angry about U.S. efforts to mediate peace in Northern Ireland, which is definitely off-topic, they are met first with silence and then abuse:[3]

> **Ex. 1** Date: Thu, 20 Apr 1995 16:22:57 -0600 (CST)
> From: Elaine Crabtree
> *Subject: re: O-KabOOOOOOOOOOOOOma*
> Hey oklabomb, any way to screen out morons like this?
> > . . . Bill Clinton sucks terrorists' cocks to get their really fucking
> > distant American relatives to vote. Meanwhile we have to bury
> > our children . . .

> **Ex. 2** Date: Thu, 20 Apr 1995 18:34:31 -0400 (EDT)
> From: Aaron L Dickey
> *Subject: re: O-KabOOOOOOOOOOOOOma*
> On Thu, 20 Apr 1995, Susan High wrote:
> > > I subscribed to this list in order to better understand what is
> > > going on in O.C. If you continue to forward this kind of
> > > garbage to me, I will unsubscribe.
> > On Thu, 20 Apr 1995, I'm Wozz wrote:
> > beggars can't be choosers, I'll be glad to remove you if you
> > don't know how to handle the delete key.
> Wozz, just drop her. I don't have time to deal with self-righteous newbies who
> don't understand the concept of mailing lists.

In this exchange, the listowner Aaron Dickey does not seem to hear the complaints of two female-presenting subscribers, Elaine Crabtree and Susan High, but he does respond to "I'm Wozz," another subscriber who sometimes served as list administrator. The listowner assumes the second woman to be a "newbie," or someone who has little Internet expertise and therefore little status, turns her comments aside, and unsubscribes her from the discussion. Even though Dickey allowed almost any topic to be discussed—which was against his own rules about staying on-topic—he asserts his authority in the above message (and he asserts his authority by not "hearing" earlier complaints). Nancy Henley and Cheris Kramarae (1994) claim that when men ignore rules or do not establish rules, they are "exercising a common prerogative of power. Those with lesser power do not have the option to ignore the other's rules, or common rules" (391). At first in the OKLABOMB discussion, Dickey ignored his own rules when it suited him, and when he and "I'm Wozz" did respond to complaints about off-topic messages, they uncloaked a structure of common rules ("handling the delete key"), which the two women with lesser status had themselves unknowingly transgressed.

Yet in many ways, rules abound on the Internet, which exists only through a hierarchy of protocols and codes, with much of its communication overseen by webmasters, dungeon masters, listowners of electronic discussions, and hackers. There is no doubt that electronic discourse possesses the potential for freedom from hierarchy and domination; and conversely, there is no doubt that hierarchy is indeed present in computer-mediated communication. In particular, hierarchy based on gender may be bolstered by flaming "games," which may increase feelings of pleasure and power of many male participants of public electronic discussions, but which may inhibit some female participants whose socialization processes do not include ritualized aggression. On the other hand, ritualized aggression may be adopted by female participants in order to adhere to group norms and to keep participating in the conversation, as in example 1. Elaine Crabtree may have decided to "play" along in a flame-for-a-flame style by calling another participant a "moron" when he posts an off-topic message, but Susan High in example 2 does not. Postmodernists such as Jean-François Lyotard and Gregory Ulmer often mention "games," "antagonism," and "play" when discussing strategies of resistance to modernist hegemonic discourse. But whose strategies of gaming and playing do they in fact mean? And do these strategies simply cloak older versions of conformity and oppression, through the work of antagonistic, playful participants seeking modernist individuality?

Women's and men's choices in this technological age may be just as murky as those constructed by Wolf for Cassandra: they may try to participate in an electronic polis but risk absorption into its discourse style, they may escape into electronic enclaves of like-minded people, or they may choose exile or be exiled. These choices are exercised by participants in the OKLABOMB discussion, as later examples demonstrate.

Resisting Ancient and Digital Heroic Narratives

Cassandra's voice subverts the heroic narrative tradition, whether in the "real" time of the Trojan War, the virtual time of the OKLABOMB discussion, or all the time in between. In Wolf's version of Cassandra's dilemma, she isolates herself from her family by briefly joining a group of women, and then returns to order the Trojans to end the war with offerings, apologies, and the truth about Helen. After her bold speech, "stalwart men turned pale as death" and they proclaimed her "mad" (75). With this final rejection, Cassandra realizes that she can no longer operate within the patriarchal system of Troy and that the heroic epic means only killing or dying. For her part in Wolf's novel, Cassandra chooses captivity over escape in order to step outside the heroic narrative that would dominate her. In the electronic discussion, participants who can be seen as following Cassandra's example did exile themselves by unsubscribing, instead of listening to and adopting the heroic discourse of the discussion group's most vocal members.

Cassandra's choices have been contemplated by many women who have sought more egalitarian speaking places, both off-line and now on-line. A repertoire of resistance strategies may be gleaned from Wolf's Cassandra: whispers, multiplicity of identity, protests, isolation, self-sufficiency, strong words, the master's tools themselves, even silence, and its contemporary on-line counterpart of lurking. Anthropologist Susan Gal (1994) argues that women's silence is an indication that, "unable to express their structurally generated views in the dominant and masculine discourse, women are neither understood nor heeded, and become inarticulate, 'muted,' or even silent" (419). Silence and mutedness, however—like lurking within computer-mediated conversations—may signify active listening and thinking and not an inactive mind.

In the OKLABOMB discussion, those who participated the most also complained about "lurkers" who had never posted messages or who posted few messages. Yet meta-talk within the discussion revealed that participants were simply inundated with messages in addition to information from mass media sources. A few lurkers finally had their say, after Rhonda complained that more than three hundred people were subscribed to OKLABOMB, with only a handful contributing:

> Can't some of you find it in your heart to participate in this list instead of sitting idly by twiddling your thumbs? Who knows, you might even be able to add something valuable, you might be able to start a discussion line that will interest others and intice (sic) them to respond, and lo-and-behold you might even teach someone something—or maybe someone else will teach you. But any way it goes, at least you will be contributing! (May 2, 1995)

Responses to her complaint are enlightening, because they validated the roles of listeners in electronic discussions. Margaret responded by posting that "your assumption that all lurkers are just sitting and twiddling their thumbs is IMHO (in my humble opinion) very offensive. When this list discusses something with substance, more lurkers will probably come out of their de-lurking mode" (May 2, 1995). Another contributor, Tom, stopped lurking to offer this: "Think of me as filtering, rather than lurking, watching, perhaps, with horror, sometimes with amusement, often with puzzlement" (May 2, 1995).

In a chain of forwarded messages, several discussion participants complain about Donna Logan, who is perceived to be participating too much and whom some wish the listowner would silence.

Ex. 3 Date: Sun, 23 Apr 1995 10:32:18 -0400
         From: "Donna J. Logan"
         Subject: Re: Michigan Militia
         > > On Sat, 22 Apr 1995, Doug Weller wrote:
     > > > This mailing list is turning into a forum for right wing
     > > > propaganda—can the listowner please shut Donna up!
     > > No, don't shut Donna up. I don't agree with a lot of what she's
     > > put out there but I'm smart enough to make up my own mind.
     > > I don't want anyone censoring the information I get in this list
     > > or anywhere else.
     > > - Cass
     > Yes, that's probably right Cass up until one person starts drowning
     > out everyone else. As long as Donna doesn't do that, I agree she
     > should be welcome. I think I overreacted to the number of
     > postings as much as anything else. But this is a worry—I've seen
     > lists and newsgroups where one or two people take over and
     > drown out the rest. Hopefully it won't happen here. (Doug)
     Don't worry Doug, I don't have enough time to do nothing else but
     drown out this list. Plus, I much prefer a DEBATE on a list, if I'm
     just going to be talking to myself, I don't have to get online to do it!
     ;->
     BTW, my political leanings (and voting history) is actually
     predominantly left-of-center . . . definitely not the right-wing nut you
     wish to portray me as . . .
         Rev. Donna, COAL
         ;->

Donna Logan here protests her labeling as a "nut," much as Cassandra confronted her subject position of being "mad" in the novel. Nonetheless, throughout this day of confrontation on April 23, Logan continues to participate, but changes to a joking identity, quite unlike her assertive presence here in example 3 and earlier in the discussion. To the majority of her messages, however, whether serious or silly, is attached a winking and smiling emoticon as in example 3, perhaps because she is powerfully manipulating discourse to suit her own ends. Logan composes other messages later on April 23, including these two in a different tone from example 3:

Ex. 4 Date: Sun, 23 Apr 1995 21:09:03 -0400
         From: "Donna J. Logan"
         Subject: Re: Islamic reaction?
         On Sun, 23 Apr 1995, Edward J. Begley wrote:
     > On Sun, 23 Apr 1995 (email address deleted) wrote:
     >   (snip)
     > > And Kennedys, Malcom X. M.I King and anti-abortion clinics
     > > bombing, LA riots, CIA political assassinations throughout
     > > the world etc, etc . . . ?
     > Excuse me? Just what is an "anti-abortion clinic?" Perhaps you
             > should watch more TV.
     Maybe it's an artificial insemination clinic? ;->

Now back to our regularly scheduled topic . . .
Rev. Donna, COAL
;->

Ex. 5 Date: Sun, 23 Apr 1995 21:47:56 -0400
From: "Donna J. Logan"
Subject: Re: Second suspect apprehended
> Can anyone cite even *one* specific source of a gun control
> > advocate who has tried to capitalise on this in any way? I've
> > been watching the news coverage extensively, and I haven't
>   > > seen any. (Samantha)
Perhaps you should be watching CNN's Crossfire, or NBC's
> Nightly News. Some are suggesting more gun control, and others > are
suggesting more control off the Internet. The Whitehouse is
>   > suggesting more control of everything. (Edward)
Now, now . . . f you caught Billy on 60 Minutes tonite, you would have heard
him making a point that he's not calling for restrictions/limitations on our
historical freedoms . . . but he IS calling for *discipline* in our ability to
practice those freedoms!
Hell, he made it sound like a new diet! We've gotten too fat and bloated with
all these freedoms, it's time to trim down to a leaner and meaner Constitution. . . .
This from a guy who stops in at McDonald's while jogging, telling us WE
should be *disciplined* . . . or perhaps he meant *discipline* in the
punishment sense?
Rev. Donna, COAL
;->

In example 4, after being publicly rebuked for posting too much, Donna Logan nonetheless continues her participation. She behaves as if she were a dominant group member, because overposting is a tactic of that group and she seems to realize her linguistic power would be diminished if she lessened her textual presence. Here and in many subsequent messages, however, her participation concerns marginal conversational threads that have drifted off-topic. Within an hour, in example 5, she posts another reaction to what others on the list have to say about the bombing and its aftermath, in contrast to many of her earlier postings that reflected her own thinking. While the level of Donna's participation did not diminish, the tone of her messages changed, from more serious contributions to meta-talk about the discussion and jokes.

Doug Weller's open complaint about Donna Logan participating too much could be interpreted as harassment, because other subscribers posted as many messages as she did or more, including at least one other female participant. He made no other complaints about overposting, except about her (and seemingly secondarily, her viewpoints). Doug's request in example 3 appears reasonable except for the inflammatory language, but another participant, Cass, notes the dampening effect his complaint will have on the conversation as a whole. After Susan High was ridiculed in example 2 (and maybe dropped from the list), she did not participate again, and Elaine Crabtree's subsequent participation was minimal. Other research about computer-mediated conversations parallels the patterns of harassment in the OKLABOMB discussion. In a semester-long study of on-line student communication (Carstarphen and Lambiase, 1998), several flame wars included sexist and racist speech of one dominating male participant and "students had vastly different perceptions of the discussion, depending on whether they felt comfortable with the topics discussed and with the tone of the discourse itself" (127). Some students never participated in the discussion after the flame wars, because, as one woman stated, "the environment was hostile. . . . I don't need the negativity nor does anyone" (130). Susan Herring (1998) plots the progression of on-line harassment episodes, in her study of the gender dynamics of an Internet relay chat and a listserv discussion group. After an initial situation occurs and harassment is initiated, next comes resistance to harassment and then escalation of harassment, after which the "targeted participants drop out and/or targeted participants accommodate to dominant group norms" (2). This pattern is very much like Wolf's own articulation of Cassandra's choices of either adapting to patriarchal discourse or disappearing.

While Donna Logan saved face within the OKLABOMB discussion by defending herself briefly and then joking her way through conversations, another active participant used strong words in a different way. Dianne Murray takes the offensive, despite her eventual apology, in responding to someone who had falsely accused her of calling him a jerk:

> I did not call you a jerk, nor would I. Actually, I've forgotten the post you are referring to, but I'm certain it had to be responding to an abstract idea of people in general with whom debate can't proceed because either/or thinking distorts the topic under discussion. If I did express myself badly, I apologize, but I wonder if you realize the extent to which you are making statements concerning the Davidian's behavior when you know nothing about them. Many of your assumptions are just not based on fact. (May 2, 1995)

Murray even critiques "either/or thinking" as causing breakdowns in communication, the kind of either/or thinking that Cassandra herself tries to resist in Wolf's novel. It could be argued, however, that Murray has succumbed to the same dividing practices through her use of accusations.

In its own resistance to dualisms, especially the binary of killing or dying, Wolf's novel responds most eloquently and convincingly to Aristotle and other thinkers who use dualistic formulas. Within the novel itself and in the essays following the novel, Wolf exposes Aristotle's seduction by a perverted question, that of whether male or female was to be the privileged sex, both inside and outside rhetorical situations. Always within his character of believing that true things "are by nature stronger than their opposites" (1991, *On Rhetoric,* 34), Aristotle responds pervertedly, dividing the essential category of human being by privileging the male in his own work. Cassandra, too long in the audience of patriarchy, at first tries to join in this perverted pattern when she dreams a riddle, that of whether the sun or moon shines more brightly. She notes:

> there was something wrong with the contest, but try as I might, I could not find out what. Until finally, disheartened and anxious, I said that of course everyone knew and could see that it was the sun that shone most brightly. "Phoebus Apollo!" a voice cried in triumph, and at the same time, to my horror, Selene, the dear lady of the moon, sank to the horizon lamenting. (87)

Cassandra regrets her decision to fall into heroic discourse by dealing in binaries, even if it is in a dream. Another dream about dualisms is imagined in another millennium by Donna Haraway (1991): "Cyborg imagery can suggest a way out of the maze of dualisms in which we have explained our bodies and our tools to ourselves. This is a dream not of a common language, but of a powerful infidel heteroglossia" ("Manifesto," 181). She envisions not conformity to the dominant discourse tradition, but instead, power based across the many texts of those who oppose that tradition. It is a collective power formed through a montage of texts. And it is the kind of localized power available to participants in computer-mediated conversations.

From Wolf's Cassandra to Haraway's Cyborg

In the digital age, will women's fingers fare better than their tongues? As the cursor blinks, electronic writers gaze at the screen to find identity. Still relying on a modernist network of the self, many aggressively write identifications for themselves. Know thyself becomes write thyself. Modernist strategies of patriarchal discourse endure and work in this digital age, despite postmodern networks of ambiguity, information excesses, and cultural politics. It is the modernist response of adapting or disappearing that deserves scrutiny.

Instead of relying on a modernist network of the self, people engaged in a struggle for electronic textual presence should perhaps exploit technology and learn what they can. A few participants in the OKLABOMB discussion seem to be doing just this sort of exploiting and learning, in their multiple messages, in their attempts to gain understanding, even in their long stretches of lurking. Technological exploitation, instead of technological determinism, may be Haraway's response to worries about a modernist-leaning technoculture that seems to engulf women as did the many pages of patriarchal print. While many promote the Internet as a space where all are welcome and may participate, the texts of the OKLABOMB discussion indicate that harmony and access are not easy to come by in computer-mediated discourse. Disputing claims of egalitarian potential for technology, Haraway says that "technology is not neutral. We're inside of what we make, and it's inside of us. We're living in a world of connections—and it matters which ones get made and unmade" (1997, cited in Kunzru, 209). In the same interview with *Wired*, Haraway directly addresses the relationship of feminism and technology:

> Feminist concerns are inside of technology, not a rhetorical overlay. We're talking about cohabitation: between different sciences and forms of culture, between organisms and machines. I think the issues that really matter—who lives, who dies, and at what price—these political questions are embodied in technoculture. They can't be got at any other way. (cited in Kunzru, p. 159)

There's a thread here of the heroic narrative found also in the traditional story of the Trojan War and in the OKLABOMB discussion, that of living and dying, and it is this commonplace narrative that Wolf resists through her own *Cassandra*. Haraway, like Foucault, points to the discourses of technology and politics as one way to uncover the power relations built inside these linguistic structures. She also realizes that technological machines are already a part of women and men; she seems to be saying that this coupling is not a choice but a reality. In fact, the texts of OKLABOMB appear to support Haraway's assertion, since many participants—women especially—joined the discussion expecting one sort of experience but got something entirely different. (It was at first a site of tragedy that quickly turned political once Timothy McVeigh was arrested.) The discussion demanded time (see headings of examples 3–5 to get an idea of how much time Donna Logan spent on-line in one day), effort, forbearance, and tolerance, requiring sometimes hours spent tethered to a computer each day to read and respond.

In "A Cyborg Manifesto," Haraway blurs the binary of human and machine, while retaining a discursive agency for her cyborg. In this way, she uses the strategies of postmodernism for disruption and salvages a subject with agency enough to resist a powerful master discourse. It is this coupling that provides one antidote for people trying to participate in on-line discussions like OKLABOMB in new ways outside patriarchal discourse. Haraway writes that "the cyborg is a kind of disassembled and reassembled, postmodern collective and personal self. This is the self feminists must code" (1991, 163). This blurring of distinctions between organism and machine, as well as of other binaries, "cracks the matrices of domination and opens geometric possibilities" (174). In other words, when "either/or thinking" is critiqued, blurred, and understood—instead of used as a default discursive strategy as it was by women and men in OKLABOMB—it will also be weakened and vulnerable to other discourse formations. This creation of alternative rhetorical situations may only happen through discourse, and participation in on-line discourse communities provides a forum for these shifts.

The tools of Haraway's subversive efforts include writing, but not the kind of writing that continues Western myth, which relies on "worship of the monotheistic, phallic, authoritative, and singular work, the unique and perfect name" (175). Instead, she advocates cyborg writing, which creates stories that "have the task of recoding communication and intelligence to subvert command and control" (175). Haraway's cyborg writers do not necessarily inhabit cyberspace, but they certainly are there, too, among those who tried to resist the dominant discourse of the OKLABOMB discussion, whether by posting public and unpopular complaints about flaming (one dominant norm) or by resisting calls for censorship of other female participants (as Cass did in example 3). For, as Haraway asserts, "writing is preeminently the technology of cyborgs, etched surfaces of the late twentieth century. Cyborg politics is the struggle for language and struggle against perfect communication" (176). It is the same struggle, Wolf might say, that she created for her narrative version of Cassandra.

It is here, in this matrix of feminism and postmodernism, that we can read across the strategies of the women writers, especially the admonitions and premonitions of twentieth-century feminists Wolf and Haraway and their implications for speaking in cyberspace. There is much to be learned from a Foucauldian-style genealogy of how an ideal (and patriarchal) rhetorical situation came into being, along with its universalizing presence in most speaking and writing spaces. Equally important are female responses to the evolution and inscription of this ideal discourse site, in order to claim it as a rhetorical space for female voices. For now, computer-mediated communication often enforces the silence of generations. When women do speak about their opportunities on the Internet, they encounter an Aristotelian legacy again and again.[4] Pamela Takayoshi (1994), for example, writes that "the medium had offered me a voice and a place for a discussion where ideas mattered more than personalities. But when I used that voice, I found that once again I was objectified as a woman, man's sexual but not intellectual counterpart" (27).

In circumstances similar to Takayoshi's, Stephanie Brail (1996) analyzes a cyberstalker's impact on her on-line life: "I've censored myself. My choice, right? Do I or do I not have the right to speak my mind in public without being harassed, stalked and threatened because of what I say?" (147). After taking elaborate precautions for her personal safety and identity, Brail pinpoints the most insidious effect, that of an energy drain: "Men don't usually have to jump through a hoop of sexual innuendo and anti-feminist backlash simply to participate. They use their energy for posting" (148). In OKLABOMB, Donna Logan had to defend herself against a charge of being a "nut" (example 3) and the listowner called another female participant a "self-righteous newbie" (example 2), simply because she had asked that the listowner's own guidelines be enforced. In dozens of postings that helped create an antifeminist climate for the discussion, U.S. Attorney General Janet Reno is attacked in grossly sexist references because of her involvement in the Branch Davidian stand-off in Waco, Texas. Overall in the OKLABOMB discussion, women did spend more time than men negotiating, deferring, and apologizing in their messages (i.e., Dianne Murray). Another example is Samantha Crouse, who broke ranks with the group and decided to help participants who wanted to unsubscribe but didn't know the commands. Other subscribers maintained a hierarchy of those with knowledge against those without, by complaining openly about participants who didn't understand listserv commands and who transgressed by seeking help by sending messages to the entire group. Despite her position in the dominant group, Crouse posted public instructions to help other participants unsubscribe. In her first message, however, she made a mistake, which she corrects in another message in order to avoid flaming: "Don't you hate people who reply to their own posts? :) Just a typo. :) . . . . I meant subscribe, so don't flame me!" (April 24, 1995). Her two smiley-faced emoticons, like Donna Logan's winking emoticons, are used along with her words to remove any assertive edge from her message.

These women and others like them have fought with their words, have risked fighting words by going against group norms, have silenced themselves, have listened, have spoken in brilliant infrequency, have longed for narrative power—much as Wolf's Cassandra does. Despite these contemporary efforts to move beyond having "unheard voices" on-line, some women are advocating that others simply adopt dominant electronic discourse conventions. Several examples may be found in the same *Wired Women* (1996) collection that contains Brail's stalking experience; a few essayists advise a modernist empowerment of writers of computer-mediated communication. Their advice, however, is predicated on the belief that Internet discourse is all right as is, that it is an effective and ethical way in which to communicate (since they advocate emulation of its style and tone), and that linguistic violence and destructive viruses are part of a natural landscape and probably cannot be altered. These female essayists assert that women on-line simply need to mimic these domineering discursive tactics, so that they will be allowed admission into an exclusive rhetorical community (even though the Internet's so-called community has been promoted as egalitarian and accessible to all). Many people participating in electronic discussions perhaps have grown accustomed to or ambivalent about these rhetorical conditions.

Yet to normalize these ways of communicating is to accept exclusion and conformity. In the OKLABOMB discussion, the exclusion and conformity of tone—a sort of kill-or-be-killed, or flame-or-be-flamed environment—did not prove successful, for the discussion ended in about a month.

Despite these realities, Haraway believes in her cyborg world, "in which the difference between machine and organism is thoroughly blurred; mind, body, and tool are on very intimate terms" (165). The binary of woman and machine is troubling, however, no matter how blurred, for woman might already be the less privileged term in this pairing. Housekeeping drudgery, data-entry tedium, and telemarketing tethers: these connections are real-world pairings of women with machines. Nevertheless, Haraway promotes "the social relations of science and technology" to deny a place for "technological determinism" and to suggest that "science and technology provide fresh sources of power, that we need fresh sources of analysis and political action" (165). Outlining methods of resistance possible in a feminist science, Haraway demonstrates how new alliances could enable progressive politics, through ventures among feminists, antimilitary action groups, women of color, and others (169). To Haraway, women's place in the "integrated circuit" brings turmoil and demands survival:

> [T]here is no "place" for women in these networks, only geometrics of difference and contradiction crucial to women's cyborg identities. If we learn how to read these webs of power and social life, we might learn new couplings, new coalitions . . . . The issue is dispersion. The task is to survive in the diaspora. (170)

To apply her progressive politics to computer-mediated communication may mean to disrupt, to be disrupted, and to endure, in order to gain a place for being and for speaking. Examples of such a rhetorical space-cum-tentative existence, as well as of the emotional cost, may be seen in some of the OKLA-BOMB exchanges. Elaine Crabtree and Susan High flamed and complained, Donna Logan joked and endured, Samantha Crouse risked helping low-status participants, and Dianne Murray defended herself while apologizing.

On-line fragmentation cannot be denied, and Internet discourse is almost monolithic in that fragmentation, hopelessly mired in discord, confusion, information excess, and enclave mentalities. It is this fragmentation that most concerns Johndan Johnson-Eilola and Stuart Selber (1996), who believe that if classrooms and political society in general do not "arrive at workable processes for public discourses that do not marginalize or remove interested participants from debate through overt or implicit means, we might realize less a global village and more a great dispersal" (289). It is only in dispersal, however, that an Aristotelian master narrative may lose its long-hoarded value. A diaspora narrative provides disenfranchised groups with on-line opportunities to craft new rhetorical situations despite fragmentation and because of fragmentation. In its embrace of diaspora, feminism would make a similar choice to Cassandra's, that of turning away from modernist killing and dying narratives and of turning toward something different and something more, unstable and ephemeral though that choice may seem. Cassandra's ancient feminism may provide a good partner for the cyborg's postmodernism, a postmodernism that is skeptical of technology and all things modern.

In its turn, this partnership brings possibilities of alternative rhetorical situations that are not predicated on stereotyped, gendered performances or ritualized patriarchal conflict. For those participating in computer-mediated communication—and who may find some parts of this "community" daunting in its hierarchy, conformity, and pettiness—this partnership of feminism and postmodernism may encourage local alliances that promote egalitarian, nonmodernist guidelines that are enforced without censorship. These discourse spaces should be pliable enough for participants to explore opinions that are not mainstream by using rules generally agreed on by group members. The work ahead will not be easy, as people negotiate their couplings with machines and struggle against authoritative discourse formations of past and present. With a more reflective and inclusive structure, however, electronic discursive forms may be able to support localized civic and civil discourse where more participants are included.

Notes

1.   Aristotle defines woman as a misbegotten man in *Generation of Animals*, which presented a view that "held sway in science, philosophy, and theology at least until the nineteenth century" (ix), according to feminist philosopher Nancy Tuana (1993), who writes that Aristotle "provided the first scientific explanation of woman's imperfection" (18).

2.   See author's empirical study, "Hanging by a Thread: Topic Development and Death in an Electronic Discussion of the Oklahoma City Bombing," in Susan Herring's (ed.) *Computer-Mediated Conversation*, forthcoming. In contrast to the formalized empirical data in "Hanging by a Thread," the figure of a cyborg Cassandra in this chapter provides an alternative riff.

3.   In electronic discussions, participants quote material from other subscribers' previous messages (or from their own previous messages) by using angle brackets. Messages contain original spelling and grammar. E-mail addresses have been deleted from message headings.

4.   Considering the Internet's patriarchal military origins, the gendered domain of cyberspace fits its parentage. Just as many women have found it difficult to join military organizations (and difficult to speak about harass-

ment, until only recently), women too have discovered that cyberspace has been colonized before their arrival in large numbers. Their narratives do not fit the reigning rhetorical structures and situations.

Works Cited

Aristotle. *On Rhetoric: A Theory of Civic Discourse.* Ed. and trans. George A. Kennedy. New York: Oxford University Press, 1991.

Brail, Stephanie. "The Price of Admission: Harassment and Free Speech in the Wild, Wild West." In *Wired Women: Gender and New Realities in Cyberspace,* edited by Lynn Cherny and Elizabeth R. Weise, 141–57. Seattle: Seal, 1996.

Carstarphen, Meta, and Jacqueline J. Lambiase. "Domination and Democracy in Cyberspace: Reports from the Majority Media and Ethnic/Gender Margins." In *Cyberghetto or Cybertopia? Race, Class, and Gender on the Internet,* edited by Bosah Ebo, 121–35. Westport, Conn.: Praeger, 1998.

Gal, Susan. "Between Speech and Silence." In *The Women and Language Debate,* edited by Camille Roman, Suzanne Juhasz, and Cristanne Miller, 407–31. New Brunswick: Rutgers University Press, 1994.

Haraway, Donna. *Simians, Cyborgs, and Women: The Reinvention of Nature.* New York: Routledge, 1991.

Henley, Nancy, and Cheris Kramarae. "Gender, Power, and Miscommunication." In *The Women and Language Debate,* edited by Camille Roman, Suzanne Juhasz, and Cristanne Miller, 388–405. New Brunswick: Rutgers University Press, 1994.

Herring, Susan. "The Discourse of Harassment on the Internet: Gender Dynamics in Two Modes of CMC." *Sociolinguistics Symposium 12.* Presentation as part of a Colloquium on Computer-Mediated Communication, Language and Society, University of London, March 27, 1998.

Johnson-Eilola, Johndan, and Stuart Selber. "Policing Ourselves: Defining the Boundaries of Appropriate Discussion in Online Forums." *Computers and Composition* 13 (1996): 269–91.

Kunzru, Hari. "You Are Borg: For Donna Haraway, We Are Already Assimilated." *Wired* (February 1997): 154–59, 209.

Lambiase, Jacqueline J. "Hanging by a Thread: Topic Development and Death in an Electronic Discussion of the Oklahoma City Bombing." In *Computer-Mediated Conversation,* edited by Susan Herring, forthcoming.

Takayoshi, Pamela. "Building New Networks from the Old: Women's Experiences with Electronic Communication." *Computers and Composition* (1994): 21–35.

Tuana, Nancy. *The Less Noble Sex: Scientific, Religious, and Philosophical Conceptions of Women's Nature.* Bloomington: Indiana University Press, 1993.

Wolf, Christa. *Cassandra: A Novel and Four Essays.* New York: The Noonday Press of Farrar, Straus, Giroux, 1984.

7

@ home among the .coms

Virtual Rhetoric in the Agora of the Web

JOHN B. KILLORAN

In a recent section of my course, professional writing and computer communications, one student developed her major course project, a web site, on the theme of Canada and the color blue. *Alternative Rhetorics* readers not familiar with Canada's rich cultural landscape should note that the symbolic connection between Canadians and that color is, to be charitable, rather modest. The student, however, commendably exposed a seeming conspiracy of blues: from the Blue Jays and Blue Bombers (sports teams from Toronto and Winnipeg, respectively) to the blue line on an ice hockey rink, the Blue Mountain ski resort, and the Bluenose (a race-winning schooner); to the blue jay, blue whale, and great blue heron; to Blue Rodeo (a rock band) and Labatt's Blue beer. Often befuddled by my students' perspectives, I struggle to learn from our work together. "Why?" I recall muttering to her. "Because," came her equally articulate response.

This chapter proposes that such irreverent work, typical of many personal home pages, is the outcome of a strategy both to create a speaking space in the crowded World Wide Web and to contest the monopoly of institutional voices in "serious" public discourse. I first develop a theoretical account, with the insights of Bakhtin and of social semioticians Robert Hodge and Gunther Kress, of why rhetors would seek recourse in irreverence. To illustrate this account, I then draw on samples of web rhetoric from an empirical study of 110 home pages and their authors. We see how that familiar trio of rhetorical appeals—ethos, pathos, logos—find virtual expression, self-conscious and parodic application, in the Web's emerging discourse. In closing, I consider how the insight we may glean from these cyberpioneers may guide those of us who find ourselves teaching writing to a generation whose lives will increasingly take them into virtual civic environments.

Sandra Stotsky (1996) observes that the writing of ordinary citizens in the public domain has received little attention from the scholarly community. This is not surprising, given how relatively little of the discourse in the public domain is authored by ordinary citizens writing as citizens. Positioned as watchers of TV, listeners of radio, readers of newspapers, and surfers of the Web, individuals have not previously been able to create a space for their own voices in the mass media. In this light, personal home pages are an unprecedented discursive innovation, not only because of the newfangled computer technology engendering them, but, more important, because of the metamorphosis in public discourse they themselves might engender. Paeans to the web rightly celebrate our greater potential exposure not just to more information but to more people, and hence to voices and perspectives that have formerly been unheard and unseen.

However, personal home pages will not easily challenge the well-entrenched preponderance of institutional voices. Selfe and Selfe (1996) warn that the new electronic media are already being shaped to limit certain kinds of participation in favor of institutional interests. In contrast with the robust producers of institutional web sites, individuals have few material, capital, and symbolic resources with which to construct competitive small-scale contributions. This imbalance of resources may partly account for the low home page authorship rate among Internet users, a rate which, according to one estimate, is around 6 percent (Buten, 1996).

Although a tiny minority, this 6 percent can help inform us about how people confront the challenge of acquiring a voice, a speaking space, on the Web. Web publishing offers students a rare opportunity for an audience beyond that of just their instructors and their classmates. In principle, it furnishes an engagement with the "worldwide" community, the often vicarious but often-enough real experience of the rhetor being acknowledged in the agora. At the same time, it throws up obstacles to its novice authors—obstacles of elusive capital and informational resources, of persuasive efficacy, of credibility. Securing a franchise in the new medium calls for a different rhetorical repertoire than that cultivated in most social and academic environments. Yet it is a rhetoric that, in our near future, will likely be required for an active literate citizenry.

Modality and Parody

In comparison with other discourses, personal home pages, as evinced by my sample, are profuse with humor, playfulness, sarcasm—in short, irreverence.

In an environment in which rhetors have, in principle, a potential "world-wide" audience to whom they can declaim, their conspicuous adoption of irreverent in lieu of earnest stances defies conventional wisdom. However, irreverence is intelligible as a sign of social disequilibrium. Irreverence calls attention to what Hodge and Kress call a text's modality: its posited fidelity or infidelity with the reality it ostensibly represents, "the status, authority and reliability of a message, . . . its ontological status, . . . its value as truth or fact" (124). Irreverence, which abandons a close fidelity with reality, has a low modality. In the framework of Hodge and Kress's social semiotics, modality is a function of the relationship between the text's producers and its receivers and, by extension, with the prevailing "system," a quality that Hodge and Kress call *affinity* (123). Textual modality and contextual affinity share a direct relationship. Thus, a text that posits a low fidelity with reality—that is, a text with low modality—is equivalently a text with a low affinity between its producer and the prevailing system, a condition of which is a lack of solidarity between that producer and that system, a difference of power.

Through this relationship between text and its social context, modality acts as a mechanism of social engagement: "Modality is . . . one of the crucial indicators of political struggle. It is a central means of contestation, and the site of the working out, whether by negotiation or imposition, of ideological systems" (1988, 123). Low modality can thus be seen as active *in opposition to* the hegemony sustaining institutional interests. In an economy in which these interests monopolize symbolic wealth, modality spreads counterfeit discourses. Its humor is humorous in part because it is related, incongruously so, to "serious" discourses.

Specifically, the irreverent texts on personal home pages are, in many cases, low-modality versions of "serious" institutional discourses: parodies of discourses of management, marketing, advertising, law, science, and so forth. Parody, according to Bakhtin, "ridicule[s] the straightforward, serious word in all its generic guises" (1981, 52) by its effect of rendering the "serious word" as itself an object, opaque (51, 61). Bakhtin observes that this obscuring effect disables the posited clear link between language and its referents: "Language is transformed from the absolute dogma it had been within the narrow framework of a sealed-off and impermeable monoglossia into a working hypothesis for comprehending and expressing reality" (61).

This distancing effect of parody is precisely in line with Hodge and Kress's characterization of modality. Parody draws as its primary target the language of "absolute dogma," language that makes a strong claim for its veracity, as its "monoglossia" admits no alternative representation of reality. Such "straightforward" usage is a defining characteristic of high-modality discourse. Once parodied, this language is rendered as a "working hypothesis," openly tentative, acknowledging its possible misinterpretations of reality. Such parodic reaccentuation, with its implied qualifications, is characteristic of low-modality discourse. Thus, we may bring into dialogue Bakhtin's perspective on parody with Hodge and Kress's perspective on modality and social affinity. Parody is essentially a lowering of the modality of a discourse and can be seen as the manifestation of a low affinity between the author of the parody and the original context of that "straight" discourse.

This conception of parody, I illustrate below, can account for some of the carnival atmosphere that animates much of the personal input to the Web. Institutional interests are quickly defining the young Web as a market to serve their interests. The ubiquity of their discourse is establishing a model of what an effective public presence in the medium should strive to achieve:

- a branding of identity
- an emotional connection with a public conceived of as consumers
- the promotion of goods, services, and information

These orientations are supported by discourses familiar from advertising, marketing, public relations, and other institutional practices. Individuals occupying positions in the mass medium for the first time would not share an affinity with such practices; individuals have little to sell and few resources with which to develop competitive public profiles. They must nevertheless establish their own presence in the shadow of institutional presences and in a tradition of media communications; such obvious precedents, after all, offer the most salient and legitimate models of contemporary public declamation. Thus, their low affinity finds ready expression in renditions of these familiar discourses, but in errant renditions, low in modality, patently made up, put on, distorted, exaggerated.

To analyze how contemporary rhetors use parody to undermine established media positions, we can explore how they adapt the traditional rhetorical appeals of ethos, pathos, and logos on the Web. In the virtual environment, these classical appeals may be better understood as *virtual*, as distinct from *real*, appeals:

- Their emergence in the public domain is contingent on the Web's virtual space. Individuals have been effectively blocked out of the "real" space of the mass media, and so have not hitherto had much occasion to exercise media appeals, "real" or otherwise. The Web's virtual space offers technological access, although not full social access, and hence necessitates a new rhetorical stance.
- Virtual appeals display, to some degree, the symbolic front of "real" authentic appeals but lack their direct suasive orienta-

tion and efficacy. Unlike the classical appeals, they do not directly construct upstanding character, emotional involvement, or compelling reasons; most individuals have few acknowledged grounds for internationally validated ethical, emotional, and rational appeals to begin with. The low modality of such appeals suggests they may index some reality but deliberately miss their mark, and hence merit the characterization of virtual in distinction from "real" earnest appeals whose high modality is not so conspicuously put in doubt.

While virtual appeals seemingly detract from whatever little *gravitas* individuals can muster for themselves, the loss is not great for the majority who have little symbolic capital to wager and little at stake to lose. Instead, with virtual appeals, their initiation to the world of institutional practices parodies that world, highlighting the boundaries between the Web's emerging classes. Virtual appeals are oblique acts of sabotage. They disrupt the hegemony of institutionally monopolized models of public ethos, pathos, and logos. They thereby reorient Web discourse to a more assertive social and political, as distinct from a referential, function.

Below, I illustrate how several participants in my study of personal home page authors made their niche on the Web with virtual appeals. In the next three sections, we look in turn at how participants fashioned a virtual ethos, virtual pathos, and virtual logos, each modeled on institutionally produced rhetoric, but parodying such rhetoric. With these virtual appeals, these participants find the means to occupy positions made available by the new medium and simultaneously to contest their lack of authentic franchise in that medium.

Virtual Ethos

The ethical appeal, in ideal circumstances, would cultivate an image of the rhetor as credible and professional. However, on the Web, personal home page authors must struggle for ethos not only against resourceful, institutionally produced sites, but also against the stigmatization of their solo and hence putatively narcissistic labors. Many apparently retreat from this struggle; for instance, close to 45 percent of the sampled sites do not make readily accessible even such basic personal information as a full name. With a virtual ethos, authors may draw instead on the credibility endowed by institutional discourses, but distance themselves from such discourses by the patently low modality of their renditions. To illustrate, consider how some participants represented themselves with the straitjacket of a genre: the form. An excerpt from one participant's form illustrates this practice:

Name: John Killoran *
Address: Esslingen, Germany
Birthday: 14 October 1965
Occupation: mechanical engineer
* My name has been substituted in place of the participant's name.

The form is most recognizable as an institutional genre, designed to optimize the information extractable from a client's or applicant's interaction with the institution. Discourse analyst Norman Fairclough reminds us that the conventions embedded in "discourse type[s] embody ideological representations of subjects and their social relationships" (1989, 157). Writing of official forms, Fairclough observes an increasingly prevalent "discourse technology" by which organizations both normalize the act of individuals revealing information about themselves and control the parameters and content of such self-revelation (218, 222). The form's anomalous appearance on personal home pages may thus be a result of the naturalization of the act of accommodating institutions and other public offerings of ourselves with structured, socioeconomic confessions. It is a discourse endowed with legitimacy. Every terse piece of data about oneself is dignified with a title. The self-representation is disciplined, Cartesian, a product not of the slovenly human body but of systematic institutional discourse. The form thus secures authors' presumptuous debut on the world stage. We can be sure we are saying the right things about ourselves if we display ourselves with such officious representations.

However, various participants resisted the expectations of a bureaucratically imbued ethos with divergent renditions of the genre. In effect, these participants struggled against being positioned as objects of institutional discourse by undermining the form's capacity to complete official representations of themselves. They did this not by disregarding the genre altogether, but by reproducing its skeleton, primarily its framework of officially sanctioned identifiers and demographic categories such as name, age, birth date, and location, and then playing against the expectations of a consummated genre, challenging its integrity with irregular, unexpected responses.

Consider how two participants represent what would otherwise be their most important institutional affiliation: their occupation. One, a twenty-four-year-old male, responds:

Occupation: Technical Support for <u>CIOE Corporation</u>, where I spout off technical information over a telephone to commputer [sic] illerate [sic] people on a daily basis (*check out my really cool <u>work page</u> that has all kinds of useless information on it . . . if you're bored*). [underlined words are hyperlinked; italics in original]

While his first five words satisfy the normative expectation for a reply to the "Occupation" category, the remainder counteracts that norm by directly challenging the validity of his occupation and undermining the public image of the prime institution of a contemporary life.

Another participant who, as a seventeen-year-old female high school student, would apparently have no socially valid response to a request for her occupation nevertheless includes the category in her self-representation, and then adapts it to her own purposes:

> Occupation: Student / Webmaster of das Spaß Haus [the title of her homepage] / part-time fiction author / original member of the Huge Quintumverate / online virtuosa / Member of the Luke Skywalker Estrogen Brigade (LSEB) / Stosh-Fu fighter (quite the Renaissance Woman, eh?)

Instead of omitting a category which, in other contexts, she may have had to leave empty, she uses the cue signaled by the genre, the cue to represent one's economic affiliation with the social system, to represent an abundance of imaginative, personal affiliations. She reveals these in the discourse otherwise reserved for those who have institutional sanction to claim proper nouns through their professional titles and affiliations: "Webmaster . . . author . . . member of the Huge Quintumverate . . . virtuosa / Member of the Luke Skywalker Estrogen Brigade (LSEB)." The juxtaposition of discourses is made especially salient by her closing parenthetical comment, with its conspicuously oral "eh?" in a passage otherwise dominated by polysyllabic proper nouns. In the responses of both of these participants, the colloquial usages, juxtaposed against the backdrop of a formal setting, foreground the lack of solidarity between individuals and institutions; they make salient that there are two kinds of discourse, ours and theirs.

The appearance of "occupation" on these two home pages illustrates how a topic that might not otherwise have been considered by a home page author or that would not have been validated if the self-representation were occurring in another context, is here cued because of the expectations embedded in the genre. Richard Coe (1987) has illustrated how form in general (as distinct from the genre of the bureaucratic form specifically) is heuristic. A form—whether it be a job application, a university admissions form, a driver's license application, a tax return—cues the frontiers of much of an individual life: birth, parentage, gender, body weight and height, education, employment, and so on. These parameters define a model of public subjecthood in a domain in which subjecthood has few precedents. The model invites authors to mold themselves to its dimensions, an invitation that these participants use as an occasion to stage their resistance. We can see this, for example, in the self-representation of the twenty-four-year-old male, who lists the category "Address" but then proceeds to deny it a response: "No, I am *not* going to give you a street address here, but I live in Lafayette, Indiana . . . right next to <u>Purdue University</u>" (bold and italics in original; underlined words hyperlink). His refusal to cooperate is made dramatic by being located within the genre. The genre and his response to it create the dialogue between the opposing statuses: the institution, represented by discursive proxy, fulfilling its usual protocol with individuals by demanding a piece of information; and the individual, staging this "dialogue" as a means of creating a speaking space for himself, explicitly rejecting the imperative of institutional practice and in so doing manifesting his capacity to answer back to the social order.

The writing of these two participants illustrates the degree to which institutional discourses exercise a prerogative in virtual space. In this case, the discourse defines the dimensions of a generic identity expected of individuals entering the domain, and yet offers little material out of which to fashion an effective personal ethos. The excesses these authors offer in response lower the modality of the genre, creating a parody of its officious model of subjecthood. To the degree that these two have fashioned an ethos, it has emerged in the agonistic challenge to the bureaucratic form, in using the genre as a foil against which to position themselves. Yet it is still a virtual ethos, constructed out of the detritus of legitimate institutional discourses in a setting in which few accessible ethical appeals carry weight.

Virtual Pathos

The Web, increasingly a commercial marketplace, is replete with pathos, emotional appeals, most notably the ostentatious stimuli of multimedia. A competitive multimedia presentation, however, demands an investment in resources—software, training, labor—that is beyond the means of many aspiring Web authors. For instance, based on a survey of home page authors, Buten (1996) reports that between 28 percent and 40 percent reported copying graphics from other sites "as they see fit." Bereft of the resources to develop pathetic appeals of their own, these authors exhibit a covetous dependence on the resources of others, especially institutionally sponsored sites, to construct a virtual pathos. In this section, I illustrate two kinds of virtual pathos: advertising and the interactivity of response forms.

Home page authors may be forgiven for sometimes sounding like advertisers; everyone else in the media does too. That much of public discourse would be dominated by advertising and promotional messages has been noted by Fairclough, who observes a trend toward a "promotional culture" overtaking other cultural practices: "The concept of promotional culture can be understood in discursive terms as the generalization of promotion as a communicative function . . .—discourse as a vehicle for 'selling' goods, services, organizations, ideas or people—across orders of discourse" (1993, 141). One cause of this "colonization" (Fairclough, 1989, 197–98) is, of course, the legitimacy that commercialism has gained in contemporary societies. It is as consumers of advertising discourse that individuals inadvertently acquire a "literacy" in how things, events, attitudes, and people are to be represented in public discourse. As individuals enter into their new situations as producers of web communication, these advertising voices are prominent among the legitimate models made available to them to appeal to their public. Promotion, after all, appears to be what one should be doing in a mass medium.

Most home page authors, of course, have little suitable to market and thus often exercise the promotional impulse in hyping their own sites. However, one participant who actually does have something very real to advertise finds herself embracing the promotional function, although at arm's length. A freelance poet, she uses part of her site to market a small-press book of her poetry. Over several separate pages, her site features a sample of her poems, scanned images of the front and back covers of her book, several brief sales pitches, and instructions on how and where to send the $6.00 payment. In the brief bio featured on the book's back cover, we learn that the poet is a single parent, earning her living "work[ing] various meaningless blue-collar day jobs," "a disenfranchised member of an indifferent society."

As someone who is on the margins of both the publishing community and middle-class America (after all, she's a poet), trying to engage in an activity—marketing—independent of the institutional networks that sanction it, she has few recognizable models to emulate. Freelance vendors commonly sell hot dogs or consulting services, but the hawking of self-published poetry has not generated its own dignified discursive precedents. Attempting to engage in an activity that is otherwise practiced almost exclusively by publishing and marketing enterprises, she uses what might appear as the unusual strategy of appropriating the most garish clichés of the advertising industry, using them as titles and slogans on the three pages directly devoted to the sale:

- "You've seen the Website - now buy the book!"
- "not available in stores! while supplies last!"
- "It makes a great gift for That Special Someone."
- "Buy this book—and rest safe in the knowledge that no animal testing was involved in the development or distribution of this product"

- "Buy one. Buy two or three."
- "Be the first (if not the only one) on your block to own this book!"

The familiar slogans nominally fulfill the ostensible purpose of this section of her site: to market her book. Yet their inappropriateness to her "product" and their excess—the irrelevance of animal testing, biodegradability, and unavailability in stores—call attention to more than just the book. As a poet, she could likely have composed a more eloquent, sincere message, but didn't. Her position is an awkward one: a poet compelled to participate unceremoniously in the "legitimate" economic practice of marketing.

Her response is to display a low-modality reproduction of that practice. Her text engages her in, but also distances her from, the act of promotion, indexing instead the perspective of the agent aware and perhaps self-conscious of the contradictions of her situation. This is what marketing is, this thing. We are not moved—nor are we entirely meant to be—by the virtual pathos of its appeals. Her parody of marketing contests not only the legitimacy it ordinarily has in its transparent form, but also her disenfranchisement as an unrecognized discourse producer whose message to the public must be promotional rather than poetical.

For the majority of web authors, without a product or service to market, a "gee-whiz" emotional appeal can be fashioned out of the Web's interactive gizmos. For instance, interactive response forms are a familiar feature of many commercial sites. They are the electronic equivalent of the print response forms commonly used by institutions to systematize their transactions with the public. Indeed, the HTML response form was no doubt inspired by an anticipated need for a tidy electronic function analogous to the print-based institutional discourse.

As mentioned above, the print-based response form is identified by Fairclough as a discursive technology by which "consumerist" and "bureaucratic" practices infiltrate the relations and subject positions of citizens (1989, 221). Citizen home page authors would seemingly have few valid purposes for posting such response forms; they do not occupy the positions that would legitimate the solicitation of formatted information from passing surfers. Institutions hold such standing through their financial, legal, and personnel resources, and institutions control the emotionally appealing goods, services, and access that surfers want or need. By contrast, individual web authors have neither the power and resources, nor the goods and services, that would entice fellow surfers to fill out a form.

However, the response form is one of the few means by which home page authors can elicit surfers' involvement. For both authors and surfers alike, previously limited to the more prosaic tools of sentences and paragraphs, the pull-down menus, radio buttons, and response windows on forms are "cool" and hence emotionally engaging. Thus, home page authors' lack of legitimate purpose in publishing the institutionally inspired genre does not restrain their appropriation of its technology, as illustrated by these excerpts from the forms of four participants:

"The Certain Distant Form(ula)," which includes ten questions such as the following:

> Do you see double?   O Yes O No
> Do you see triple?   O Yes O Yes O Yes   O No O No O No

On the "Cyber-Divorce" site, the divorce application form, which includes the open-ended question,

> State all reasons (and it doesn't matter what the reasons are, all cyber-divorces shall be granted) this cyber-divorce is needed.

A form on the index page used to provide haphazard access to the various pages of the site, depending on which combination of three multiple-choice options are selected:

> Sex   O Male
>   O Female
>   O Yes
>   O No
> Occupation: O President of the United States
>   O Student
>   O Vice President
>   O Cult Member
> School Attending:
>   O Mills College
>   O Oxford

"The Weird Gauge," designed ostensibly to assess one's personality and social and cultural disposition, which includes a long list of questions about pop culture, such as the following:

> If someone was talking about No Doubt (random choice . . . I couldn't care less 'bout 'em), you would say:
> O I'm not a poser like you guys! I've liked them since '88. (Even if you are now only 13 years old.)
> O They are soooo rockin'! Ska puppies like me love "I'm just a girl" and . . . er . . . the other stuff they do.
> O Who?

These questions and their answers obviously transgress the normal conventions and expectations of the bureaucratic genre from which they originate. Some questions appear obscure and unanswerable or, if serious, are followed by multiple-option answers that include incongruous options and fail to accommodate a full range of likely answers. The neutrality presupposed of multiple options is violated by options clearly made to sound undesirable. The standard English and formal tone expected of written forms is juxtaposed with colloquial usages or transcriptions of spoken utterances, the private voices of unofficial speakers. Effectively excluded from authentic, credible uses of the technology, these four participants instead adopted the technology for ostentatiously inauthentic, playful uses. They elicit the involvement of surfers by staging a mutual intercourse of fanciful question-and-answer banter.

Although such humor might be the refuge of those who have little recourse to a wider palette of emotional appeals, it can be seen not merely as a playful indulgence, a toying with the technology, but also as a political move, a means by which the excluded can contest their exclusion. Revealingly, all four participants are between the ages of fifteen and twenty-four. They would likely only have filled in forms, never having achieved the status to produce and distribute one of their own invention. They would also likely share little solidarity with the institutions, such as schools, employers, and governments, that have elicited completed forms from them. Included in the excerpts listed above, for instance, and in the many other questions and answers on these response forms, are passages that draw not just on any question-answer exchange but on discourses that are recognizable from institutional contexts: legal discourses (e.g., the Cyber-Divorce application); administrative discourses (e.g., the options for sex and occupation); psychological discourses (e.g., the "Weird Gauge" of personality); and medical discourses (e.g., the question about seeing double). In drawing on these voices, participants create an intertextual presence for powerful official practices, practices that have the sanction to ask serious questions and to compel serious answers. Yet their distorting responses to these official voices render these voices effete, recasting them as fodder for lighthearted pathetic appeals. These participants' parodies contest the default model of relations between institutions and the public that is reinforced by the genre. The transcribed spoken utterances and the "trivial" content that mark their virtual appeals manifest a solidarity with other users of informal speech and trivia: fellow individuals who can share casual, informal relations.

Virtual Logos

Though sometimes considered the first among the classical rhetorical appeals, logos has been left for last because it is the most problematic of the three to find contemporary application. Logos is, of course, the contribution of rational argumentation in support of a claim. On the Web, however, claims are not so much argued as asserted. The purposes and modular design of many sites restrict argumentation to what I call "data-bytes," the cyber equivalent of television sound bites. As well, much of the Web is more pre-occupied with the appeal of status that comes from a web presence (ethos) and with multimodal, sensory appeals (pathos). As is suggested by the moniker "Information Superhighway," we might conceive of the logos of a web site as the caliber of its information offering. For home page authors, displaying information or, more precisely, validating whatever trivia they have to offer as indeed informative constitutes their sites' virtual logos.

As Michel Foucault (1979) demonstrates with his fusion of power-knowledge, knowledge and information emerge in conjunction with applications of power. Universities and corporations, with their power to marshal material, capital, and labor resources, can produce and dispense what is popularly recognized as legitimate knowledge and information and can construct and maintain sites that are perceived to be continuously informative. With this monopoly of the Web's symbolic currency, institutions thus dominate the web economy. With little capacity to establish new information, and hence with little capacity to offer high-modality messages that matter, individuals are left with trivia. Some draw on the kinds of discourses that are widely credited as being valuable, informative, and official, but undermine such discourses with a low modality, using material that is trivial, fallacious, and fraudulent.

This application of virtual logos can be seen on the home page of a male participant in his late twenties. His site is an archive of esoteric "information," especially mathematical discourse, consisting almost entirely of inside jokes, fabricated documentation, and sham mathematical data, such as the following:

- a fictitious letter from the "President" of the specious organization POACH (Protection of Animal Cruelty Hibernians) objecting to the author's use of animal names in writing and conversation. The letter issues the following warning: "[W]e do not mean to dog you, but we might have to turn you in to the pigs. We hope that you try to break this habit and don't duck the issue."
- a sophisticated but spurious mathematical calculation of the profligacy of houseflies
- a glossary mostly of quasi-mathematical terms, including
      umpteen
            47,012
      a lot
            265,503.12

a wicked lot
3,451,540.5

Two-thirds of the site, in volume, comprises "The Studley Encyclopedia (or Dictionary)," a "complete and unabridged" work, which even includes the requisite © symbol for verisimilitude.[1] The following are typical of the more comprehensible entries, many of which are otherwise based on esoteric inside jokes:

Guslike Jobs
the three professions that guses strive for. They are corner pencil vending, umpiring, and Studley lawnmowing.
Snarf
to exhale food through one's nose, especially when spontaneously laughing at something funny just said.
Yes
to attend gym class when not required to do so

This participant's eccentric site is entertaining and obviously the product of an intelligent, creative mind. In describing how he arrived at the theme of his site, the participant explained, "[I] [t]hought about what I could write about myself without sacrificing privacy." His work indeed protects his identity with its consistent abstention from earnest revelations or believable information. Using instead a bogus mask of specious text that resembles information, he satisfies the "Information Superhighway's" demand not for the presence of individuals but for certain kinds of information offerings. His penchant for numerical data, and especially his 35 Kb "Encyclopedia," results in a presentation that resembles those of larger organizations, with their resources to produce and control masses of data. By occupying a niche analogous to those of such information providers, this home page author puts his ostentatious work in dialogue with authentic constructions of logos. The main difference is, of course, the vacuity of his "information" displays. They constitute an elaborate parody of logos, one inspired by the veneer of "real" information resources but which does not aspire to the high fidelity of those resources. His voluminous "Encyclopedia," in particular, mocks the more sober versions of that genre. His site shows up "real" information for its situated condition. Logos is seen to be a private property of certain information owners. His virtual logos contests the exclusivity of that ownership.

Educating Citizen-Rhetors

In the three sections above, we have seen illustrations of what I identify as the virtual appeals of the web texts of ordinary web authors. On the surface, these may look like the frivolous pursuits of computer junkies with too much time on their hands. They invent fanciful titles for themselves, try to engage their readers in apparently fruitless question-answer exchanges, and post material that bears the intellectual caliber of doodles in the margins of textbooks. Their sites bespeak "attitude."

However, in light of the social environment in which these virtual appeals are made, and of the marginal positions and paltry resources of their makers, we can appreciate how, in the mass media, such apparent frivolity offers individuals one of their few viable public stances. My hope is that this chapter will bring some understanding to the tenuous positions of these individuals, and by extension, of all of us, as the juggernaut of the World Wide Web develops with or without our participation. Despite its promise of a new worldwide agora, the Web threatens to induce an agoraphobia among citizen-rhetors. We are small figures in its environment. As prohibitive as Internet access is for many, even more so is access to a sense of voice and agency. For the estimated 94 percent of Internet users who apparently feel they have no legitimate web stance to take up, a virtual rhetoric can be an inviting opening gambit; the low modality of virtual appeals manifests the lack of affinity individuals hold for their institutionally dominated environment. Individuals' mouthing of familiar institutional discourses reorients, and undermines, the suasive effect of such discourses. Parody inserts their voices, virus-like, into the commerce of the mass media, while at the same time redressing their estrangement. It contests the otherwise secure precedence and monopoly of institutional agents and practices in the public domain.

Imitation is one of the oldest pedagogical methods, and parody, which Linda Hutcheon characterizes as "a perfect postmodern form" (1988, 11), is a fitting contemporary application of it. Hutcheon locates some of parody's impulse among the demographic of "those who are marginalized by a dominant ideology," including writers of postcolonial nations and those outside the white-heterosexual-male demographic (35). I would add to this population individuals who, despite their privileged access to the new technologies, are seen to have little business being in the public forum, especially the young. Parody creates a speaking space for student publishers, usually receptacles of learned and literary and commercial discourse, who would otherwise be dwarfed by their society's Shakespeares and Microsofts— the unmatchable eloquence of the literary canon (e.g., Ruszkiewicz, 1979) and the unattainable power of institutions. Parody offers students a way to rub shoulders with, and to rub against, some of the loudest figures of their environments.

Through parody, students may exercise the resources of their discursive environment to gain a franchise in the public forum, without implicitly committing themselves to the ideology sustaining much of that forum. A successful student project, for instance, might not so much emulate Microsoft as expose Microsoft. A pedagogy engaging students with the Web would thus not position them to compete with professional sites on commercial terms—where rhetorical efficacy follows from a corporate ethos, a commodified pathos, and a data-thick logos—but in terms of the representations feasible for democratic citizenship: a critical engagement with public discourse and a position in the ongoing public conversation.

In this light, composing web parody is one answer to a call by many scholars for greater critical awareness of the role of new technologies (e.g., Johnson-Eilola, 1997; Selfe, 1999) and a greater role for our students as technologically supported agents of social change (Wahlstrom, 1997). The Web must not be left to brand itself as an electronic shopping mall, and our students certainly must not be positioned just as its shoppers and shopkeepers. More than two decades ago, Frank D'Angelo (1975) celebrated the critical potential of the graffitist. More recently, Selfe and Selfe called for electronic landscapes to be occupied by our "*nomadic, feminist, cyborg guerilla*" alter egos engaged in small-scale "tactical" actions (1996, 354). Some manifestations of these stances are already familiar among habitués of the Web, www.whitehouse.net being perhaps the best known of these. The emerging genre of web parody can help deflate the otherwise ebullient but uncritical ideology sustaining much of the Web's institutional interests. Its critical orientation performs an important counterbalancing function to the ubiquity of institutional, especially commercial, voices in the public domain. A virtual ethos, pathos, and logos can be cultivated as part of our objectives to develop such critical literacy, a literacy that would construct ironic distance between the prerogative of institutional practices and our students' voices as citizen-rhetors.

How we bring students onto the Web will influence the profile of the new medium as it develops over the next generation. In just a few years, the web population has grown from an obscure techno-subculture to the mainstream of society's principal institutions. While nominal diversity slowly increases, much of that diversity remains well hidden and seldom visited. The virtual landscape in public consciousness is increasingly indistinguishable from the real landscape sprawl of skyscrapers and shopping malls. Raising the public authorship rate above the paltry 6 percent may help relieve the new medium from the homogeneity congesting other mass media. My hope is that, as the Web develops, my former student with the quaint fixation on the color blue will have yet more to say to the world. Individuals like her can potentially add to the Web a self-reflective and critical dimension that institutionally sponsored sites cannot. Their voices thus take up a civic responsibility for our future virtual agora.

Notes

1. "Studley" appears capitalized throughout the site as an all-purpose, quasi-official adjective. It is defined in the site "Encyclopedia" as "awesome, funny, friendly, tricky, unique, etc." As far as can be discerned, it bears no relation to the name of the participant.

Over a hundred parodic sites, many targeting specific companies, may be found at dir.yahoo.com/Entertainment/Humor_Jokes_and_Fun/By_Topic/ Computers_and_Internet/ Internet/Website_Parodies/

Works Cited

Bakhtin, Mikhail M. From the Prehistory of Novelistic Discourse. In *The Dialogic Imagination*, trans. C. Emerson and M. Holquist, 41–83. Austin: University of Texas Press, 1981.

Buten, John. "The First World Wide Web Personal Homepage Survey." [Online]. Available: http://www.asc.upenn.edu/usr/sbuten/phpi.htm. (Cited June 17, 1998.) 1996.

Coe, Richard M. "An Apology for Form: or, Who Took the Form Out of the Process?" *College English* 49, no. 1 (January 1987): 13–28.

D'Angelo, Frank J. "Oscar Mayer Ads are Pure Baloney: The Graffitist as Critic of Advertising." *College Composition and Communication* 26, no. 3 (October 1975): 263–68.

Fairclough, Norman. *Language and Power*. New York: Longman, 1989.

———. "Critical Discourse Analysis and the Marketization of Public Discourse: The Universities." *Discourse and Society* 4, no. 2 (1993): 133–68.

Foucault, Michel. *Discipline and Punish*. Trans. A. Sheridan. New York: Vintage, 1979.

Hodge, Robert, and Gunther Kress. *Social Semiotics*. Ithaca, N.Y.: Cornell University Press, 1988.

Hutcheon, Linda. *A Poetics of Postmodernism: History, Theory, Fiction*. New York: Routledge, 1988.

Johnson-Eilola, Johndan. "Wild Technologies: Computer Use and Social Possibility." In *Computers and Technical Communication: Pedagogical and Programmatic Perspectives*, 97–128. Greenwich, Conn.: Ablex, 1997.

Ruszkiewicz, John J. "Parody and Pedagogy: Explorations in Imitative Literature." *College English* 40, no. 6 (February 1979): 693–701.

Selfe, Cynthia L. "Lest We Think the Revolution is a Revolution: Images of Technology and the Nature of Change." In *Passions, Pedagogies, and 21st Century Technologies*, edited by G. E. Hawisher and C. L. Selfe, 292–322. Logan: Utah State University Press and NCTE, 1999.

Selfe, Cynthia L. and Selfe, Richard J., Jr. "Writing as Democratic Social Action in a Technological World: Politicizing and Inhabiting Virtual Landscapes." In *Nonacademic Writing: Social Theory and Technology*, edited by Ann H. Duin and Craig J. Hansen, 325–58. Mahwah, N.J.: Erlbaum, 1996.

Stotsky, Sandra. "Participatory Writing: Literacy for Civic Purposes." In *Nonacademic Writing: Social Theory and Technology*, edited by Ann H. Duin and Craig J. Hansen, 227–56. Mahwah, N.J.: Erlbaum, 1996.

Wahlstrom, Billie J. "Teaching and Learning Communities: Locating Literacy, Agency, and Authority in a Digital Domain." In *Computers and Technical Communication: Pedagogical and Programmatic Perspectives*, 129–46. Greenwich, Conn.: Ablex, 1997.

PART III

Resisting Labels, Promoting Change

Taking a New Look at Rhetorics of Race and Ethnicity in Literature, Poetry, and Film

Until recently, rhetorics of race and ethnicity received far too little attention in rhetorical studies. Likewise, the role of raced and ethnically diverse representations in film and on television have often remained outside the mainstream of rhetorical inquiry, reserved more for the arena of cultural studies. This section seeks to put issues of race and ethnicity at the center of our investigations and to broaden rhetorical inquiry across a range of text types. In doing so, we implicitly suggest that close readings of representations of race and ethnicity across genres are critically necessary. While this can be done in a number of important ways, the chapters in this part highlight how we might theorize race and ethnicity through methods that challenge previous histories of rhetoric. As such, these chapters offer new rhetorical studies and histories of the discipline that do not simply include issues of race and ethnicity but place them at the crux of our investigations. Doing so has implications for how we reconceive of the history of rhetoric. As Jacqueline Jones Royster and Jean C. Williams have called for, "Instead of always measuring progress and achievement by the tape of mainstream experiences . . . and discounting viewpoints that do not match them, we have the opportunity to set the terms of historical engagement with a more critical view, to shift locations, and to raise questions, previously unasked, that might more fully animate knowledge and understanding" (581). We need to see that rhetorical studies that make raced representations crucial to our inquiry will not only change issues such as inclusion and exclusion. They will also alter our "social, political, and cultural" landscape (583).

These chapters challenge not only our received histories of rhetoric from which interrogations of race and ethnicity are often largely absent.

They also disrupt what has been the general trend in rhetorical studies about race and ethnicity. In other words, they call for what Keith Gilyard calls "theorizing race." While there are many "personal, albeit necessary reflections in classrooms and professional outlets," Gilyard suggests that we need to theorize representations of race and ethnicity more fully. This means not falling back on personal interrogations of race relations, but placing race and its representations within social, political, and cultural contexts. These chapters, then, seek to construct spaces in which peoples who have been marginalized, ghettoized, or labeled Other gain empowerment and agency through their speech. As Scott Lyons indicates, creating such spaces involves supporting the idea of sovereignty: "For indigenous people everywhere, sovereignty is an ideal principle, the beacon by which we seek the paths to agency and power and community renewal. Attacks on sovereignty are attacks on what it enables us to pursue; the pursuit of sovereignty is an attempt to revive not our past, but our possibilities." Lyons argues for "rhetorical sovereignty" or the "right and ability of *peoples* to determine their own communicative needs and desires in this pursuit, to decide for themselves the goals, modes, styles, and languages of public discourse" (450). These chapters reveal a support of sovereignty and a willingness to press against techniques that limit agency or result in further forms of marginalization.

Drawing on such calls to historicize, theorize, value, and question representations of race, these chapters attempt to continue these discussions about race and ethnicity in important ways. They ask questions such as: What does it mean to examine representations of race within different genres? How do representations of race and ethnicity operate within texts not often discussed when constructing histories of rhetoric? From what alternative theoretical modes for understanding race and ethnicity represented within our discipline might we draw in conducting such inquiry and why? How can we teach an appreciation and understanding of the rhetorics used by different cultural groups? The following chapters challenge traditional ways of thinking about ethnicity, race, and culture, and about the influence of rhetoric in the construction of identity.

Works Cited

Gilyard, Keith, ed. *Race, Rhetoric, and Composition*. Portsmouth: Boynton/Cook Heinemann, 1999.

Lyons, Scott Richard. "Rhetorical Sovereignty: What Do American Indians Want from Writing?" *College English* 51, no. 3 (February 2000): 447–68.

Royster, Jacqueline Jones, and Jean C. Williams. "History in the Spaces Left: African American Presence and Narratives of Composition Studies." *College Composition and Communication* 50, no. 4 (June 1999): 563–84.

8

Geographies of Resistance

Rhetorics of Race and Mobility in *Arna Bontemps'* Sad-Faced Boy *(1937)*

LAURA GRAY-ROSENDALE

Blow your whistle, Mr. Railroad Train. Me and my two
bubbers is all got itching feet. We got them bad, and we
aims to see the place they call Harlem. Blow your whistle,
sir. Take us away from here, if you please.
                                   —Bontemps, *Sad-Faced Boy*, 8

While relatively well known for his Harlem Renaissance poetry and
novels, Arna Wendell Bontemps has yet to receive adequate attention
for the complicated rhetorical tactics of his 1930s children's literature.
Largely ignored because these texts' intended audiences were children and
their political perspectives challenged both traditional and dominant leftist
paradigms,[1] Bontemps' books are quite discursively complex. They act primarily as sites of conflict and contestation in which hegemonic power relations popular during the time of their cultural productions are proffered and
then actively though temporarily resisted from within. In doing so, they
behave as "no mere verbalization of conflicts and systems of domination"
but rather, as Foucault indicates, the "very object of men's conflicts."[2]
Raising a variety of consonances and dissonances, what Mikhail Bahktin
terms "a multitude of concrete worlds, a multitude of bounded verbal-ideological and social belief systems," Bontemps' texts present a multiplicity of
verbal-ideological belief systems simultaneously.[3] In this essay I explore one
particular text, *Sad-Faced Boy* (1937), to show how Bontemps couples the
motif of physical mobility, transportation from a rural to an urban landscape and economy, with an associated theme of psychological mobility.[4] I
argue that mobility and immobility within the terrain of Bontemps' text are
complicated: both are at times positive and empowering, contributing forms

of resistance to the status quo and serving to forward problematic conformi-
ties, lack of resistances, and forms of oppression. *Sad-Faced Boy*'s geography
of mobility capacitates the characters to temporarily confront existing power
relations through challenging consumer markets and capitalism in their move
from the south to the north, use of music, development of multiple literacies,
and participation in a parade. Such examples sanction the characters to resist
urban modernism, dislocation, and confusion as they experience the problematics of associated with technology and urban capitalism.

Reading Bontemps' text divulges an alternative rhetorical perspective
and, more precisely, an oppositional text: (1) It contributes a rhetorical reading of a text not often read as rhetorical, revising the view of this text as
strictly apolitical. Although Bontemps has been often criticized as an assimi-
lationist "Southern chivalric," a "rationalist, analyst, and educator, a status-
seeker in the middle class,"[5] his textual choices, under close scrutiny, emerge
as highly political. (2) It announces complex realignments of the values frequently attributed to cultural and linguistic forms (including mobility and
conformity). As Violet Harris advises, Bontemps' text "contradicts traditional portrayals" of African Americans in ways that "might alter the group's
status, or at least change some perceptions of the group."[6] And (3) it discloses
the possibilities for agency extended by the narrative itself to a population
generally overlooked—children—making explicit that their socialization and
politicization ought to be valued.

In his 1937 *The Negro in American Fiction* Sterling Brown asserts that
in working against racist stereotypes Bontemps in effect constructed a new
audience that failed to impose middle-class white traditions onto black children, enabling them to create their own value systems.[7] As such, Bontemps'
text is able to expose and undermine economic, social, and political tactics as
well as intricate operations of power relations prevalent during the period.
While Bontemps' text conforms to the traditional migration narrative (of a
catalyst to migration), initial confrontation with the urban landscape, navigation of the landscape, and construction of the urban subjectivity, it also supplies an unexpected deconstruction of that very subjectivity and a return to
the original, although altered, location. As a result, in contrast to its por-
trayal in most migration narratives, the South is represented multiply, not
only as a site of dispossession and disenfranchisement due to slavery, and
not solely as a site of romanticism for an agrarian past. Additionally, the
North is represented ambiguously as a space of rabid consumerism and a
problematic capitalist economy that nevertheless holds adventures and possibilities which bring agency and empowerment.

Initiating a complex symbolization system that is polyvocal and ambiguous, destabilizing binary economies such as black/white, poor/wealthy, rural/

urban, and the like in favor of simultaneous differences, *Sad-Faced Boy* utilizes several innovative rhetorical techniques that afford linguistic defiance of economic and cultural assimilation. Aimed primarily at capturing an audience of African American children, this emphasis on physical and psychological mobility was concordant with the demographics of the 1930s, when many Southern black families relocated to the North. This was due in part to Northern industries' desires to produce a new labor and consumer market. Bontemps' book disrupted the notion that a shift to the North would easily abolish the oppressions of the South such as Jim Crow, lynchings, and sharecropping, specifying that there were comparable perils to be encountered in the North that had to do with the firmly entrenched operations of a market-driven economy.

Bontemps' text employs rhetoric on two levels: the local or sentence level, and the global or narrative level. At the sentence level, Bontemps assembles rhetorical figures of speech such as antithesis, apposition, alliteration, assonance, anaphora, climax, metaphor, metonymy, rhetorical questions, and simile that help support the larger cultural rhetorical choices that the text makes. At the narrative level the text behaves rhetorically to affirm as well as disrupt conventional binary oppositions that result in insidious forms of oppression, thereby contributing possibilities for empowerment and temporary freedom from alienation and marginalization.

Rural and Urban Landscapes: Consumer Markets and Capitalism

Sad-Faced Boy concentrates particularly on the adventures of three African American brothers ages eight through eleven, Slumber, Rags, and Willie Dozier, and their migration from the rural South of Alabama to the Northern city of Harlem.[8] Slumber, the eldest brother and main character, commences the story in a state of literal immobility. We find him lying on a freight station platform next to bales of cotton and sacks of grain readied for export. Using anaphora and apposition, the narrative characterizes the plight of a "sad-faced boy": "Slumber, the sad-faced boy, drew his harmonica lightly across his lips. What should he play next? Ho-hum, it was almost too hot to think. . . . He was a sad-faced boy, that Slumber. He was sad-faced and he never laughed."[9] The use of these sentence-level rhetorical techniques heightens the reader's sense of the bleakness of Slumber's situation and reinforces the extent to which Slumber is immobile both physically and psychologically.

Quickly the narrative's rhetorical choices illustrate that Slumber's paralysis and sadness are due in large part to the adversities that this young African American male has endured within the rural South. Slumber has already experienced the hardships that await him as a future Southern black sharecropper. Likewise, Slumber appears acutely aware of his own exploitation as a child worker. Slumber has spent many a summer working for his family, picking cotton, hoeing fields, and driving mules. As the narrative clarifies, exercising the rhetorical device of a climactic series, Slumber "knew what it was to work in the fields where old Mr. Sun was putting out all the strength he had. . . . He was used to hoeing cotton when the ground was hot enough to fry an egg."[10] This rhetorical tactic operates to reinforce the many and often proliferating tasks for which Slumber has been responsible and therefore helps to perpetuate the reader's sense of Slumber's static immobility. Likewise, at the local level the narrative adopts paradoxical language to further communicate the arduous nature of Slumber's childhood: "He always thought about sad things like sick kittens and cows who had seen their pretty calves sold to the butcher and buzzards sitting on fence posts because they were too tired to fly anymore."[11] At the cultural rhetorical level of the narrative, the juxtaposition of "sick" to "kitten" and "pretty calves" and "sold to the butcher" also makes unmistakable the extent to which what should be a time of childhood innocence and leisure has been anything but that. The socio-cultural contextualization concerning the rural South further reveals the psychological and political effects of sharecropping, hard manual labor, and racial segregation.

Slumber's state of social, cultural, psychological, and identity-based immobility changes, however, when he and his brothers make a calculated decision based on Slumber's own newly emerging "powerful thoughts" to jump a freight train in the hopes of reaching Harlem. As a result of this proactive choice, Slumber's music suddenly becomes "sweet" and imaginative since, as he claims, using metonymy to substitute "way" for train or movement out of the South, "I'm on my way, big shorty, and it make me feel kind of good inside."[12] The sentence-level use of this term "way" and other key words that substitute for it within the language of the text transform what has been the character's rhetoric of immobility and sadness to one of mobility and potential freedoms.

Bontemps' choices do not remain on this simplistic level, however. As Violet Harris has disclosed, there is a "certain precariousness" about the oppositional images Bontemps' work utilizes.[13] As swiftly as the rural South has been denigrated for its social oppressions, the narrative works rhetorically to resurrect and reconstitute it, destabilizing binary conceptions of North and South, revaluing the South in terms of its resistances to urban capitalism. After the boys leave the train, they catch a ride on a truck. During this second leg of the brothers' journey, despite Slumber's own suffering within the South, he apprehends that his own experiences of the rural South do indeed present him with a great deal to teach people from the

North. Slumber pauses, however, understanding that he might have trouble explaining their value since his experiences perform outside the machinations of urban capitalism in city life. While Slumber recalls his home in Alabama descriptively as "a small brown cabin, not much taller than the high green corn that grew around it," he also foregrounds the merit of appreciating the simplicity of this small home.[14] According to Slumber, one should value the land on which one grows all that one needs in order to sustain livelihood, and the aesthetic beauty of nature. Using assonance, the repetition of similar vowel sounds preceded and followed by different consonants, the narrative recounts "rows of sunflowers . . . how sweet the world smelled when that lilac bush bloomed . . . the blue trumpet-shaped flowers that hung in clusters like bunches of grapes on the vine . . . how the fields of cotton seemed to roll like waves."[15] The positive valuation of attributes of the Southern life builds through Bontemps' rhetorical choices of repetition and assonance.

Bontemps juxtaposes these representations of the rural South to Slumber's first impressions of Harlem. While the North has fewer overt forms of oppression, it does employ more covert forms, such as noise, technology, and alienation. The continued rhetorical practice of assonance and simile renders this situation all the more palpable: "The clamor grew louder and louder. There were bells ringing, motors popping, wheels rattling, voices shouting . . . trains passed with a roar like thunder."[16] "So many wagons and trucks and automobiles and streetcars jostled down below that Slumber expected them to smash into one another any minute."[17] While the rhetorical techniques of assonance and repetition are adopted to build a positive valuation for the South, Bontemps makes use of the very same rhetorical techniques to revalue the North as potentially frightening and frenetic.

The North's other forms of oppression include the effects of the operations of a market-driven economy on its populations. The boys witness the overabundance of goods for sale in the outdoor markets, and ask a rhetorical question so as to implicitly assert the emphatic statement that there is something wrong with this situation: "What did folks want with so many kinds of cabbage?"[18] This permits Bontemps to contend that there are indeed problems within the Northern economy without having his characters or his narrator say so directly. The boys also discern that this overflow of goods produces problematic competition (the boys witness a fight between two chefs over a bunch of turnips), and that the economic situation impacts negatively on small businesses as they struggle to sell their goods.[19]

The North as a site of liberation or freedom and mobility is further called into question as the boys settle into life in Harlem. They apprehend that they are no longer observers of this economy but participants in it. As such, they are forced to work mopping floors and carrying sandwich signs.

The boys seem none too happy with the economic operations of the North, which produce large levels of unemployment: "there were always many boys and men who wanted jobs."[20] Given such high unemployment, the struggle to maintain their jobs becomes more intense. Using the feeling of exhaustion and bleakness that comes from the repetition of similiar sentence structures, onomatopoeia, the sentence level of the narrative announces that in the North "people didn't have much patience. . . . They wouldn't waste many words talking about it. They could always find, and very easily too, somebody to take your place."[21] Even within their mobility, then, we learn that immobility still exists: despite the North's fast-moving pace and the boys' own movement within its landscapes, the city terrain still holds other forms of immobility for them.

Music and Resistance to Urban Capitalism

While the first part of the narrative works to deconstruct traditional conceptions of North and South, highlighting their internal contradictions, the subsequent parts of the narrative impart discursive tactics one might take to counteract such complex forms of oppression, particularly within the Northern terrain. It is perhaps through their roles as musicians that the Dozier brothers thoroughly achieve mobility by not partaking of middle-class white values, or market-driven motivations. Music acts as a rhetorical force that sanctions the construction of the boys' new black urban subjectivities that both challenge urban experience and yet give voice to it. Music crops up many times in the book as disruptive to immobility, assimilation to the market economy, and conformity to Northern culture. It furnishes a resistant space that presents moments of order, stability, and community amid the estrangement wrought by the urban landscape.

There are a number of critical instances aside from Slumber's early use of the harmonica during which this occurs. First, after finding a temporary home with their Uncle Tappin in Harlem, the Dozier boys proceed to the roof of the building and Slumber plays a new song he wrote about "three country boys in a great big city" which the boys play together repeatedly during the course of the book.[22] In particular, during this early stage in the narrative, music becomes a method through which the three brothers make sense of their own experiences of proceeding from the rural South to the urban North and the differences between the two places. Music also functions to afford a way for the boys to understand the differences and similarities between their situations within the two locations. Rags, for instance, dances to the music, whistles, and creates words to go along, singing, "Aw, blow your whistle, Mister Railroad Train . . . Blow your whistle on the Dixie line. Sun in the sky, not a tree in sight. Country boys in a big man's town."[23] At the cultural rhetorical level, fragmented sentences and repetition help to cement the ways in which the boys hope to keep their own values and realities intact in the midst of living in a landscape which does not immediately value them but which challenges and disputes them.

Second, music finishes a way for the boys to dwell in Harlem and partake of the market economy while not becoming captives to it. This emerges as very important since Harlem creates desires in the boys which they have never experienced before and which they cannot satiate. At the sentence level, the narrative's recurrent use of "you" manages rhetorically to entice the child reader into becoming an active participant rather than a passive recipient: "Harlem made you want things you never wanted before—like water ices and Eskimo pies and popsicles—but it didn't help you to get the money to buy these things."[24] As Rags elucidates, music itself works rhetorically to aid the boys in combating the various pressures of this market economy, to "forget about what we has and what we hasn't got" (90). The sentence-level use of polyptoton, the repetition of words derived from the same root, assists in reinforcing the ways in which materialism and possession are key to the boys' interactions with the Northern economy and therefore must be contested. At the level of the cultural rhetoric of the text, the boys are able to exploit music to accomplish this through fashioning alternative realities within the words they set to music and through the power they acquire while playing together. Music also becomes a critical safe space through which the boys can assert their own cultural heritage since the other activities which they adopted in the South to achieve psychological mobility, magic and conjuring, "didn't do a bit of good in New York.[25] As the narrative describes, "He [Slumber] found that in the big city to which he and his brothers had come even a rusty bent horseshoe or a rabbit's left hind foot wouldn't help you to get a cool water ice when you didn't have the nickel."[26]

Finally, toward the book's close, the boys apply music to counteract the market economy's inculcation of wants and desires in them while still working within that economy. They accomplish this by locating an audience for their music and establishing a full fledged, self-sustained and -operated band complete with a harmonica, a washboard, and a tin can. At first the Dozier brothers play for the people in a building where their Uncle Tappin works as a janitor, sending their music through the air shaft as residents shower them with coins. While they certainly participate within the economy here, their actions and verbalizations make it explicit that they are not *of* the economy. Instead, the brothers utilize the economy's operations to their own personal and political ends. Later the boys play their music outside on the streetcorners in the evenings. Bontemps' narrator gives directions about how to get to the city streets on which the boys played: "You will pass beneath the shadows overhead as the black men of the jungle used to pass beneath the trees of Africa."[27] These "directions" and the use of simile reveal the extent to which at both cultural and rhetorical levels Bontemps wants African American child readers to not only see themselves in the city but to equate the experience of the boys' city music with their own cultural pasts. At last the brothers play their music downtown during intermissions from plays and films: "Little Willie caught the time and began beating the drum. The theatre people seemed delighted. They drew around the boys, forming a half circle."[28] Eventually their music, which brings them a bit of money, affords the boys freedom from assimilation to this Northern market economy and its fabricated desires. Interestingly, rather than spending their money on the many products the North offers, they deplete their money on their return trip home on the train, this time leaving by passenger car.

Not only does the narrative indicate that music contributes a way to avoid physical and psychological immobility and to resist economic and cultural adaptation in the North. Music also helps the boys challenge the social injustices prevalent within the Northern economy. In particular, it affords the opportunity to flip the conventional racist construction of the minstrel show on its head. When Willie becomes sick with a sore throat and can't sing, Rags and Slumber deliberate about whether to disband the musical group. Instead, they agree to recruit a new drummer. The only drummer they can locate, however, is a young white Jewish boy named Abie. In order for him to function as a member of the band, the boys demand that Abie look "black" by painting his face and body with shoe polish, echoing the ways in which "black face" was utilized in racist ways by white performers before African American people were allowed to be performers themselves. Although the boys finally abandon this idea, they reverse the market-conceived situation through which black people were made to assimilate to white consumer desires and challenge the history of the minstrel show. Interestingly, the brothers choose in the end to abandon this project because they determine that it is dehumanizing to Abie.

Mobility and Literacy

The narrative provides several other critical rhetorical tactics at both the sentence and narrative levels through which the Dozier brothers defy cultural adaptation to Northern market-driven desires. They often deploy language coupled with action to accomplish this. When the boys ride what they term the "down-under-the-ground car" (subway), they learn that what con-

stitutes an "ordinary" experience in which money exchanges hands for transportation to these Northerners is altogether foreign to them: "They went
down the steps slowly. All of the boys were puzzled by the strange lay-out of
things in the subway station, so they took their time and noticed carefully
what the other people did."[29] Bontemps' long sentence structure and the repetition of key terms such as "slowly," "puzzled," "strange," "time," "noticed,"
and "carefully" helps to suspend the narrative in much the same way as the
narrative reveals the boys themselves have paused so as to fully experience
their new environment. Rather than going through and depositing his money,
Willie, the smallest of the brothers, deliberately decides not to pay and runs
under the wheel, resisting conformity to the parameters of travel in the North.
The narrative reads: "And there he was, inside with his brothers, laughing
about what he had done and holding up his coin to show them what he had
saved by ducking under the turnwheel."[30] Bontemps' rhetorical use of commas
as well as "and" help to break up the sentence, divulging something palpable
about the glee Willie experiences at circumventing the Northern rules.
Although he ends up having to pay the fine, Willie's conscious choice reveals
the extent to which he is willing to challenge those experiences which seem to
limit his mobility in the North rather than merely acquiescing to them.

The boys similarly resist cultural conformity and Northern conventions
of social decorum through their use of language and action when they
encounter a public library for the first time. They become captivated by all
of the children going in and out of the building carrying books. Rather than
remaining quiet and diminutive, the boys enter the library and read a book
they have never encountered before entitled *The Gingerbread Man*—a book
about a darkly colored cookie-man who comes to life, takes swift action,
and begins to run swiftly down the street away from his white baker. As they
read the story, the boys can't restrain their emotions and begin to laugh hys-
terically, rolling on the floor. Slumber cries, "Oo-wee! Look at him go! Hee-
hee-hee! He's an old gingerbread man, and see there, he's done hopped out
of the oven and started down the street. Oo-wee! Go it, Mister Gingerbread
Man!"[31] The image offered through Bontemps' rhetorical choice here is one
of mobility and resistance to conformity. The language is short, choppy,
filled with verb forms, operating in the imperative mode, and indicating
rapid movement. This, of course, echoes the boys' own choices within the
narrative as well. Because the boys are loud, the librarian demands that
they go home, saying imperatively, "Boys, this is a public library. We can't
have noise in here."[32] In this section of text, the librarian's sentences are
short and tight, mirroring restriction to the boys' own movement they
require. Although the brothers are forced to leave the library, thereby learning something about the limits imposed on them in city libraries for keeping
a certain kind of decorum, the boys also depart happy to have discovered

the book about a brown man who strategically escapes consumption by a white baker and his hungry customers.

The Parade: Consumer Culture Under Scrutiny

The last telling example of the boys' rhetorical resistance to economic and cultural conformity in the North occurs when they witness a parade. Here the brothers observe people dressed in "shiny shoes" and "well-pressed clothes," products that appear oddly and unnecessarily "brand new" to the boys, a result of market pressures more than need. Likewise, while watching "the human fly" scale buildings, Slumber declares that the man "will do anything for money."[33] As with the boys' incredulity about the market-driven desire to have new clothing, Slumber emphatically asserts that *he*, unlike these Northerners, would *not* do just *anything* for money. Instead, Slumber reasons that one should only partake in the market economy for justifiable reasons.

In addition, throughout their experiences of the parade, the boys' conceptions of the other aspects of the parade resist the problematic elements of Northern culture. For instance, after seeing a man on stilts, Slumber insists that this man is tall because of what he eats, and refuses to believe the explanation given by Daisy Bee, an African American girl from Harlem, that he is standing on platforms. In addition, after noticing a horse who resisted "behaving," the boys feel glad and happy for the horse's personal strength and conviction against the men "breaking" him: "That horse was a case, for sure. He seemed to be almost empty inside, and once or twice it looked like he would break down in the middle. . . . And the more the two men tried to make him behave, the more foolishness he carried on."[34] Here Bontemps employs language to paint a particular visual image. Just as he announces that it seems as if the horse would "break down in the middle," Bontemps' sentence does this as well, coming to a brief halt with a comma. Only later do the boys realize that the horse is not a real horse but several men dressed in a horse outfit. In the end, the brothers join the march themselves. They do so much as they played music earlier in the text. The brothers aim is not to perform for a white audience but rather to help those in the parade who appear weary, agreeing to take up their positions. Slumber takes on the role of the drummer: "The man was so happy to be rid of his tight shoes and the hot coat that his face was covered with smiles. He helped Slumber get into the things and handed Slumber's other shoes to Rags." Although the shoes were "too big and hard to walk in . . . Slumber was too happy to think about them."[35] Bontemps' hyperbolic terms ("so," "covered with smiles," and "too") draw further attention to the parodic and carnivalesque nature of the parade itself.

Conclusion: Teaching Bontemps' Work in Rhetoric Courses

This text, along with Arna Bontemps' many other rarely read children's books, recommends strategic ways in which rhetorics of physical and psychological mobility can afford agency to characters.[36] In doing so these texts present critical resistances to the social, political, and institutional forces that pressed on African American child readers amid the rampant racism of the 1930s. Offering up an oppositional politics, Bontemps' *Sad-Faced Boy* also aided in constructing subjectivities for these child readers, most often African American children, that afforded them agency and empowerment.[37]

Since examining rhetorical choices within children's texts is rarely done within rhetoric classrooms, in teaching courses that center on cultural rhetorics in African American literature during the early twentieth century, I often expose my students to Bontemps' texts. I find that reading these texts in small groups helps accomplish the following: (1) It gives students a good chance to apply rhetorical reading skills to literary texts and to recognize the complexities of rhetorical features within any texts. It also enables students to explore what rhetorical readings can offer that mainstream literary readings alone might not. (2) It allows students to recognize that many forms of literature can have political potentialities, even if they do not ascribe overtly to political platforms. Rhetorical tactics used within the narrative or by the narrative's characters can themselves have political import. Since students are often resistant to "politics," recognizing the extent to which politics are always already embedded within rhetorical choices and possibilities can be a very useful exercise for our students. (3) Students can come to see that texts within or related to the Harlem Renaissance can be far more rhetorically complicated than they at first appear. These texts, they learn, struggle to serve the purposes of different and sometimes conflicting audiences, market needs, and political agendas. Recognizing these factors can aid students in realizing that the most seemingly benign of texts are always already rhetorical, or constructive of specific yet often changing audiences, exigencies, and constraints. (4) Students can come to perceive that everything from word choice to the construction of audience and exigence can be deployed critically so as to advance persuasive tactics, promoting radical effects.

Reading Bontemps' children's books within the contexts of rhetorical criticism and Harlem Renaissance authors, then, helps provide new ways to read the Harlem Renaissance's contradictions, politics, and possibilities, making rhetoric come alive for our students in new, captivating ways. Doing so also opens up our research to the potentialities of reading how conflicts and contradictions operate within these texts as well as the ways in which narrative- and sentence-level rhetorical tactics work in concert with each other to produce politicized prose.

Notes

1.   Although rhetorical readings of adult-centered literary texts have frequently been offered, rhetorical readings of children's literature are scarce. However, I would argue that it is just as critical to examine the rhetorical tactics employed in children's literature as it is in adult literatures. Not surprisingly, many American radical literary histories have had little room for Bontemps' children's literature because it does not correspond to the general definition of "radicalism": it is not party-based, not class-based, not adult, not rationalist (but fantasy), and not overtly sociological. Instead, the writers of such histories have concerned themselves mainly with a broad exclusion of the politically "left" literary tradition from the received canon of American literary classics (see Rideout's 1956 *The Radical Novel in the United States 1900–1954: Some Interrelations of Literature and Society*, Aaron's 1964 *Writers on the Left: Odysseys in American Literary Communism*, and Foley's 1993 *Radical Representations*). As a result, such works have focused largely on the novels and poetry of Communists and fellow-travelers to construct their corrective contributions to American literary history and criticism. Four major treatments of African American children's literature have also neglected the import of Bontemps' contribution to the American literary history. These include Dorothy M. Broderick's 1973 *Image of the Black in Children's Fiction*, Bob Dixon's 1977 *Catching Them Young: Sex, Race, and Class*, Rudine Sims's 1982 *Shadow and Substance: Afro-American Experience in Contemporary Children's Fiction*, and Dianne Johnson's 1990 *Telling Tales: The Pedagogy and Promise of African American Literature for Youth*.

2.   Michel Foucault, "The Discourse on Language," in *The Archaeology of Knowledge and the Discourse on Language*, trans. A. M. Sheridan Smith (New York: Pantheon, 1972), 216.

3.   Mikhail M. Bakhtin, *The Dialogic Imagination: Four Essays*, trans. Michael Holquist (Austin: University of Texas Press, 1981), 288.

4.   This theme of mobility is depicted through Virginia Lee Burton's illustrations as well. Charcoal renditions of the Dozier Brothers in action are provided, representing them while playing in their band, running down crowded streets, traveling on subways, or wearing sandwich signs. In all of the illustrations for this book, the African American characters are portrayed attractively and in strategic ways. There are no denigrating images of African American people, only carefully and thoughtfully rendered ones. In the very last visual image in the book, the boys are looking up at falling leaves and crying with loneliness for their country home, an image which cements the boys' resistance to economic and cultural assimilation with the Northern market economy.

5.   James Miller, "Black Images in American Children's Literature," in the *Masterworks of Children's Literature* (London: Allen Lane, 1986), 114.

6.   Violet J. Harris, "From Little Black Sambo to Popo and Fifina: Arna Bontemps and the Creation of African-American Children's Literature," *The Lion and the Unicorn: A Critical Journal of Children's Literature* 14, no. 1 (1990): 127.

7.   Sterling Brown, *The Negro in American Fiction* (Port Washington, N.Y.: Kennikat, 1937), 167.

8.   *Sad-Faced Boy*'s favorable and unfavorable reviews since its initial publication are themselves telling. One May 9, 1937 review, entitled "Stories of Now and Long Ago from Mathematics to Movies: 'Sad-Faced Boy,'" proposes that the book resists stereotyping the characters' personalities and speech. Another 1937 assessment by Ellen Lewis Buell entitled "A Review of 'Sad-Faced Boy'" praises Bontemps' book, this time for his use of "crisp humor" and his "real understanding of boyhood" (79). However, nearly thirty years later, a review published in 1961 disapproves of the book, reading it now within the context of civil rights and radicalism. In "Realistic Fiction: 'Sad-Faced Boy'" the writers claim that while the book is well written and well conceived, it also falls short of being "realistic fiction." They write: "Although [the boys'] first trip to New York is plausible, their confidence in exploring the city seems somewhat improbable." Ironically, it is precisely the mobility exercised by the young boys in the book despite their psychological and physical oppression that makes the book seem "unrealistic" to these writers.

9.   Bontemps, *Sad-Faced Boy*, 1.

10.   Ibid.

11.   Ibid., 3.

12.   Ibid., 7.

13.   Harris, "From Little Black Sambo to Popo and Fifina: Arna Bontemps and the Creation of African-American Children's Literature," 126.

14.   Bontemps, *Sad-Faced Boy*, 11.

15.   Ibid.

16.   Ibid., 14.

17.   Ibid.

18.   Bontemps, *Sad-Faced Boy*, 15.

19.   Ibid., 16.

20.   Ibid., 37.

21.   Ibid.

22.   Ibid., 32.

23.   Ibid., 33.

24.   Ibid., 88.

25.   Ibid., 90.

26. Ibid.
27. Ibid., 100.
28. Ibid., 102.
29. Ibid., 51.
30. Ibid., 53.
31. Ibid., 67.
32. Ibid., 58.
33. Ibid., 81.
34. Ibid., 82.
35. Ibid., 85.

36. See 1932 *Popo and Fifina: Children of Haiti*; 1934 *You Can't Pet a Possum*; 1942 *The Fast Sooner Hound*; 1946 *Slappy Hooper: The Wonderful Sign Painter*; 1951 *Sam Patch, The High, Wide, and Handsome Jumper*; 1955 *Lonesome Boy*.

37. Eleanor Nolen's 1942 "The Colored Child in Contemporary Literature" and Marjorie Hill Allee's 1938 "Books Negro Children Like," both early reviews of Bontemps' text, make clear that publishers were beginning to realize the extent of the African American child readership (Nolen 347) Bontemps had captured in the 1930s and the need for books about African American children which were not problematically stereotypical in their depictions but realistic and more politically aware. These texts also evidence the extent to which Bontemps' books were used in Southern grammar school classrooms comprised mainly of African American students and white teachers during the late 1930s and the 1940s (Allee 81). As Allee suggests, African American children were drawn to *Sad-Faced Boy* precisely because it did not rely on "stories of old plantation life" or providing "grotesque" characterizations but instead gave children adventures they could hold onto while also making them aware "of their own background" (85).

Works Cited

Aaron, Daniel. *Writers on the Left: Odysseys in American Literary Communism*. New York: Avon, 1961.

Allee, Marjorie Hill. "Books Negro Children Like." *Horn Book Magazine* (March 1938): 81–87.

Baker, Augusta. *Books About Negro Life for Children*. New York: The New York Public Library, 1963.

Baker, Houston A., Jr., and Patricia Redmond. *Afro-American Literary Study in the 1990s*. Chicago: University of Chicago Press, 1987.

———. *Modernism and the Harlem Renaissance*. Chicago: University of Chicago Press, 1987.

Bakhtin, Mikhail M. *The Dialogic Imagination: Four Essays*. Trans. Michael Holquist. Austin: University of Texas Press, 1981.

Bassett, Jon E. *Harlem in Review: Critical Reactions to Black American Writers, 1917–1939*. Selinsgrove: Susquehanna University Press, 1992.

Becker, Anne T. "Early Railroad Days." *New York Times Book Review*, November 15, 1942, 8.

———. "Sad-Faced Author." *The Horn Book Magazine* (January-February 1939) 15, no. 1: 7–19.

———. *Sad-Faced Boy*. Boston: Houghton Mifflin, 1937.

Bontemps, Arna, and Jack Conroy. *The Fast Sooner Hound*. Boston: Houghton Mifflin, 1942.

———. *Lonesome Boy*. Boston: Houghton Mifflin, 1955.

———. *The Unpublished Papers of Arna Bontemps, 1927–1968*. Arents Special Collections. Syracuse University.

———. *Sad-Faced Boy*. Boston: Houghton Mifflin, 1937.

———. *Sam Patch, The High, Wide and Handsome Jumper*. Boston: Houghton Mifflin, 1951.

———. *Slappy Hooper: The Wonderful Sign Painter*. Boston: Houghton Mifflin, 1946.

———. *You Can't Pet a Possum*. New York: William and Morrow, 1934.

Breed, Clara E. "Books That Build Better Racial Attitudes." *The Horn Book Magazine* (1945): 55–61.

———. "Negro Character as Seen by White Authors." *Journal of Negro Education* 2 (1933): 179–203.

Brown, Sterling. *The Negro in American Fiction*. Washington, D.C.: Kennikat, 1937.

Buell, Ellen Lewis. "A Review of 'Sad-Faced Boy.'" *New York Herald Tribune Books*, May 9, 1937, 12.

Dixon, Bob. *Catching Them Young: Sex, Race, and Class in Children's Fiction*. London: Pluto, 1977.

Foley, Barbara. *Radical Representations Politics and Form in U.S. Proletarian Fiction, 1929–1941*. Durham and London: Duke University Press, 1993.

Foucault, Michel. "The Discourse on Language." In *The Archaeology of Knowledge and the Discourse on Language*, trans. A. M. Sheridan Smith, 215–37. New York: Pantheon, 1972.

Gates, Henry Louis, Jr. *"Race", Writing, and Difference*. Chicago: University of Chicago Press, 1986.

———. *The Signifying Monkey: A Theory of African-American Literary Criticism*. New York: Oxford University Press, 1988.

Gilyard, Keith, ed. *Race, Rhetoric, and Composition*. Portsmouth: Boynton Cook and Heinemann, 1999.

Grant, Robert B. *The Black Man Comes to the City: A Documentary Account from the Great Migration to the Great Depression, 1915–1930*. New York: Nelson Hall, 1972.

Griffin, Farah Jasmine. *"Who Set You Flowin'?" The African-American Migration Narrative*. New York: Oxford University Press, 1995.

Harris, Violet J. "African American Children's Literature: The First One Hundred Years." *Journal of Negro Education* 4, no. 59 (1989): 540–55.

———. "From Little Black Sambo to Popo and Fifina: Arna Bontemps and the Creation of African-American Children's Literature." *The Lion and the Unicorn: A Critical Journal of Children's Literature* 1, no. 14 (1990): 108–27.

Huck, Charlotte S., and Doris Young Kuhn. "Realistic Fiction: 'Sad-Faced Boy.'" In *Children's Literature in the Elementary School*, 261. New York: Holt, Rinehart and Winston, 1961.

Johnson, Dianne. *Telling Tales: The Pedagogy and Promise of African American Literature for Youth*. Westport, Conn.: Greenwood, 1990.

Jones, Kirkland C. *Renaissance Man from Louisiana: A Biography of Arna Wendell Bontemps*. Westport, Conn.: Greenwood, 1992.

Mikkelsen, Nina. "Censorship and the Black Child: Can the Real Story Ever Be Told?" In *Proceedings of the Ninth Annual Conference of The Children's Literature Association: The Child and the Story, An Exploration of Narrative Forms*, edited by Priscilla A. Ord, 117–27. New York: The Children's Literature Association, 1983.

Miller, James. "Black Images in American Children's Literature." In *Masterworks of Children's Literature*, 112–22. London: Allen Lane, 1986.

Nolen, Eleanor Weakley. "The Colored Child in Contemporary Literature." *The Horn Book* (September 1942): 348–55.

Olson, Gary A. and Lynn Worsham eds. *Race, Rhetoric, and the Postcolonial*. Albany: State University at New York Press, 1999.

Rideout, Walter. *The Radical Novel in the United States 1900–1954: Some Interrelations of Literature and Society*. New York: Hill and Wang, 1956.

Rollock, Barbara, ed. *The Black Experience in Children's Books*. New York: New York Public Library, 1984.

Sims, Rudine. *Shadow and Substance: Afro-American Experience in Contemporary Children's Fiction*. Urbana, Ill.: National Council of Teachers of English, 1982.

"Stories of Now and Long Ago from Mathematics to Movies: 'Sad-Faced Boy.'" *New York Herald Tribune Books*, May 9, 1937, 10.

Vaughn-Roberson, Courtney, and Brenda Hill. "The Brownies' Book and Ebony Jr.!: Literature as a Mirror of the Afro-American Experience." *Journal of Negro Education* (1935) 4, no. 58: 494–510.

Williams, Helen E. *Books by African-American Authors and Illustrators for Children and Young Adults*. London: American Library Association, 1991.

Wintz, Cary D. *Black Culture and the Harlem Renaissance*. Houston, Tex.: Rice University Press, 1988.

Young, James O. *Black Writers of the Thirties*. Baton Rouge: Louisiana State University Press, 1973.

9

Visual Rhetorics and Classroom Practices

Negotiating 'Contact Zones' in Julie Dash's Daughters of the Dust

ANTHONY J. MICHEL

The question of how to make cultural rhetorical theory "work" in the composition class remains perplexing. We can still see a contradiction in existing research in composition studies that continues to support a "skills"-based approach to reading and writing on the one hand, and that tries to incorporate cultural theories and a "critical" approach to learning on the other hand. While there has been a good deal of recent attention to the intersections of cultural and rhetorical approaches within English studies, there has been little discussion, with the exception of "social-epistemic" rhetorics,[1] of how we might make cultural theories relevant to the contemporary classroom.

Explicating Julie Dash's 1991 film, *Daughters of the Dust*, as a specific type of visual rhetoric, this essay seeks to develop one alternative to traditional classroom practices and social-epistemic rhetorics that too often incorporate popular texts into existing pedagogical practices, and ignore the specific academic context in which visual texts are produced and consumed. Postcolonial criticism, with its stress on the location in which language is circulated, affords an important set of assumptions for exploring rhetorical practices that challenge tendencies to "write" marginalized peoples as colonial objects. In an interview with Gary Olson and Lynn Worsham, Homi Bhabha suggests,

> Too often writing—in the broadest sense—is treated as a communication medium where the subjects of that communication are

constituted prior to the writing, where the objects of the communication are also constituted prior to the writing, where the objects of that communication are also constituted prior to that writing. (9)

As one specific type of cultural rhetoric, alternative visual rhetoric is defined here as the use of media such as film, television, and hypertext that disrupt dominant codes which inscribe colonial subjectivities. Drawing on the strengths of cultural studies and rhetorical analysis, alternative visual rhetorics incorporate postcolonial criticism to conceive of writing as "oppositional and reiterative textual responses of post-colonial cultures in dialectical relation to their colonialist precursors."[2] Careful analysis of postcolonial texts enables students and instructors to conceive of writing as more than the communication of predefined writing subjects. Dash's film, this essay argues, is an excellent model of a postcolonial visual rhetoric that allows students to view their own writing from locations within the colonial-postcolonial dialectic. An analysis of the film serves as a point of departure for students' own visual rhetorics. It can foreground the terms through which their own writing is mediated in the contemporary academy, which often views students as objects of, rather than producers of, academic discourse. Before developing specific practices of visual rhetorics, however, it is useful to locate these practices in the increasing body of scholarship called "cultural rhetorics" that seeks to bridge traditional concerns of rhetoric with cultural criticism.

Cultural Rhetorics

Recent analyses of the intersections of cultural and rhetorical studies help point to the importance of both close readings and the consideration of the cultural politics shaping production and consumption. As Sloop and Olson caution, in incorporating cultural and rhetorical critique, it is important to avoid privileging a close reading to the exclusion of an analysis of a text's production. It is equally important, they argue, not to "dilute" the close readings on which rhetorical studies are based. While acknowledging the importance of "social-epistemic" rhetorics and the ideological, the implications of social-epistemic rhetorics for the contemporary classroom suggest that we need to revisit the two theoretical strands to consider alternative approaches that decenter ideology as the structuring concept of cultural rhetorics.

Although it gives little attention to the pedagogical implications of this convergence, Thomas Rosteck's anthology, *At the Intersection: Cultural Studies and Rhetorical Studies*, outlines critical distinctions between the two bodies of knowledge. Cultural studies, Rosteck suggests, focuses on the "larger structural issues of ideology, race and gender" without paying adequate attention to the rhetorical focus on close reading (13). While cultural studies may overemphasize structural concerns, rhetorical studies, Rosteck argues, traditionally lacks "a true sense of the broad social forces involved in producing discourses" (14). Rosteck sees promise in blending these different emphases into a methodology that bridges the formerly separated areas of "cultural production, textuality, and consumption" (14). As John M. Sloop and Mark Olson contend, the convergence of cultural studies and rhetoric enables consideration of the "cycle" from production to consumption, and calls for attention to "more active and public forms of politics" associated with cultural studies and rhetoric's "focused inquiry into the available means of persuasion" (249). They, however, caution against the "conflation of cultural studies and rhetorical studies" that might limit the political potential which they associate with cultural studies and rhetoric's ability to provide "insights into the process of carrying out those politics" (250). Importantly, rhetoric's role implies that "public politics" are necessarily a part of a stated methodology and not merely an effect of rhetorical practices. This elision is particularly important if we view the role of the composition instructor as already part of public politics. What is needed is a cultural rhetoric that incorporates "close reading" practices of ideologies alongside analyses of the cycles of production.

The Culture Industry: Visual Rhetorics and the U.S. Film Industry

Julie Dash's *Daughters of the Dust* (1991) reveals interesting rhetorical tactics that can provide a useful model for classroom practices. It challenges linear or unified perspectives of history, undercuts colonial practices, and challenges traditional aesthetic conventions. It speaks to the production of privileged historical knowledge as it is impacted by particular cultural places and material circumstances.[3] The following analysis of the film focuses on cultural locations from which to explore the politics of production and consumption of contemporary cinema: the culture industry, technologies of historical representation, and authorial subject position.

The film centers on the Gullah culture, ancestors of slaves, living on islands off the coast of South Carolina. It focuses on a single day in 1902, and concerns strife in the Peazent family as some members prepare to leave their geographically isolated culture and migrate to the mainland United States.[4]

First, I provide a close reading of Dash's film that offers insights into dominant ideologies by looking at the specific conditions Dash faced as she attempted to get her film produced. I then analyze the culture industry to identify the implications of this reading on questions of aesthetic value and historical validity. Finally, I extend these issues to a discussion of classroom practices and the value of student writing.

Dash's film can be read as a strategic response to specific contemporary institutional constraints that repress "subversive" films. Initially the audience is positioned to view the day in which it takes place as historically significant through references to a particular date, August 19, 1902, and a particular location, IBO Island. As the film progresses, however, it becomes clear that the reason for the day's significance is contested and subject to each family member's perspective. The matriarch Nana Peazant, for example, is upset that her family is "coming apart" because of the move. On the other hand, her daughter, Viola, attributes historical significance to the family's move toward "progress" and "civilization." Several other characters add their own layers of meaning. Eula, another of Nana Peazant's daughters, is distraught over her pregnancy resulting from rape, and her husband Eli's perceived threat to his manliness. Yellow Mary, a prodigal daughter, returns from Cuba "ruint" with cynicism and disdain for Viola's idealism. The interplay of these perspectives, often dramatized in heated exchanges, argues against a single historical perspective. As the day unfolds, Dash's use of vivid and dynamic visual images and dialogue dramatizes the inability of traditional historical forms of representation to offer anything more than a reduction of a collective history. Dash's sense of history is linked, as Nana Peazant says, to "those who came before and those that will come." The question of significance, then, becomes a multivoiced challenge to the idea of a single perspective historical accounting, inviting a series of generative questions: For whom is this day significant? Is this day meant to be historically significant? Is the film historically significant? Indeed, is the film historical at all?

The text itself presents an ideological challenge to the colonial practices that represented African American history as static and univocal. Ideological critiques, as Stephen Slemon suggests, are "mediated through the colonialist educational apparatus," including the film industry, to effect "cultural domination by consent."[5] The Gramscian notion of domination by consent is particularly important to understanding the U.S. film industry as a set of ideological practices that can be read through the cinematic texts. Although no text is ever either totally subversive or totally hegemonic, some—and frequently these films make less money and might be less popular—consistently challenge normative Westernized conceptions. *Daughters of the Dust* is one compelling example of an oppositional film that rigorously subverts normalized Western concepts of storytelling.[6]

This text also challenges traditional conventions of aesthetics. Dash, who had spent ten years researching the Gullahs, found it extremely difficult to secure the funding for the film's production. When she approached the major Hollywood production companies, all refused to fund the film. She ultimately had to secure production money from non-Hollywood sources, such as the Corporation for Public Broadcasting, in exchange for broadcast rights after the film's release in public cinemas. Additional difficulties arose as Dash attempted to distribute the finished project. Even after entering the film with some success in the Toronto and Sundance Film Festivals, it was ignored by large Hollywood distributors. Finally, a small distributor, Kino International, agreed to distribute the film through small "art" theaters. Although it eventually became very popular among primarily African American middle-class audiences, the lack of advanced billing and limited distribution channels suggest that the film suffered from a tendency in the U.S. film industry to ignore films that veer too widely from mainstream conventions.[7]

Dash's experiences reflect a historical pattern in Hollywood, guided by market conditions, of not financing unconventional films.[8] Mark Crispin Miller suggests that the film industry took a significant turn in 1985, when anti-trust legislation opened the doors for large corporate acquisitions of independent film companies such as Lorimar, Cannon, New World, Atlantic, De Laurentis, Alive, and Island. The legislative act, Miller contends, put control of cinematic production in the hands of corporate giants like Disney and Time Warner for whom the movie industry constitutes one segment in an overarching industry guided by a desire for profit. The effect was a shift from films with "a tragic or subversive view to a posture both reverential and promotional" of national and corporate interests.[9]

Yellow Mary's and Viola's stories in *Daughters* offer examples of Dash's willingness to subvert Hollywood's marketing standards, especially Viola's traditional celebratory immigrant narrative. Taking a different stand than that of her mother's, Viola wholly accepts the promises of the mainland to provide "education, wealth and civilization." On the other hand, Viola's sister, Yellow Mary, returns from the mainland with a caustic cynicism about both the promise of the mainland and the "salt water Negroes" to whom she's returned.

However, Viola's idealism, which resonates with the rhetoric of Christianity and U.S. nationalism, is ultimately deflated in a crucial scene where she is asked to kiss a Bible which Nana Peazant has wrapped with one of her voodoo religious icons. At this point, Viola has come to realize that her family is a part of her identity that she can no longer totally dismiss. Furthermore, her willingness to finally embrace the dual religious icons calls into question the exclusivity on which Western historical teleologies are built. To dismiss voodoo as heresy would be to do violence to Viola's past, a dangerous act in a society that embraces a circular conception of history in which past and future are interminably connected. While she is willing to embrace Christian ideals and to associate them with a move forward, Viola is unwilling to live with the implications of a faith that denies her connection to her mother and her ancestors.[10] This overlaying of alternative perspectives is consistent with what Stephen Slemon argues is the primary strategy of postcolonial literary texts: "to position the oppositional and reiterative textual responses of post-colonial cultures in dialectical relation to their colonialist precursors."[11]

Further, Viola is what Homi Bhabha calls an "enunciatory subject—which is a subject in performance and process" (19). In other words, Viola's willingness to kiss the Bible signals a critical shift in her sense of self, undermining her earlier willingness to categorically embrace American nationhood. Hollywood seems to perpetuate a certain "type" of immigrant who basically desires to assimilate, but Viola ultimately develops a hybrid identity that overlays the past with the present, allowing neither to stand wholly static from the other. Overall, these market conditions provide insight into Dash's film and her conscious rhetorical decision "to subordinate market forces to spiritual forces as determining criteria for *Daughters*."[12]

Ultimately we gain a good deal from reading Dash's film in relation to dominant ideologies that ignore or marginalize African American experiences. However, while this conception benefits from a sophisticated understanding of the way texts operate as ideologies to effect "domination by consent," it doesn't encourage the reader to view the text itself as the outcome of a long, frequently formidable process of legitimization and silencing. Reading Dash's aesthetic through local production processes shows that one level of "significance" in the historical film is to be found in its irreverent response to the endorsement of contemporary celebratory immigration/migration stories. In contrast to the tendency to consider a film that takes place in the American past as divorced from the present, production analysis encourages an awareness of how history and historical knowledge emerge only as part of an ongoing process of elimination, reconstruction, and sanctification.

Technologies of Visual Rhetorics

The film also dramatizes the technologies that organize and legitimize particular types of knowledge in unique ways. In *Daughters of the Dust*, cinematic technology enables Dash to explore how the relationship between power and knowledge is organized and disseminated. In particular, *Dust* focuses on technologies of photographs and writing as colonial apparatuses that attempt to produce historical records. While it is important to read these technologies as they are explicitly portrayed in the film, it is equally important to consider Dash's film as a particular type of contemporary technology that impacts our understanding of the past. This section analyzes how Dash represents and employs technologies in the film to subvert traditional notions of historical authenticity. It then explores these uses as critiques of contemporary representational politics. The implications of Dash's text for classroom practices are particularly important and will be developed in the final section of this chapter.

The rhetorical depiction of Mr. Snead, the photographer, offers a critique of the notion that the photograph presents an unbiased representation of the past. Mr. Snead is an African American from the mainland, and is viewed as an outsider. He becomes a symbol of science and rationality, but his awareness and authority are narratologically subverted. For example, his camera cannot fix on the character of a supernatural unborn child that recurs throughout the film as a reminder of the interconnectedness of past and present. The child debunks Snead's rigid faith in the merits of modern technology and rationale. Dash, however, uses film as a means to shift the focus from the photographic record to the colonizing features inherent in the process of photographing itself. Thus, her text works to critique history's tendency to obscure the processes and subjectivity inherent in its own production.

Moreover, Dash's film can be viewed as a self-referential critique of a contemporary tendency to view cinema as a reflection of reality. Dash reveals the illusionary technology of film through her representation of a child's manual movie camera, where a series of images of a city in the United States are turned with a lever to provide the illusion of movement. The constant movement between photograph and motion picture suggests a self-conscious critique of all forms of representation to render a static, "true" reflection of reality. In contrast to the scientific forms of representation associated with Mr. Snead, these images demonstrate the limitations of science's ability to reproduce reality, giving added credence to Nana Peazant's haunting shouts, "I remember and I recall," as viable sources of historical significance. Moreover, through Nana Peazant, Dash presents an overall rejection of history as stored coherently in the past. Nana refers to "those eighteenth century Africans watch[ing] us." This statement suggests that the past and present overlap and that history is recursive rather than linear.

Dash's focus on photographic processes and her self-referential critique of the moving picture can also be viewed as an argument against the exclusive nature of contemporary media practices. Dash alludes to these practices of exclusion, stating, "In my film, I'm asking the audience to sit down for two hours and listen to what black women are talking about. When have we been asked that before, from a female point of view?"[13] Read in the context of dominant cinematic practices, Dash's challenge to the politics of representation of the past establishes a necessary connection to contemporary colonizing practices that still exclude alternative historical accounts.

Displacing the Colonial Subject

The concept of the unified narrational voice has important implications for the way visual rhetorics are used to legitimize and challenge particular types of knowledge. The unified subject is a modern ideal that posits some core or essence to each individual, regardless of her or his historical or social context. Through the disruption of narrative conventions, Dash critiques these modernist notions and, in particular, the notion of the single, unified authorial voice that presumes to tell "the" story. Dash also critiques the unified voice of the narrator by depicting history as the producer of subjective interpretations, limited by vantage points and cultural biases. This section focuses on two instances of Dash's challenge to this concept. First, I explicate her critique of the authorial or ethnographic subject position that has historically presumed the authority to speak for the Other. I then explore Dash's development of the concept of fragmented subjectivities. While it is important to read these critiques as they are explicitly portrayed in the film, it is equally important to consider Dash's film as a challenge to contemporary adherence to the autonomous subject. Such cinematic treatments are especially useful for helping students understand complex notions of subjectivity.

To disrupt the historical and contemporary pretense of cinematic objectivity, Dash effectively and perhaps ironically employs conventions specific to mainstream cinema to initially assume an authoritative, objective stance. Specifically she supplies apparently objective textual signposts that seem to moor the viewer to a particular place of origin by presenting written text:

> At the turn of the century, Sea Island Gullahs, descendents of African slaves, remained isolated from the mainland of South Carolina and Georgia.

This segment is a convention in much mainstream U.S. cinema, which tries to pose an objective, authoritative voice to orient the viewer. It supplies the reader with seemingly relevant contextual and historical information without providing its source or a sense of where it came from. It's such a common cinematic convention that we don't always consider its suggestion of objectivity, but it is especially striking in this movie because Dash seems to introduce it in order to subvert it.

This objective authorial subject position is established only to be displaced through a sequence of written, audible, and visual images that disassemble and fragment the authoritative subject. The presumably objective background information creates the expectation that the narrative to follow will correspond to the way empirical reality has been formally disseminated in Western cultures. This orienting voice, however, is supplemented by another written statement that begins to reveal a crack in objective stance:

As a result of their isolation, the Gullahs created and maintained a distinct, imaginative and original African American culture.

In contrast to the descriptive information of the first lines, this evaluative language reveals a slight shift in narrative perspective. Words like "imaginative" and "original" suggest that the group being described has its own agency, indicating that this group was responsible for creating their own culture. Their culture is presumably not a projection of colonial imagination.

The third phrase provides an even more forceful disruption of the authority of ethnographer to "write" another culture. Informing the audience that "Gullah communities recalled, remembered and recollected much of what their ancestors brought with them from Africa," Dash presents an alternative to empirical histories and undercuts the authority of the omniscient historical subject. The posture of ethnographic objectivity is subverted through this suggestion that history is a product of the people's own acts and not a static entity to be described by others. Moreover, this sequence of narrative perspectives constitutes what Stephen Slemon calls an "oppositional and reiterative textual response" to colonial logics (4).

This assertion of authority over one's own history is further demonstrated through the film's visual rhetoric. In the first shot is a brief, slow-motion closeup of two hands cupping dust, a disorienting departure from the black-and-white words with which the film began. The following images of the community's matriarch, Nana Peazant, fully clothed and immersed in water, provide a brief hint that perhaps she will be the source of such "remembrances." Her words, however, suggest an alternative to familiar conventions of a centralized narrative perspective:

> I am the first and the last,
> I am the honored one and the scorned one.
> I am the whore and the holy one.
> I am the wife and the virgin,
> I am the barren one
> And many are my daughters.
> I am the silence that you cannot understand
> I am the utterance of my name.

This pattern of visual disorientation and written words that continues throughout the film's narrative reveals the multiple subjectivities inhabiting Nana Peazant's "I." While she is a primary character in the unfolding debates over migration, the film dramatizes, through the sequence of images, a sense of communal identity at odds with the conventional singularity of the traditional Western cinematic narrative. The shot of Nana Peazant is followed by a sequence of misty images: a woman in a white dress, a couple floating on a

boat, and a man praying. These images further suggest a radical deforma-
tion of the authoritative text with which the film began. Nana Peazant's
words, moreover, establish a shift in subjectivity from the ethnographic "the
Gullahs" as a community known by its place and time, to a collective, circular subjectivity where one voice is both "first" and "last," "wife" and "virgin."
Dash again calls attention to the limitations of all historical accountings with
her reference to "the silence that you cannot understand." Yet this silence is
different from the silent voice of the ethnographer who speaks for the Gullahs.
It underscores that the limitations of understanding any group of people are
inherent to all histories that attempt to establish a single story of what happened. The film accepts this limitation, and because it regards all histories as
contingent, seeks to establish the credibility of alternative, circular, historical
accounts through recollection and imagination.

The text presents the limits of "recollection, remembrance, and recall"
along with the disorienting series of images in the opening sequence of
Daughters of the Dust to provide a linkage to the past buried by the traditional history or, more metaphorically, dust. Importantly, a mixture of visual,
audio, and verbal images dramatizes the apparent limitation of any image to
convey the "truth." In effect, the multiplicity of forms enabled by the visual
medium ruptures meaning from conventional (Western) systems of logic,
with its testaments to truth, and the viewer is left to determine the "significance" of infinite possibilities for meaning. The images then provide the basis
for the unconventional narrative perspective of the unborn child, who represents the link among past, present, and future. Over shots of the community
the unborn child asserts another claim to subjectivity through her extended
links to the family through time and space: "My story begins on the eve of
my family's migration. My story begins before I was born. My Great-Great
Grandmother, Nana Peazant, saw her family come apart. Her flowers to
bloom in a distant frontier. And then there was my Daddy's problem."

This close reading of the text provides rich insights into the film's ideological critique of dominant colonial and neo-colonial formations. Yet the
focus on multiple subjectivities inhabiting Nana Peazant must also be considered as a response to the colonial power dynamics that remain masked by
third-person authorial subjects. Through relentless fragmenting of the narrative subject, Dash provides a commentary on past and present practices of
writing the Other. Read outside the context of contemporary racial and gendered politics in the film industry, the film may actually reinscribe a sense of
disconnectedness between past and present, under the assumption that contemporary society has progressed beyond colonialism. So-called postcolonial
discourses argue forcefully that a view of the historical past as a separate,
knowable object, rather than as sites of ongoing contestation and debate, is

in danger of simply repressing those colonial logics and related material conditions that exist in contemporary society.

The belief that the past can be known as a separate entity, I argue, operates in writing classrooms that rely on unexplored distinctions between student writing processes and sanctified knowledges. Susan Miller's distinction between process writing and "actual" practices is one example of this tendency to rely on too great a separation between student writing and other, more legitimated forms of knowledge. Concentration on a visual rhetoric, as I stated above, seeks to complicate such pedagogical distinctions, emphasizing a critical approach that places student rhetorics in relation to multiple rhetorical forms. Visual rhetorics, moreover, provide a particularly rich starting point because of the increasing occurrence of multiple visual media forms in students' everyday lives. In the following section, I explore the broader pedagogical implications of this rhetorical emphasis by offering specific strategies for using visual rhetorics in the classroom. These practices seek to demystify the complex processes of negotiation that ultimately inform all forms of textual production.

Classroom Implications of Visual Rhetorics:
Negotiating Subjectivities in Student Writing

In *Shooting for Excellence* (1998), Jabari Mahiri argues that "as educators we ask students to study things we have seen to be important in our world, but our success with them also depends on our efforts to understand things they have deemed important in theirs."[14] To understand the "things" students value and that we, as educators, value ourselves, we might start by acknowledging the terms on which such exchanges take place. Reading *Daughters of the Dust* as a visual rhetoric provides an alternative to conventional rhetorical tendencies to avoid the impact of production on textual practices. By combining ideological critique with an analysis of production constraints, we get a richer view of the material, institutional, and ideological terms Dash negotiated. While the film provides an excellent source for reading the particularities of cinema and cinematic production, the ultimate purpose of using visual rhetoric for pedagogical reasons is to encourage students to view their own writing practices as effects of negotiations that emerge from specific cultural locations.

Rather than suggesting that we somehow equate the capital-intensive processes of cinema production with student writing, this approach uses a reading of film to encourage students to explore the terms on which they engage with instructors to negotiate their own material and ideological constraints.

Classroom practices should then be flexible enough to encourage students' self-conscious negotiations of the terms of exchange on which they read and write. What follows, then, are specific practices surrounding students' linking Dash's text to their own engagement with the culture industry, technologies and subjectivities.

The Culture Industry: Visual Rhetorics, the Academy, and Student Writing

Dash's film's unique institutional setting, demonstrated in the discourses surrounding it, provides a provocative framework for discussing the hierarchy of textual values within the academic institution. Dash's film read in relation to the material and institutional conditions influencing students' reading and writing invites a series of questions concerning the terms of exchange on which the student writes in the classroom. I consider academic definitions of aesthetics and history that shape their readings of cinema in the classroom, and conclude with a discussion of a classroom practice that questions the criteria for "good" student writing. What, for instance, does a grade represent regarding a student's ability to strategically negotiate academic expectations? What does it represent to students about their relationship to the academy as a discursive site? And how do expectations about future skills reflect a complex understanding of the terms on which students negotiate the contemporary academy?

An investigation of visual rhetorics can challenge the perceived stability of institutional definitions through asking such questions and by introducing alternative definitions that frame aesthetic value and historical legitimation as open questions that students will have to negotiate. A postcolonial visual rhetoric, like Dash's film, is part of a pedagogy that opens up questions of aesthetics in relation to the historical and material conditions influencing what counts as knowledge for the academy and for students. *Daughters of the Dust* provides just one source in an ongoing interrogation of the conditions attendant to all forms of textual production. In a cultural context where creative texts are often viewed and read as unified, autonomous expressions—as something that the student should "get"—I have found it useful to begin the course by calling assumptions regarding aesthetic value and legitimate historical knowledge into question.

Before introducing the film, students discuss two definitions of historical and aesthetic texts each. Historical texts are defined as (1) objectivist: those texts that seek to present as close a reproduction of facts, events, and people from the past; and (2) culturalist: texts defined as historical by those in a position to make distinctions between historical and nonhistorical texts. After some discussion of the limitations and possibilities of each definition, we turn to definitions of literary/aesthetic texts that are similarly introduced as (1) formalist: those texts that employ creative devices to elicit emotional or intellectual responses, and (2) culturalist: those texts that are called literary/aesthetic by those in positions of influence.

While these definitions are problematic in terms of contemporary theoretical developments, they provide a taxonomy from which the class may begin to frame the relationship between their own valued texts and those that the academy implicitly or explicitly privileges. This taxonomy was particularly useful, for example, in a recent discussion of Makaveli's (Tupac Shakur) "Me and My Girlfriend."[15] Many of the students decided that aesthetic concerns are highly personal yet at the same time acknowledged the institutional tendency to marginalize rap lyrics. By calling these texts into question, students get ready to broach the relationship between aesthetics and material constraints at work in *Daughters of the Dust*.

The questions that emerge from a discussion of aesthetic value and historical legitimacy in Dash's film provide a promising framework for exploring the relationship between perceptions of aesthetic and historical value and the circumstances surrounding the production of texts. Students who research questions surrounding the production of Dash's text begin to locate institutional and material constraints that too often go unnoticed in rhetorical analysis. Rather than supplying definitive answers regarding institutional politics, the difficulties associated with Dash's text, framed in relation to the definitions presented, generate promising lines of inquiry: What do her difficulties suggest about the racial politics of the film industry? What other visual forms support or complicate Dash's claim that there is an "aura of invisibility around black women film makers"?[16] Does the film itself comment on the contemporary politics of cinematic production?

An important shift in the class takes place when students are asked to explore similar questions regarding their own written productions. While there is no shortage of ready responses for what constitutes "good writing," questions surrounding the mechanisms that influence these conceptions are much more complex. Ultimately the dichotomies presented in my definitions of aesthetic and historical texts provide the framework from which student rhetorics will be negotiated. Discussions of what defines good writing, then, are cast in terms of a similar dichotomy: (1) traditional definition: good student writings are those texts that employ proper narrative conventions to clearly develop a sustained coherent argument; and (2) culturalist definition: good student writing is that which is called good writing by those who are in positions of power.

The class presents a series of assumptions or definitions from which their own writing will be evaluated. In the context of the writing classroom, the perception of subjectivity is often a good starting point, and students will inevitably argue that grading policies in writing are often subjective. When asked to clarify, they begin to approach something similar to a "culturalist" definition of good writing—that which those in power determine to be good writing. At the same time, I encourage students to consider those factors, which they might argue make all writing good or which are essential to good academic writing. A list from a recent class reads as follows: "clarity, interesting, good grammar, addresses audience." This "formalist" or "objectivist" definition presents the source for classroom discussion of the terms on which their writing will be graded. However, as our analysis of the film suggests, such questions are often complicated by factors external to the finished project.

Reading Dash's film through these definitions, then, helps generate questions directly related to student writing. For example, it is important to ask students what factors influence their desire to write a certain way in the classroom. It is often difficult to extend this conversation beyond grading and classroom concerns. However, the vocabulary provided by an analysis of *Daughters of the Dust* proves useful. Students, for example, are encouraged to consider the following questions: What are the material or monetary factors involved in your own textual productions? What are the cultural relationships between you and your perceived audience? Is there a "dominant" idea of good writing to which the classroom, instructor, or institution subscribes? Is there room for you to subordinate such an idea for alternative purposes? These questions often place the instructor in the dubious position of opening up grading criteria to student debate. Yet this position is preferable to the tendency to obscure the terms of exchange on which students are asked to produce texts.

Conclusion

Discussing visual rhetorics is equivalent to arguing for multiple rhetorics. This enables students and instructors to explore the unique ways alternative discursive forms are circulated through specific institutional settings, with distinct technologies, and with alternate assumptions about what constitutes legitimate knowledge. The analysis and use of visual rhetorics in classroom practices, then, encourages students to explore how visual media attain effects in relation to nonvisual rhetorics. A visual rhetoric operates in the classroom as an alternative to a rhetorical tradition that privileges writing over visual medis. As our culture is becoming increasingly saturated by visual imagery through media such as movies, MTV, the Internet, and television, it seems only appropriate, therefore, that we as instructors engage students with textual forms that they mediate in their everyday lives. The objective here, however, is not to displace one form of rhetoric with another. It is to incorporate multiple rhetorics that more adequately represent the many ways legitimate knowledge is debated and institutionalized through invisible logics. Jabari Mahiri's claim that instructors hope to engage students by understanding "things they value" also suggests that we understand specific rhetorical questions surrounding the multiple discursive forms students negotiate daily.

Notes

1. With social-epistemic rhetorics, I refer to James Berlin's definition of this term: "the real is located in a relationship that involves the dialectical interaction of the observer, the discourse community (social group) in which the observer is functioning, and the material conditions of existence. Knowledge is never found in any one of these but can only be posited as a product of the dialectic in which all three come together" (490)

2. Stephen Slemon, "Past the Last Post," in *Past the Last Post: Theorizing Post-colonialism and Postmodernism*, ed. Ian Adam and Helen Tiffin (Hemel Hempstead: Harvester Wheatsheaf, 1991), 4.

3. *Daughters of the Dust* employs a number of conventions of postcolonial fiction. Postcolonial texts are especially useful sources for visual rhetoric because they focus on the specific mechanisms by which knowledge is produced about marginalized groups. They tend to look at historic geographical and temporal conditions surrounding textual production. Critiquing the gaps of traditional scholarship, writers such as Toni Morrison, and Gabriel García Márquez and José David Saldívar stress that texts operate as strategic responses to colonial logics that continue to naturalize dominant ideologies along lines of race, class, gender, and ethnicity. However, postcolonial discourses have also tended to focus on strategies located within the written texts, ignoring production, so this line of inquiry could use further exploration.

4. *Daughters of the Dust*, Dash.

5. Slemon, "Past the Last Post," 4.

6. Although "oppositional" or postcolonial films provide excellent sources for visual rhetorics because they often foreground issues surrounding the politics of representation, I have also used texts that are less subversive. For instance, other movies I've found useful for these purposes are *Mississippi Masala* and *The Quick and the Dead*. Although alternate arguments could be made for ways in which these films reinscribe traditional norms of gender, sexuality, class, and race, this concern does not limit their potential for providing insights into various ways that dominant knowledges

are subverted. Indeed, 'mixed' texts often engage the most spirited and thoughtful inquiries into the relationship between politics and knowledge.

7.   Sheila Rule, "Director Defies Odds with First Feature, *Daughters of the Dust,*" *New York Times,* February 12, 1992, C15, C17.

8.   Vietnamese filmmaker and critic Trinh T. Minh-ha describes the invisible relationship between media and aesthetics as follows: "standardization and sameness in variation is the unacknowledged agenda of media suppliers and consumers . . . the goal is to render power sufficiently invisible so as to control more efficaciously the widest number down to the smallest detail of existence." For an excellent discussion of the relationship between cinema and market conditions, see Trinh, Minh-ha, *When the Moon Waxes Red: Representation and Cultural Politics* (New York: Routledge, 1991), 86–91.

9.   Mark Crispin Miller, *Seeing Through Movies* (New York: Pantheon, 1990), 6–10.

10.   *Daughters of the Dust*, Dash.

11.   Slemon, "Past the Last Post," 4.

12.   Greg Tate, "La Venus Negre," *Artforum* (January 1992): 90.

13.   Rule, "Director Defies Odds with First Feature, *Daughters of the Dust,*" C15, C17.

14.   Jabari Mahiri, *Shooting for Excellence: African American and Youth Culture in New Century Schools* (Urbana, Ill.: National Council of the Teachers of English, 1998), 116–17.

15.   Makaveli. "Me and My Girlfriend," *The Don Killuminati: The 7 Day Theory*, Death Row Records, 1996.

16.   Rule, "Director Defies Odds with First Feature, *Daughters of the Dust,*" C15.

Works Cited

Berlin, James A. "Rhetoric and Ideology in the Writing Class." *College English* 50, (September 1988): 477–94.

Dash, Julie. *Daughters of the Dust*. Perf. Cora Lee Day, Barbara-O, Cheryl Lynn Bruce, Tommy Hicks, Kaycee Moore, and Alva Rogers. Geechee Girls, 1991.

Geissler, Kitty, ed. *American Identity/American Explorer*. New York: McGraw Hill, ed. 1997, CD-ROM.

Mahiri, Jabari. *Shooting for Excellence: African American and Youth Culture in New Century Schools*. Urbana, Ill.: National Council of Teachers of English, 1998.

Miller, Mark Crispin, ed. *Seeing Through Movies.* New York: Pantheon, 1990.

Miller, Susan. *Textual Carnivals: The Politics of Composition.* Carbondale: Southern Illinois University Press, 1991.

Olson, Gary A., and Lynn Worsham. "Staging the Politics of Difference: Homi Bhabha's Critical Literacy." In *Race, Rhetoric and the Postcolonial,* edited by Gary A. Olson and Lynn Worsham, 5–22. New York: State University of New York Press, 1999.

Rosteck, Thomas, ed. *At the Intersection: Cultural Studies and Rhetorical Studies.* New York: Guilford, 1999.

Rule, Sheila. "Director Defies Odds with First Feature, *Daughters of the Dust.*" *New York Times,* February 12, 1992, C15, C17.

Saldívar, José David. *Dialectics of Our America: Genealogy, Cultural Critique, and Literary History.* Durham, N.C.: Duke University Press, 1991.

Slemon, Stephen. "Past the Last Post." In *Past the Last Post: Theorizing Post-colonialism and Post-modernism,* edited by Ian Adam and Helen Tiffin, 4–13. Hemel Hempstead: Harvester Wheatsheaf, 1991.

Sloop, John M., and Mark Olson. "Cultural Struggle: A Politics of Meaning in Rhetorical Studies." In Rosteck, 248–65.

Tate, Greg. "La Venus Negre." *Artforum* (January 1992): 90.

Trinh, Minh-ha. *When the Moon Waxes Red: Representation and Cultural Politics.* New York: Routledge, 1991.

10

Audience in Afrocentric Rhetoric

Promoting Human Agency and Social Change

DANIEL F. COLLINS

> [T]he introduction of writing and all the subsequent stages
> of its development, are intrinsically new forms of social
> relationship.
> —Williams, *Writing in Society*, 3

Introduction

A lternative rhetorics (i.e., rhetorics that are open and accepting of different and alternative presentations of language and discourse) problema-
tize the assumption that rhetorical discourse fits into "easily recognizable
categories or modes" (introduction, this collection). Given that specific
groups define themselves and their worlds differently—for particular reasons and toward multiple ends—alternative rhetorics provide the means to
construct and reconstruct the worlds in which we live. Rhetorics are social
inventions, James Berlin explains, informed by conceptions of reality, language, and human nature.[1] Rhetorics relate to lived realities; they are products of economic, social, and political conditions of historical moments.
Rhetorics have roots. Exploring alternative rhetorics, then, can unsettle and
challenge common assumptions about rhetoric and foster reconsideration of
what has been taken for granted in the rhetorical tradition.[2]

In this chapter, I explore multiple understandings of a particular rhetorical construct—audience—through a comingling of Western and non-Western
theories.[3] I relate Western views of audience to those operating within
Afrocentric rhetoric (roughly, a rhetoric informed by African and African
American philosophies and worldviews),[4] identifying the kinds of social
relations they establish and the ways in which these relations are employed

in the production and use of human knowledge. In no way do I wish to essentialize these categories, however. The traditions of Western rhetoric and Afrocentric rhetoric are rich, varied, and fluid and are comprised of diverse theories. Instead of binary distinctions, unchangeable tenets, and nonporous borders, I enumerate each tradition according to historical trends that will, no doubt, change over time. For comparative purposes, though, I delineate characteristics reflective of their different rhetorical orientations.

The conceptualization of audience I offer highlights rhetoric as a process enabling human agency and social change without reducing rhetorical interaction to discursive combat. As James Berlin argues, a rhetoric tells people about who they are, their position in the social order, and the nature of the order itself.[5] A rhetoric thereby endorses certain social and political relationships and particular ways of being in and with the world. The question I am going to ask, then, is the following: Can an examination of audience across two largely distinct rhetorical traditions (i.e., Western and Afrocentric) help writing teachers consider the rhetorics of social relations in new ways?

Through my explorations, I want students to develop enriched understandings of important issues and therefore encourage them to use rhetoric as a form of inquiry, as a way of connecting with others, even across differences. Such exploration engages different perceptions, ideas, and implications of the many sides of an issue. I want students to identify and acknowledge informing assumptions behind competing claims in their writings and the writings of others, to see past calls for objectivity, to conceptualize themselves and their views in a constellation of others, and to discover the importance of gaining a social understanding of self. To attain these goals, I argue for a more fluid, dynamic category of audience. Using this approach, rhetor and audience are no longer considered autonomous and static, but affiliated with and transformed by larger social arenas and created through the rhetorical act. In the following section, I discuss the limitations of Western notions of audience and agonism and the need for a more dynamic interpretation of audience.[6]

Agonism and the Western Rhetorical Tradition

Although agonism is not the only form of social relations manifest within Western rhetorics, it is nevertheless an informing tenet. R. J. Willey, for example, cites Heraclitus's view of audience as empty receptacles in need of filling as the origins of agonism within pre-classical Western rhetoric.[7] According to Willey, this subservient role, based on a deficit model of humanity, is furthered to varying degres in the work of Parmenides, Empedocles, and Democritus. For Robert J. Connors, the history of Western rhetoric from the classical period through the eighteenth century is unquestionably agonistic. Connors identifies Western rhetoric as an assertion of self, explaining that any "public display of extrapersonal knowledge is agonistic."[8] As such, Western rhetoric borders on a contest wherein one combatant offers her or his views at the expense of others. Connors forecasts that even as Western rhetoric struggles to move beyond its agonistic past (in part through nurturing relationships between instructors and students and through "personal" observation and narrative writing assignments), "agonism is not gone from the teaching of writing, and in a pedagogically pluralistic world, it can never —and should never—be gone."[9]

According to Connors, agonism will—and rightfully so—remain a part of rhetorical education. That is, agonism is dependent on the perceived separation of the rhetor and his or her potentially antagonistic audience. This hierarchical distance (i.e., rhetor as separate from and superior to the audience) produces agonistic essays that often appear too quick to judge the opposition and too readily dismiss other sides of an issue without full consideration of their merits. In Western rhetoric, then, agonistic relations between writer and audience become standard practice, thereby fashioning a writer whose rhetorical success is dependent on the exclusion of other viewpoints.[10]

By merely positing an either/or duality regarding complex issues, agonism minimizes the grounds for the production and use of knowledge. According to agonism, people either agree or they don't, and with little intermingling of ideas, no fruitful exchange is created from which to construct new knowledge. Carole Blair and Neil Michel, for example, argue that Western rhetoric treats audience in "only perfunctory or assumptive ways."[11] Barry Brummett and Detine L. Bowers agree, stating that "the traditional conception of audience assumes stable subjects already 'in place,' ready to be swayed by a text that moves but does not constitute them."[12] Robert G. Roth maintains that "we see the audience solely as others out there upon whom writers must figure out how to work their wills."[13] To create new rhetorical spaces within disagreements, an alternative, dynamic, social sense of audience is needed.

Although Western rhetoricians struggle against notions of audience as a stable, textual entity, the conceptual vocabulary describing audience is informed by an agonistic history. Roth, Lunsford and Ede, Louise Wetherbee Phelps,[14] Gregory Clark,[15] and James Porter[16] all seek to constructively break down the boundaries between audience and rhetor; all seek in various ways to interrogate lockstep notions of audience indiscriminately following the lead of a writer. However, the lingering effects of an agonistic history—a hierarchical, antagonistic separation between rhetor and audience—inform these conceptualizations. For example, Gregory Clark writes:

Although made in response to the conversation of a community, every rhetorical statement necessarily claims independence from that process when it portrays one person's preferred version of the knowledge shared by the people it addresses as a truth that is already authorized by their consent. In essence, the private purpose of every rhetorical statement is to isolate itself from the collaborative activity that is the public function of rhetoric to sustain.[17]

Although Clark offers a vision of rhetoric as collaborative, social interaction, Clark's rhetor must distance herself or himself from others, thereby creating the initial conditions for agonism. Agonist relations are further reinforced by identifying rhetorical success as the exclusion of other viewpoints. For Clark the goal of writing is "to persuade others to believe what we believe."[18] The rhetor's objective is "to present what is only someone's belief by portraying that belief as if it carried the authority of shared, social knowledge."[19] Rhetoric remains a competition between enumerating one set of beliefs, values, and actions and denying the validity of others' ideas. Although audience is perceived as active and social, its agonistic overtones eliminate any possibility for a coexistence of differing claims.

To conclude, agonism denotes a combative response, reflecting a tendency to approach topics as polarized debates leading to inordinate competition. By agonizing opponents, by writing to engage in war, we lose sight of what it means to compose: to order, to create connections, lasting connections that develop into deeper relationships and more comprehensive truths.

Without dismissing good work done within Western rhetoric, I examine Afrocentric rhetoric as a reminder that the world can be reconstructed if we talk about rhetoric differently. Specifically, I show that Afrocentric rhetoric conjoins certain precepts and cultural values that distinguish it from Western rhetorics, including a legitimization of divergent viewpoints used to uphold multiple frames of reference. These tenets forge social relations between rhetor and audience that highlight a sense of obligation to one another regardless of divergent outlooks. My analysis shows that this rhetorical obligation is based on traditional African values, such as harmony and balance.

Exploring Afrocentric Rhetoric

Briefly, Afrocentricity uses as its conceptual base an African worldview (i.e., the placement of African and African American ideas and ideals at the center of inquiry) to examine African cultures and behaviors.[20] Under this rubric, African modes of being are understood from a foundation of African philosophy, history, and mythology. As such, African ideas and concepts are subjects and not objects of educational practices, culture, and history,[21] in turn positing Africans and African Americans as subjects of education, culture, and history. Afrocentricity, then, "strives to generate, sustain, and perpetuate viable and dynamic communities of African peoples. It simultaneously wishes similar objectives to all global communities."[22] Based on the belief in the existence of "polycenters of culture and history" from which knowledge is generated, distributed, and used, Afrocentricity is projected as a synthesis: "a nonhegemonic and polycentric synthesis" that centers groups in their own histories and cultures and connects them holistically with one another.[23] Intended to expand the continuum of human knowledge to include ideas native to African culture (and, by extension, other neglected cultural traditions), Afrocentric values can be used to examine the effects of Eurocentrism and the constitutive effect of language on knowledge.

Afrocentric Rhetoric: Audience and Agency

By way of definition, Asante poetically explains, that "rhetoric, in an Afrocentric sense, is the productive thrust of language into the unknown in an attempt to create harmony and balance in the midst of disharmony and indecision. The uses of rhetoric are varied, and it is necessary to include the production of disharmony in its utility."[24] By offering ways to forward and uphold divergent views in the face of rhetorical challenges, Afrocentric rhetoric is a mutually transformative relationship between audience and rhetor, a relationship that works according to its intrinsic power to open new rhetorical ground and expand perspectives on human knowledge. Contrary to traditional assumptions and values associated with Western ways—namely, an emphasis placed on a linear, individualistic, rationalistic, materialistic worldview[25]—Afrocentric rhetoric provides another perspective on reality, a framework based on harmony and balance from which to understand and (re)create the world.[26]

To begin with, Afrocentric rhetoric is informed by a conception of the human being different from that endorsed by Western rhetoric. Whereas a Western perspective generally isolates the self as an autonomous individual rather than a social phenomenon, Afrocentricity frames the individual in relation to the collective: "[E]mphasis is placed on those communication patterns and behaviors that will promote the bonds of strong and productive coexistence of groups in the community."[27] One such pattern is the African concept of *nommo*. *Nommo*—based on intonation and style, theme and wordplay—creates an immediacy between interlocutors through a collective vision and voice, turning rhetoric into an interactive and revitalizing force. Through *nommo*, the connection between the individual and the collective is established. Enmeshed in the cultivation of life, meaning, and communal understanding,[28] *nommo* attempts to bring opposing forces into harmonious relation. *Nommo* is that rhetorical element that energizes, linking all living beings, providing the impetus and the path toward collective responsibility.[29]

Paul Carter Harrison offers storytelling as one possible example of an active rhetorical practice designed to make manifest the power of the word. According to Harrison, the story grounds its speaker and audience in the realities of experience, and the ethos of the speaker—garnered through sound and gesture, style and performance—orders the world materially and cosmically to reinforce human connections and community as revitalizing forces.

With an emphasis on the collective, Afrocentric rhetoric also conceptualizes audience differently than Western rhetoric. Whereas Western rhetoric separates and privileges the rhetor over the audience, Afrocentric rhetoric proposes a more active, involved audience, one that designates equal participatory roles to both rhetor and audience:

> [T]raditional African philosophy cannot make the distinction of "speaker" and "audience" to the same degree found in rhetorical traditions of Euro-American society. Separateness of speaker or artist from audience in Euro-American society is based upon the degree of participation. But in African society the coherence among persons and things accords, so that music, dance, or nommo must be a collective activity.[30]

Within the collective cosmology of Afrocentricity, the rhetor attempts to augment preexisting communal ties through greater understanding between interlocutors. The importance of preexisting connections cannot be underestimated: the source of rhetorical exigence and possible social change is not seen as one well-wrought, highly sophisticated, agonistic text, but as a communal investment in others. Audience responses are seen as "joint creations of the text . . . in which collective experience is valued over individual needs."[31] Furthermore, affective approaches to knowledge—those that value feeling, emotion, and intuition—are just as important as rational approaches. Affective and holistic means of knowing and understanding the world promote the kind of interconnectivity valued within Afrocentric frameworks.[32]

Based on a desire for participatory democracy and open public discourse, Afrocentric notions of audience offer a model of a social, collective self that presupposes and utilizes rhetorical and cultural agency in the struggle for (rhetorical) power. In this way, the concept of audience stands as a synecdoche for the whole of Afrocentric rhetoric. What I mean is this: whereas audience and rhetor are defined according to an active engagement with one another, so, too, are multiple rhetorics. Alternative rhetorics, seen as "parallel frames of reference," are used to highlight multiple truths.[33]

Thus, Afrocentric rhetoric offers ways of "disidentifying from controlling structures" in order to decrease coercion and open up ground for alternative views.[34] Asante offers the example of an African American protest speaker: not only is the speaker constrained by racism in America (influencing how the speaker is represented, received, and responded to), she or he is also constrained by the nature of social protest in wider society (i.e., the language and syntax, and so on, of protest). Both circumstances inform the rhetorical condition and influence the nature of the rhetorical strategies available. To be heard, the rhetor must interrogate the rhetorical structure itself and show it to be an artificial construct. Afrocentric rhetoric emphasizes this structuring (thereby becoming a rhetoric of structure) in order to expose the effects of power relations on rhetorical situations and the subsequent production of knowledge within such acts.

To conclude, Afrocentric rhetoric offers a different conceptual framework and vocabulary to use with students to talk about audience conceptualization, what it is and how it works. Most apparent in this reconfiguration is the importance of rhetoric as a collective enterprise and the generation of multiple frames of reference in the construction of knowledge.

Pedagogical Implications

Based on this juxtaposition of Western and Afrocentric audiences, I offer the following pedagogical points, not as prescription, but instead to open a dialogue about audience as a rhetorical concept. Although we cannot presuppose the Afrocentric tradition of spiritual and rhetorical collectivity exists in our classrooms, we can help students move beyond preformed impressions and generate new knowledge within their compositions by creating fresh connections across entrenched positions. Can such an examination illuminate, theoretically and pedagogically, rhetoric as intersubjective understanding "that comes with the willingness to see through the eyes of those least like oneself"?[35] With this question in mind, I offer the following suggestions.

First, audience can be introduced to students as a social construct that is part of the rhetorical situation. This audience is not docile, but pervasive and active throughout the rhetorical act. Both rhetor and audience offer valuable insights and perceptions worthy of consideration and further deliberation; neither is empty or passive. As such, rhetorical success is no longer dependent on the exclusion of other voices; instead, other voices are used to enumerate the complexity of the issue under investigation. As other voices become important, the utility of agonism as the predominant means of argument diminishes. Because of this connection between rhetor and audience, different processes are used to analyze audience as a rhetorical construct.

Audience members are seen as knowledgeable; the rhetor's task is to understand her or his audience, why they believe what they do and how such
views seem sensible to them, and how these views intersect with other views.
Granting such legitimacy to views other than one's own need not imply that
we merely accede or cede to other claims. Instead, as Erika Vora explains,
we should "listen to each other more effectively, to see the world not only
through our own cultural lens but through those of others, without being
blown off our feet by any other culture."[36] Based on an understanding that
all perspectives are limited, endorsing a need to ask questions and resist clo-
sure by allowing conflicting ideas to coexist side-by-side, we frame rhetoric
as a means to a participatory worldview.

Concomitantly, teachers of composition can use the language of "balance" and "harmony" instead of the language of winning and losing. This
will allow students to see the complexity of political, social, or economic
issues according to the ways in which certain communities stake their claims
within the debates. Instead of dismissing other sides as paranoid, stupid, or
just plain wrong, students begin to understand why other sides comprehend
issues as they do. Students see their detractors not as the opposition but as
co-creators of knowledge mutually energizing one another. As Asante writes,
"[W]e can never truly know ourselves without the knowledge of others; or
more precisely, that we truly experience our own harmony in the productive
engagement with others. This is the *sudic* ideal."[37] As students begin to see
their positions according to a context of conflicting views, they will begin to
grow in their perception of themselves as social beings.[38] Such self-perception
reduces the perceived efficacy of agonism simply because multiple truths will
exist as realities to these students.

Toward such ends, when I teach argument-based writing, I ask students
to examine their views relative to those shared by other classmates.
Specifically, groups form around paper topics, and after students have indi-
vidually written synthesis papers mapping the intricacies of their topics, and
argumentative papers forwarding specific claims relative to those of others,
they work together on a project. The goal of the project is to have students
examine their individual argument papers in relation to one another and
resolve their differences to form a consensus position—*or* to identify the differing assumptions and arguments across group members and to articulate
the nature of these differences (i.e., determining and explaining the reasons
why consensus cannot be reached).

If a group chooses the first approach, they identify the consensus position reached and present it with the pertinent supporting information.
Narrating how the consensus was reached and why they felt it the most
appropriate position, students convey new understandings of their issue generated from their group interactions. They explain, in other words, what

their struggle across divergent ideas teaches them about their topic. If consensus is not reached, groups present the different arguments forwarded by their members, highlighting the pertinent supporting information for the various positions. From these arguments, students identify and discuss the different assumptions behind these positions. Each group explains why they cannot reach consensus, and students are asked to highlight new understandings of their issue generated from their group interactions (i.e., what they learned about the value of the positions enumerated).

In either case, such analysis motivates students to consider their interests, ideas, and experiences according to those of others. Differences potentially begin to make more sense when idealized rhetorical patterns give way to exploring actual situations (i.e., when our interests, ideas, and experiences—and those of others—are considered according to their cultural, social, and economic underpinnings). Students begin to see that differences matter simply because they are reflective of lives led and the wider social arrangements that shape our worlds. The negotiation of different subject positions also involves understanding conflict according to "positioning and power—conflicts in which students can discern that something is at stake, someone is affected, and someone has been silenced for reasons that can be determined."[39] Discerning the ways in which power arrangements bind debates within specific boundaries, students may be less likely to uphold one set of views at the expense of all others. They may, in other words, begin to see agonistic arguments as limited and question what information has been omitted or rejected. Furthermore, they may be more likely to value multiple realities and argue their views without denying the legitimacy of competing claims.

To offer another example, when my students write argumentative essays, I ask them to include a formulation and an analysis of likely future scenarios by answering questions similar to the following: Given the current state of affairs within a debate, what predictions can be made about the texture and shape of the debates to come? What issues will remain at the forefront of complicated debates? What discrepancies might get agreed on? What new exigencies or complications might arise? Such questions help students consider multiple facets of complicated social issues. Such questions ask them to consider various sides of a debate and forecast what might happen next without the agonistic exclusion of other views. Such speculation offers students the opportunity to excavate new rhetorical ground by moving beyond present positions to see other viewpoints as parallel frames of reference. Projecting future scenarios requires an understanding of the issues involved and suggests the importance of factoring in the longevity of divergent views.

We can also begin to help students appreciate non-Western ways of knowing the world. For example, we can discuss Afrocentric rhetoric's value of affective knowledge. Questions to help students generate affective knowledge

include the following: "How do I feel about the knowledge I gained? . . .
Does the knowledge I gained make me feel good about myself and the society to which I belong? How practical is the knowledge I gained? What are
the moral implications of the knowledge I gained? How can the knowledge I
gained be used to improve humanity?"[40] Answers to such questions would
generate further understanding of one's rhetorical condition, and not simply
from a rational perspective but from a more holistic view of the world. As
James Porter explains, "A writer does not 'analyze' an audience so much as
become one with the audience; a writer must not simply 'analyze' the emotions but must share the emotions, be of one mind and heart with the audience. . . . To change my audience, I have to be willing to change, too."[41]
Porter admits, though, that such a social view of audience comes at a certain
expense: "Treating audience in such terms may threaten a cherished assumption—the belief in the autonomous status of the writer as privileged ground
of discourse, as independent *cognito*."[42]

    To further an understanding of affective rhetoric, I ask students to go
into the community and interview heads of local agencies. Students, for
example, interview supervisors of soup kitchens and homeless shelters; they
speak with environmental advocates and administrators of women's shelters. They then write up these profiles or incorporate them into larger explorations of their issues. By profiling local agencies and the people who work
in these places, students develop firsthand knowledge of the ways in which
broad debates impact fellow community members. Hopefully, complex
issues become less abstract through their contact with people that have
vested interests in them. By experiencing complexity firsthand, students can
begin to see the trappings of looking at things through objective lenses. I do
hope they begin to see themselves as connected to issues with which they
may disagree, if only by beginning to understand the emotive sides of various debates.

Conclusion

To conclude, James Berlin points to a need for an increased awareness of the
role of rhetoric in democratic society. According to Berlin, "[S]tudying a
rhetoric in its relationship to society reveals a great deal about both a rhetoric and the society producing it."[43] As sensitive indicators of the nature of
any society, rhetorics also project desired futures of any society. That is,
rhetorics can create new kinds of relationships, relationships out of which
different patterns of human inquiry may arise. Why not shape our classrooms and our study of rhetoric around the need for greater levels of understanding between individuals and larger collectives that make up society? If

we believe that rhetorics are plural, if we see social realities reflected and constructed in rhetoric, then rhetorical action involves seeking out other positions and engaging in ongoing dialogue. If we believe competing claims to knowledge potentially lead to multiple ways of seeing and expressing the world, then individual achievements are weighed against collective perform-ance. Researching and teaching Afrocentric rhetoric (along with other rhetorical traditions) can put interpersonal relationships to constructive rhetorical use. Introducing Afrocentric rhetoric to students offers other ben-efits as well. To those already initiated, it offers a chance to reinforce the validity of Afrocentric tenets. For the novice students, introducing Afro-centric rhetoric provides the opportunity to see another version of rhetoric (and reality) and equips them with further choices to make as they compose their worlds.

Notes

1. James A. Berlin, *Writing Instruction in Nineteenth Century Amer-ican Colleges* (Carbondale: Southern Illinois University Press, 1984), 1.

2. Sonja K. Foss, Karen A. Foss, and Robert Trapp, "Challenges to the Rhetorical Tradition," in *Contemporary Perspectives on Rhetoric*, 2nd ed., ed. Sonja K. Foss, Karen A. Foss, and Robert Trapp (Propsect Heights, Ill.: Waveland, 1991), 273.

3. George A. Kennedy, *Comparative Rhetoric: An Historical and Cross-Cultural Introduction* (New York: Oxford University Press, 1998), 1.

4. Derek Owens makes an important point that Afrocentric rhetori-cal traditions have had direct and indirect influence on African American rhetoric, although differences do exist. My focus is on rhetorical patterns labeled as Afrocentric. For a discussion of the differences, see Owens, *Resist-ing Writings (And the Boundaries of Composition)* (Dallas, Tex.: Southern Methodist University Press, 1994), 72–105.

5. James Berlin, "Rhetoric, Poetic, and Culture: Contested Boundaries in English Studies," in *The Politics of Writing Instruction: Postsecondary*, ed. Richard Bullock and John Trimbur (Portsmouth, N.H.: Heinemann Boyn-ton/Cook, 1991), 35.

6. The tradition of agonism in Western rhetoric is well documented. See, for example, James J. Murphy, "A Roman Writing Instruction as Described by Quintillian," in *A Short History of Writing Instruction: From Ancient Greece to Twentieth-Century America*, ed. James J. Murphy (Davis, Calif.: Hermagoras, 1990), 19–76; S. Michael Halloran, "From Rhetoric to Composition: The Teaching of Writing in America to 1900," in *A Short His-tory of Writing Instruction: From Ancient Greece to Twentieth-Century America*, ed. James J. Murphy (Davis, Calif.: Hermagoras, 1990), 151–82;

and Deborah Tannen, *The Argument Culture: Moving from Debate to Dialogue* (New York: Random House, 1998). Murphy demonstrates the importance of imitation within rhetorical education as it relates to an agonistic tradition; Halloran identifies how belletristic rhetoric emphasized the genius and autonomy of the individual author, solidifying a disconnection between audience and rhetor at a time when audience was receiving proper attention; and Tannen explains how agonism has become a contemporary model for good civic behavior even as its adversarial stance instills inadequate patterns for social relations.

7.   R. J. Willey, "Pre-Classical Roots of the Addressed/Invoked Dichotomy of Audience," in *A Sense of Audience in Written Communication*, ed. Gesa Kirsch and Duane H. Roen (Newbury Park, Calif.: Sage, 1990), 28.

8.   Robert J. Connors, *Composition-Rhetoric: Backgrounds, Theory, and Pedagogy* (Pittsburgh: University of Pittsburgh Press, 1997), 65.

9.   Ibid., 67.

10.   Recently, Andrea Lunsford and Lisa Ede question such standards of rhetorical success that exclude other voices and viewpoints. Because Western rhetoric "casts misunderstanding, miscommunication, disagreement, resistance, and dissent as failure," Lunsford and Ede name Western rhetoric as a tradition of exclusion in its attempts to suppress conflict, minimize debate, and silence conflicting views through agonism. Lusford and Ede lament such exclusion and call for a need to create *new* rhetorical spaces within disagreements. See Andrea A. Lunsford and Lisa Ede, "Representing Audience: 'Successful' Discourse and Disciplinary Critique," *College Composition and Communication* 47 (1996): 173.

11.   Carole Blair and Neil Michel, "Commemorating in the Theme Park Zone: Reading the Astronauts Memorial," in *At the Intersection: Cultural Studies and Rhetorical Studies*, ed. Thomas Rosteck (New York: Guilford, 1999), 68.

12.   Barry Brummett and Detine L. Bowers, "Subject Positions as a Site of Rhetorical Struggle: Representing African Americans," in *At the Intersection: Cultural Studies and Rhetorical Studies*, ed. Thomas Rosteck (New York: Guilford, 1999), 136.

13.   Robert G. Roth, "Deconstructing Audience: A Post-Structuralist Rereading," in *A Sense of Audience in Written Communication*, ed. Gesa Kirsch and Duane H. Roen (Newbury Park, Calif.: Sage, 1990), 176.

14.   Louise Wetherbee Phelps, "Audience and Authorship: The Disappearing Boundary," in *A Sense of Audience in Written Communication*, ed. Gesa Kirsch and Duane H. Roen (Newbury Park, Calif.: Sage, 1990), 153–74.

15.   Gregory Clark, *Dialogue, Dialectic, and Conversation: A Social Perspective on the Function of Writing* (Carbondale: Southern Illinois University Press, 1990).

6effffff f

16. James E. Porter, *Audience and Rhetoric: An Archaeological Composition of the Discourse Community* (Englewood Cliffs, N.J.: Prentice Hall, 1992).

17. Clark, *Dialogue, Dialectic, and Conversation*, 61

18. Ibid., 50.

19. Ibid.

20. See Molefi Kete Asante, *The Afrocentric Idea*, rev. and exp. ed. (Philadelphia: Temple University Press, 1998), xv. Asante offers Cheikh Anta Diop, W. E. B Dubois, Ida B. Wells, George James, and David Walker as sources of inspiration for Afrocentricity. Other influences include Na=im Akbar, Wade Nobles, Linda James Myers, Kobi Kambon, Maulana Karenga, and Franz Fanon. See also Jerome H. Schiele, "Afrocentricity: Implications for Higher Education," *Journal of Black Studies* 25 (1994): 150–69; and Ayele Bekerie, "The Four Corners of a Circle: Afrocentricity as a Model of Synthesis," *Journal of Black Studies* 25 (1994): 131–49 for other works that inform Afrocentricity.

21. Bekerie, "Four Corners of a Circle," 137.

22. Ibid.

23. Ibid.

24. Asante, *Afrocentric Idea*, 46.

25. Jerome H. Schiele, "The Contour and Meaning of Afrocentric Social Work," *Journal of Black Studies* 27 (1997): 802.

26. Asante, *Afrocentric Idea*, 186.

27. R. L. Nwafo Nwanko and Chinelo G. Nzelibe, "Communication and Conflict Management in African Development," *Journal of Black Studies* (1990): 259.

28. Jeffrey Lynn Woodyard, "Locating Asante: Making Use of the Afrocentric Idea," in *Molefi Kete Asante and Afrocentricity: In Praise and in Criticism*, ed. Dhyana Ziegler (Nashville: James C. Wilson, 1995), 39.

29. Paul Carter Harrison, *The Drama of Nommo* (New York: Grove, 1972). Music, dance, and preaching also can exhibit *nommo*. See also Owens, *Resisting Writings*, 72-105.

30. Asante, *Afrocentric Idea*, 78.

31. Foss, Foss, and Trapp, "Challenges to the Rhetorical Tradition," 288.

32. Schiele, "Contour," 805.

33. Asante, *Afrocentric Idea*, 183.

34. Ibid., 31.

35. Kurt Spellmeyer, *Common Ground: Dialogue, Understanding, and the Teaching of Composition* (Englewood Cliffs, N.J.: Prentice Hall, 1993), 263.

36. Erika Vora, "Asante's Contribution to Intercultural Communication," in *Molefi Kete Asante and Afrocentricity: In Praise and in Criticism*, ed. Dhyana Ziegler (Nashville: James C. Wilson, 1995), 82.

37.   Asante, *Afrocentric Idea*, 204.
38.   Deborah Brill, "Issues of Audience: Egocentrism Revisited," In *Rebirth of Rhetoric: Essays in Language, Culture, and Education*, ed. Richard Andrews (New York: Routledge, 1992), 81–101.
39.   Dennis Lynch, Diana George, and Marilyn Cooper, "Moments of Argument: Agonistic Inquiry and Confrontational Cooperation," *College Composition and Communication* 48 (1997): 66.
40.   Asante, *Afrocentric Idea*, 158.
41.   Porter, *Audience and Rhetoric*, 116.
42.   Ibid., 115.
43.   Berlin, *Writing*, 3.

Works Cited

Asante, Molefi Kete. *The Afrocentric Idea*. Rev. and exp. ed. Philadelphia: Temple University Press, 1998.

Bekerie, Ayele. "The Four Corners of a Circle: Afrocentricity as a Model of Synthesis." *Journal of Black Studies* 25 (1994): 131–49.

Berlin, James. "Rhetoric, Poetic, and Culture: Contested Boundaries in English Studies." In *The Politics of Writing Instruction: Postsecondary*, edited by Richard Bullock and John Trimbur, 23–38. Portsmouth, N.H.: Heinemann Boynton/Cook, 1991.

———. *Writing Instruction in Nineteenth Century American Colleges*. Carbondale: Southern Illinois University Press, 1984.

Blair, Carole, and Neil Michel. "Commemorating in the Theme Park Zone: Reading the Astronauts Memorial." In *At the Intersection: Cultural Studies and Rhetorical Studies*, edited by Thomas Rosteck, 25–83. New York: Guilford, 1999.

Brill, Deborah. "Issues of Audience: Egocentrism Revisited." In *Rebirth of Rhetoric: Essays in Language, Culture, and Education*, edited by Richard Andrews, 81–101. New York: Routledge, 1992.

Brummett, Barry, and Detine L. Bowers. "Subject Positions as a Site of Rhetorical Struggle: Representing African Americans." In *At the Intersection: Cultural Studies and Rhetorical Studies*, edited by Thomas Rosteck, 117–36. New York: Guilford, 1999.

Clark, Gregory. *Dialogue, Dialectic, and Conversation: A Social Perspective on the Function of Writing*. Carbondale: Southern Illinois University Press, 1990.

Connors, Robert J. *Composition-Rhetoric: Backgrounds, Theory, and Pedagogy*. Pittsburgh: University of Pittsburgh Press, 1997.

Foss, Sonja K., Karen A. Foss, and Robert Trapp. "Challenges to the Rhetorical Tradition." In *Contemporary Perspectives on Rhetoric*, 2nd ed., edited by Sonja K. Foss, Karen A. Foss, and Robert Trapp, 273–314. Prospect Heights, Ill.: Waveland, 1991.

Halloran, S. Michael. "From Rhetoric to Composition: The Teaching of Writing in America to 1900." In *A Short History of Writing Instruction: From Ancient Greece to Twentieth-Century America*, edited by James J. Murphy, 151–82. Davis, Calif.: Hermagoras, 1990.

Harrison, Paul Carter. *The Drama of Nommo*. New York: Grove, 1972.

Kennedy, George A. *Comparative Rhetoric: An Historical and Cross-Cultural Introduction*. New York: Oxford University Press, 1998.

Lunsford, Andrea A., and Lisa Ede. "Representing Audience: 'Successful' Discourse and Disciplinary Critique." *College Composition and Communication* 47 (1996): 167–79.

Lynch, Dennis, Diana George, and Marilyn Cooper. "Moments of Argument: Agonistic Inquiry and Confrontational Cooperation." *College Composition and Communication* 48 (1997): 61–85.

Murphy, James J. "Roman Writing Instruction as Described by Quintilian." In *A Short History of Writing Instruction: From Ancient Greece to Twentieth-Century America*, edited by James J. Murphy, 19–76. Davis, Calif.: Hermagoras, 1990.

Nwanko, R. L. Nwafo, and Chinelo G. Nzelibe. "Communication and Conflict Management in African Development." *Journal of Black Studies* (1990): 253–66.

Owens, Derek. *Resisting Writings (And the Boundaries of Composition)*. Dallas, Tex.: Southern Methodist University Press, 1994.

Phelps, Louise Wetherbee. "Audience and Authorship: The Disappearing Boundary." In *A Sense of Audience in Written Communication*, edited by Gesa Kirsch and Duane H. Roen, 153–74. Newbury Park, Calif.: Sage, 1990.

Porter, James E. *Audience and Rhetoric: An Archaeological Composition of the Discourse Community*. Englewood Cliffs, N.J.: Prentice Hall, 1992.

Roth, Robert G. "A Deconstructing Audience: Post-Structuralist Rereading." In *A Sense of Audience in Written Communication*, edited by Gesa Kirsch and Duane H. Roen, 175–87. Newbury Park, Calif.: Sage, 1990.

Schiele, Jerome H. "Afrocentricity: Implications for Higher Education." *Journal of Black Studies* 25 (1994): 150–69.

———. "The Contour and Meaning of Afrocentric Social Work." *Journal of Black Studies* 27 (1997): 800–19.

Spellmeyer, Kurt. *Common Ground: Dialogue, Understanding, and the Teaching of Composition*. Englewood Cliffs, N.J.: Prentice Hall, 1993.

Tannen, Deborah. *The Argument Culture: Moving from Debate to Dialogue*. New York: Random House, 1998.

Vora, Erika. "Asante's Contribution to Intercultural Communication." In *Molefi Kete Asante and Afrocentricity: In Praise and in Criticism*, edited by Dhyana Ziegler, 80–92. Nashville: James C. Wilson, 1995.

Willey, R. J. "Pre-Classical Roots of the Addressed/Invoked Dichotomy of Audience." In *A Sense of Audience in Written Communication*, edited by Gesa Kirsch and Duane H. Roen, 25–39. Newbury Park, Calif.: Sage, 1990.

Williams, Raymond. *Writing in Society*. London: Verso, 1983.

Woodyard, Jeffrey Lynn. "Locating Asante: Making Use of the Afrocentric Idea." In *Molefi Kete Asante and Afrocentricity: In Praise and in Criticism*, edited by Dhyana Ziegler, 27–44. Nashville: James C. Wilson, 1995.

PART IV

Other People, Other Customs

*Defying Traditional Rhetorics of Gender and
Class in Asian Literatures and Cultures*

This part specifically examines the traditional roles of gender, class, and race in our construction of non-Western rhetorical theory and history. While many histories of rhetoric are driven by patriarchal conventions about women's roles in histories of rhetoric, and by Western understandings of gendered and classed behavior, the chapters in this part are specifically concerned with the rhetorics in non-Western literatures and the rhetorics used by non-Western cultures. These essays recognize the prevalence of Eurocentric forms of rhetoric as they converge with sexism, racism and classism. They also recognize that rhetoric, and with it literate behaviors, is always linked to cultural and power structures and is "saturated with ideology" (Street, 9). Thus, it is important to look at the cultural, sociological, and ideological conditions that are part of the rhetorical situation. It is especially important to look at different rhetorical situations in non-Western cultures, since, as George Kennedy points out, "some might argue that 'rhetoric' is a peculiarly Western phenomenon" (2). To move beyond such notions, the authors in this part ask us to rethink preconceived ideas of rhetoric as the prerogative of Western culture.

These chapters then push against the traditional views of Western rhetoric that dominate the discipline of rhetorical studies. The authors blend together traditional rhetorical readings of literary texts as well as readings of visual and cultural texts that are informed by feminist theory, poststructuralist theory, and cultural studies. As such, they seek answers to critical questions about the relationship among gender, class, race, and rhetoric: How does a feminist, poststructuralist, or cultural studies interrogation of the rhetoric used in the texts analyzed reveal investments we would otherwise be unable to see? How do gendered, classed, or raced forms of rhetoric work together to shape or change the rhetorical force of the text in question? Do rhetorical strategies differ according to the cultural understanding of peoples from different countries and nationalities? What is distinctive about the rhetorics employed in Asian literatures and films, and by Asian people from different class backgrounds? How is gender and gendered rhetoric perceived by Asian women and men? In these pieces, the authors assume that, as Joy Ritchie and Kate Ronald argue, "feminist theories offer alternative stances for working in and against the male-dominated canon of rhetoric, for questioning assumptions about the relationships between readers and writers, for demonstrating ways of rereading rhetoric, and for expanding received definitions of discursive authority and effective communication" (219). As such, the following interrogations of rhetoric provide new lenses through which to read non-Western rhetorical choices. Specifically, the chapters call for layers of multiple inquiry and suggest that rhetorical investigations cannot and should not be separated from other modes of theoretical inquiry, such as feminist studies, postmodernism, poststructuralism, postcolonial inquiry, and class-based analyses. The essays in this part look at alternative rhetorical forms used by Asian women, female characters, and people in lower-class positions to reveal their possibilities for rhetorical agency and their modes of empowerment.

Works Cited

Kennedy, George A. *Comparative Rhetoric: An Historical and Cross-Cultural Introduction.* New York: Oxford University Press, 1998.

Ritchie, Joy, and Kate Ronald. "Riding Long Coattails, Subverting Tradition: The Tricky Business of Feminists Teaching Rhetoric(s)." In *Feminism and Composition Studies: In Other Words,* edited by Susan Jarratt and Lynn Worsham, 217–38. New York: MLA, 1998.

Street, Brian. "Introduction: The New Literacy Studies." In *Cross-Cultural Approaches to Literacy,* edited by Brian V. Street, 1–29. New York: Cambridge University Press, 1993.

11

Rewriting the Butterfly Story

Tricksterism in Onoto Watanna's
A Japanese Nightingale *and*
Sui Sin Far's "The Smuggling of Tie Co"

HUINING OUYANG

In her introduction to *Tricksterism in Turn-of-the-Century American Literature* (1994), Elizabeth Ammons highlights some of the "fundamental questions" underlying the volume: "What are the possibilities and strategies for self-assertion, self-definition, and voice for the writer who is a person of color in a racist, imperial context? How does a writer occupying a liminal position—as does trickster—survive"?[1] The focus on the trickster in this set of questions suggests powerful implications for contemporary rhetorical inquiries. Underscoring the close relations among language, power, and knowledge, this invites us to question the presumed universality and objectivity of language and to explore the possibilities for resistance and change within the hegemonic discourse.

Since the development of poststructuralism and the social-epistemic rhetorical theories, critics have argued that rather than being universal or transcendent, language is a discursive terrain where different cultural meanings and practices compete for hegemony. As Michel Foucault suggests, discourse is power in itself, and those who have the right to participate in discourse exercise power by privileging certain statements in place of others in the production of knowledge.[2] On the other hand, to Foucault, power is not limited to a ruling body but permeates the entire discursive field, which, as he indicates, is multiple, uneven, and constantly changing.[3] It is this Foucauldian notion of discourse and power that informs my examination of revisions of the Butterfly narrative. While the Orientalist discourse underlying the master plot assumes authority in speaking about and for the Orient, Foucault's understanding of power as diffuse and productive prompts us to investigate the possibilities for alternative discourses to gain voice and validity and to transform the terms of the dominant discourse.

Connected with language, particularly with "the power to create or deceive by the word," in the phrase of Annette White-Parks,[4] tricksterism became one such alternative way of speaking for Sui Sin Far (Edith Maude Eaton) and Onoto Watanna (Lillie Winnifred Eaton) in their attempts to negotiate with the dominant discourses of race and gender at the turn from the nineteenth to the twentieth century. Although culturally specific, the concepts of trickster and trickstering share universal meanings. Typically characterized by disguise, ambiguity, disruption, and adaptation, tricksterism refers to the rhetorical and cultural strategies practiced by the powerless to achieve some vindication, validity, or balance of the scales. American literary tricksterism, for example, as White-Parks suggests, grew out of the marginalization and exclusion of women and minority writers and has come to serve as a means of "achieving voice and visibility in a context of oppression, even of overturning the established hegemony."[5] As women of Chinese and English descent writing in the era of Chinese exclusion, a period of severe Sinophobia in North America, the Eaton sisters relied on tricksterism not only as strategies of authorship but also as narrative and rhetorical tactics in their writings.[6] In their (re)presentations of Asian/white love and marriage, in particular, both writers reappropriated popular formulas so successful in the literary marketplace of their time and yet subverted many of the ideologies and stereotypes within these formulas. In the following readings, I examine how the Eaton sisters contest or accommodate the Orientalist discourse in their retellings of the Butterfly story. Through my analyses of Watanna's novel *A Japanese Nightingale* (1901) and Sui Sin Far's short story "The Smuggling of Tie Co" (1900), I focus on how tricksterism functions rhetorically as both form and theme in these texts, in which authorial manipulation of dominant language intertwines with motifs of the trickster. I argue that although they speak within the dominant language structure and thus do not ultimately transform the racial and gender status quo, in their efforts to reconstitute the power relations as constructed within the master plot, both sisters achieve voices of their own and thereby disrupt the Orientalist discourse of domination.

Through this focus, I hope to contribute an alternative view of rhetoric. Rather than examining audience, exigence, constraints, and purposes alone, the traditional rhetorical elements, I am interested in how narrative tactics work rhetorically to resist or accommodate hegemonic power relations. As a result, my inquiry affirms the call in recent years for combining the study of rhetoric with cultural studies. This means that we move away from readings of individual texts toward discourse analysis, examining how texts operate as ways of speaking about a subject, how they produce knowledge, and how they relate to other discursive practices. This in turn allows us a greater understanding of the language-power nexus and thus opportunities for resistance and change.

The Butterfly Story

Critics have long pointed out the intrinsic links between nation and sexuality, imperialism and desire, sexual politics and the politics of colonial rule. Some scholars, such as Robert Young and Ann Stoler, have demonstrated how nineteenth- and early-twentieth-century scientific, administrative, and medical discourses exercise sexual control to maintain the categories of colonizer and colonized, master and slave, white and nonwhite.[7] Others, like Edward Said, emphasize the symbolic function of sexuality in literary representations as a signifier of colonial domination. The signifying role of sexuality is certainly played out in turn-of-the-century Orientalist narratives of exotic romance, or what has come to be known as the Butterfly story,[8] in which the sexual possession and domination of Asian women by white men figure as a metaphor for, as Said puts it, "dominating, restructuring, and having authority over" the Asian Other.[9]

Set in the far reaches of the Orient, such as Turkey, China, and most frequently Japan, and usually authored by white male writers, the Butterfly story operates according to a major Orientalist discursive strategy. Namely, the romantic involvements depicted in this type of narrative are, without exception, between a white man and a native woman, rather than the reverse. Further, the white-male/Asian-female paradigm rests on a hierarchical relation of domination and submission, realized typically through the stereotypes of the childlike, willing doll-woman and the condescending, manipulative white hero. More important, this hierarchy is naturalized through the trope of Asian self-sacrifice. Whether it be in the narrative of transcendent love or the novel of desertion, the Asian woman readily sacrifices all—her family, ancestry, country, and sometimes even her own life—for the sake of love. The figure of Asian sacrifice finds its ultimate expression in the character of Madame Butterfly, whose Japanese ritual suicide immortalizes her as a martyr of romantic love and an exemplar of feminine submission.

Appearing at a time of Western imperial ascendancy with the rise of Japan as a burgeoning colonial power threatening Western dominance in Asia, the Butterfly story embodies not only an avowal of white male desire for the exotic Oriental female, but as an Orientalist discursive practice, it also produces and manages knowledge about an "Oriental" Other and thereby maintains and legitimizes power for the white male hegemony. However, although such narratives seek to represent white masculine authority as legitimate, fixed, and stable, they also reveal the inherent anxieties underlying the attainment of colonial power. The simultaneous assertion of and uneasiness with Western domination in John Luther Long's "Madame Butterfly," for example, indicate that the story is, as Gina Marchetti puts it, "far from being an unproblematic affirmation of the ideological status quo."[10]

The ambivalences and inconsistencies in the Butterfly story provide important opportunities for discourses of resistance. As Homi Bhabha reminds us, by "reveal[ing] the ambivalence at the source of traditional discourses on authority," we "[enable] a form of subversion, founded on that uncertainty, that turns the discursive conditions of dominance into the grounds of intervention."[11] That the elucidation of the unstable moments of the dominant discourse can become a powerful critical tool is similarly noted by Lisa Lowe. Such an attempt, she explains, "may prove useful in terms of both method and political strategy" because it is these moments that mark the places where this discourse is "vulnerable to challenge" and from which resistance may be articulated.[12] Indeed, it is precisely from these emergent spaces of opportunity that the trickster speaks.

Of Trickster and Butterfly: *A Japanese Nightingale*

Perhaps the most famous among Watanna's best-selling "Japanese" romances, *A Japanese Nightingale* (1901) was adapted in 1903 into a play that shared the limelight on the Broadway stage with David Belasco's long-running hit *Madame Butterfly*. According to Earl Miner, while the stage representation of Watanna's novel was "popular enough" because of its "genuinely Japanese" settings, "everybody compared it unfavorably with *Madame Butterfly*."[13] The ambivalent reception of the Broadway production of *A Japanese Nightingale* may well have reflected its ambiguous treatment of the Butterfly fantasy. Indeed, the novel on which the play was based reveals that *A Japanese Nightingale* is a complex text in which the Orientalist discourse is first simulated and then problematized through trickster strategies.

A story about the contractual marriage between an American man and a Japanese geisha, Watanna's novel appears to be another formulaic Butterfly story. However, although it is equipped with the usual trappings of Oriental exoticism—a Japanese setting with exotically charming gardens, tea-houses, and geishas and a feminine, "Oriental" print design with a cherry-blossom decorated cover, floriated pages, and color illustrations by a Japanese artist— it tells a distinctly different story of the Japanese-American romance. In the place of a Japanese innocent manipulated and dominated by a Western male is a heroine whose trickster maneuvers ultimately displace the white male protagonist from his position of dominance and destabilize the established power structure within the master plot.

Such play with audience expectations entwined with the trickster motif becomes evident in the very first chapter, in which the sensual storm dance of Yuki Burton, the Eurasian heroine, signifies a major trickster tactic for narrator and heroine alike. Through what Michel de Certeau calls "polymorphic simulations" and characteristic trickster mischief,[14] Watanna/Yuki teases her audience with Oriental exoticism and then frustrates them with her elusiveness.

Trickster play certainly characterizes the Japanese-American marriage that drives the narrative. From the moment that she offers to become the wife of John Bigelow, the richest Western man in Tokyo, Yuki plays a duplicitous role. She presents herself as an exotic Japanese innocent and then turns the tables, or, to borrow Min-ha Trinh's words, "beat[s] the master at his own game."[15] During the "look-at meeting" with Jack, Yuki appears to be a typical doll-woman—at once virginal and alluring. Standing in front of the man with her head "drooping bewitchingly" and her "exquisite, delicate" hands clasped before her, she stirs his desire with her "little affected pose" as well as her "thrilling, elfish laughter" and "entrancing" "ingenuousness."[16] And yet, Yuki is no Butterfly. Instead of being deluded by illusions of a fairy-tale American marriage, Watanna's heroine enters the contractual union with guile and cleverness. When a fascinated Jack asks her why she wants to marry him, she disturbs his fantasy by replying nonchalantly, "I mus' make money" (26). Indeed, her motive, as we discover later, is to help pay for her brother's educational expenses in the United States and his passage home. Playing on the desires of "foreigners who for a short, happy, and convenient season take unto themselves Japanese wives, and with the same cheerfulness desert them" (17), she reassures Jack that he needs to marry her "jus' for liddle bit while—as you desire" (30). Even though Jack, obviously tempted and yet seemingly scrupulous, initially withdraws his consent to the marriage, she succeeds in making him "[take] a fancy to her" (45), and, exploiting white male rivalry, she eventually persuades him by making it known that two other American men are also considering her. Yuki displays her trickster shrewdness again when she bargains during the marriage settlement, insinuating that Jack should pay more for a young girl like her, a virgin, not a formerly married woman. And once they are married, she constantly wheedles money out of him with her "little arts and witcheries" (60).

It is with such trickster maneuvers that the Eurasian heroine gradually displaces the white male protagonist from his position of power and privilege. If Jack's fantasy to objectify the Asian woman has already been interrupted by Yuki's "reference to money" (54), her periodic disappearance after their marriage undermines his power even further. Each time she procures a considerable sum of money from him, she will, without warning, return to her mother's house and leave him behind for days. While he has fantasized about his wife "adding wonderfully to the appearance of things . . . in his little house" (39), he discovers that in reality she is not a passive aesthetic/erotic object he has thought her to be and that, left alone in the house waiting for her return, he has become that passive "woman" himself. Indeed, each time she leaves him, he "long[s] ardently for her return" (59), knowing "all the time" that "he [is] waiting for her, and in the waiting doubling his misery" (83). Thus, by portraying the American husband as a left-behind lover constantly longing for his wife's return, Watanna transforms him into a passive, masochistic Butterfly and thus effectively reverses the power relations.

White masculine power is mocked once again when Jack attempts to restore his sense of dominance. After a day of vicarious experience of Western masculine display of power during his attendance at the parade of the Westernized Japanese imperial army, he returns to his wife and wonders if "she [is] sitting up waiting for him" (117). However, he finds that she has fallen asleep instead. Suddenly struck with her "extreme youth," Jack muses: "She seemed little more than a tired child, who had grown weary and had fallen asleep among her toys" (117). Under his masculine gaze, Yuki is infantilized and rendered supine. Simultaneously, she is refetishized into an object of desire as he imagines her to be "a tiny wild bird that he had caught in some strange way and caged—caught, though she had come to him, as it were, for protection" (118). However, Jack's fantasies are once more interrupted when he discovers, not long after, that Yuki has packed her belongings. He realizes instead that "it was now her intention to desert him utterly" and that "[he] had served her purpose, apparently, and she was through with him" (128). Although Yuki has fallen in love with her husband by this point, her imminent leaving once again relegates him to the role of a cast-off lover.

Watanna's attempt to inhabit and subvert the master plot is also evident in her reconstruction of a major Orientalist trope—Asian female sacrifice. Through what Henry Louis Gates calls "semantic appropriation," a typical trickster rhetorical move,[17] Watanna supplants the Orientalist concept of Asian self-sacrifice at its connotative level. Although Yuki makes "a sister's sacrifice" for her brother,[18] her self-abnegation involves neither the cultural violence nor the self-destruction that constitutes the sacrifice of Butterfly. Moreover, while the master plot sanctifies Butterfly's sacrifice by elevating her to the status of martyr, Watanna's text resists ennobling its heroine's self-abnegation. Rather, through Yuki's mixed feelings about her sacrifice and her brother's deep regret that "there is no such thing as justice in this land for the woman" (162), the novel reveals an unmistakable ambivalence toward female sacrifices. Recast in a different cultural context and from a different authorial stance, the Japanese heroine's sacrifice thus subverts the Orientalist construction of Asian otherness, which, as Min-ha Trinh puts it, "records in [the master's] language while pretending to speak through mine, on my behalf."[19]

In light of these transgressive revisions of the master plot, it is small wonder that *A Japanese Nightingale* compared unfavorably with *Madame Butterfly* on Broadway. At the same time, the tremendous success of Watanna's text in the marketplace also attests to the effectiveness of its trickster stylistics, which paradoxically both enables and masks its subversion from within. Aside from its Oriental exoticism, or its simulation of an "authentic" Japanese sentiment, and its subtle reversals of power, however, the novel's trickster inhabitation of the dominant cultural form is also evidenced by its reappropriation of the stereotypical ending of the romance plot. By having the heroine fall in love and by transforming the American male protagonist into a conscience-stricken "pilgrim of love" in the final chapters (188), the narrative shifts from subversion to mediation. Given that "complex mediation between and among conflicting value systems" is an important function of the trickster,[20] the happy ending of Watanna's text can perhaps be understood as a trickster strategy to deflect attention from the racial and gender power play at the center of the novel. In other words, to placate her white, middle-class readers, Watanna devises an ideological "solution" by creating a utopian fantasy of interracial harmony achieved through romantic love. To be sure, such an ending undeniably defuses the novel's subversive power, but it by no means nullifies the earlier destabilization of terms. Although ultimately Watanna's novel does not transcend the dominant discourse, by making alternative statements about race, gender, and power, it exemplifies nonetheless what Rachel Duplessis calls "a poetics of rupture and critique" that defines women's and minority writing.[21]

Border Crossings: "The Smuggling of Tie Co"

Sui Sin Far's story first appeared in *Land of Sunshine*, a major Californian periodical, in July 1900, coincidentally the same year as Belasco's production of *Madame Butterfly* began its run in New York. Writing at a time when the Butterfly narrative had become increasingly popular in Western culture, Sui Sin Far was prompted, as was Watanna, to compete with and challenge dominant representations of Asian/white romance. While her sister appropriates the exotic setting and the formulaic romance plot, Sui Sin Far transplants the Butterfly story to a North American context and radically alters the original story line. On the other hand, like Watanna, she engages in such forms of rhetorical play as ironic reversals and the trickster motif in her attempt to contest the master narrative.

Set in eastern Canada near the U.S. border during the early years of Chinese exclusion, "The Smuggling of Tie Co" tells the story of Tie Co, a cross-dressed young Chinese woman, who sacrifices all for love. The plot unfolds when Tie Co, as a "young Chinaman," offers to give up "his" laundry business partnership and be taken across the border by Jack Fabian, a white Canadian who smuggles Chinese laborers into the United States.[22] During their trip over, Tie Co confesses to Fabian: "I like you. . . . I like you so much that I want to go to New York, so you make fifty dollars" (107). To save the white smuggler from the punishment of law, Tie Co makes the ultimate sacrifice. While crossing the bridge over a river, s/he suddenly jumps over the rail after catching sight of two customs officers. When the body is brought out of the river, to everyone's confusion, it turns out not to be Tie Co, for "Tie Co was a youth, [but] the body found with Tie Co's face and dressed in Tie Co's clothes [is] the body of a girl—a woman" (108).

A tale of an Asian woman sacrificing herself for the sake of a white man, "The Smuggling of Tie Co" appears to be yet another reproduction of the white masculine fantasy of Asian submission. However, Sui Sin Far's story reimagines the white-male/Asian-female relationship in a radical way. By transforming the Butterfly figure into a cross-dressed "man," this text ventures into a gender-passing fantasy that, to borrow Judith Butler's phrase, "destabilizes the naturalized categories of identity and desire" underlying the master narrative.[23]

Narrated apparently by one of Jack Fabian's followers, "The Smuggling of Tie Co" opens with a laudatory portrait of Fabian and elevates him from a mercenary smuggler to an "unimmortalized Rob Roy."[24] With the appearance of Tie Co, however, the vainglorious first-person narrative voice shifts to that of a third-person narrator, and the boastful account of white masculine adventures is displaced by a new fantasy that reveals Tie Co to be the true trickster hero of the story.

The seamlessness of Sui Sin Far's shift of the narrative voice for the effects of ironic reversals is paralleled by the adroitness of her heroine's border crossings in her attempts to challenge the racial and gender status quo. In spite of her ill-fated crossing from Canada to America, Tie Co has successfully crossed other kinds of borders. "[Having] come out to Canada with a number of other youths" during the years of Chinese exclusion (109), she has traversed geographical, national, and, above all, gender boundaries. In *Gender Trouble: Feminism and the Subversion of Identity* (1990), Judith Butler suggests that gender parody, such as cross-dressing, "deprives hegemonic culture . . . of the claim to naturalized or essentialist gender identities," and reveals instead "gender's performative character and the performative possibilities for proliferating gender configurations outside the restricting frames of masculinist domination."[25] In this light, Tie Co's gender-crossing is particularly subversive and enabling. Although Sui Sin Far offers no explicit explanation for her heroine's behavior, the specific historical and cultural context of her story suggests that for Sui Sin Far, as well as a number of women writers of her time, the trope of transvestism is deployed, in the words of Sandra Gilbert and Susan Gubar, as "a way of addressing and redressing the inequities of gender categories."[26]

One such major inequity that Sui Sin Far seeks to redress is the overwhelming maleness of the Chinese population in North America during the early decades of Chinese immigration.[27] While the circumscription of women in Chinese patriarchy played a key role in limiting the number of Chinese female immigrants, the anti-Chinese movement in North America and restrictive immigration laws targeting Chinese women were also a significant factor.[28] Characteristic of her commitment to giving visibility to Chinese immigrant women in her fiction, Sui Sin Far's figuring of a female trickster in "The Smuggling of Tie Co" both challenges Chinese female exclusion and underscores the possibility of usurping or subverting masculine authority. Through gender performance, the Chinese heroine is able to circumvent the constrictive gender roles in Chinese patriarchy as well as the restrictive immigration laws in North America. Moreover, it enables her not only to migrate to Canada but to do so on her own terms.

Tie Co's gender-passing, however, serves another significant rhetorical purpose. Namely, her performance of drag denaturalizes the role of Asian Woman as the exotic female Other in the Butterfly fiction. If, as Andrew Parker and others suggest, the dress of the national subject may "identify, disguise, distort or enhance the desired body politic,"[29] the volatility of attire certainly functions as a central sign in the (re)construction of national and gender identities in "The Smuggling of Tie Co."[30]

When Tie Co, "dressed in citizen's clothes," sets out with Fabian across the Canadian/U.S. border on a dark night,[31] she is doubly disguised. Unknown to her white companion, dress has long become for her a camouflage. In male attire, she has passed for a man and thus been able to develop a longterm friendship with Fabian. Indeed, whether it is when Fabian confides to "the nice-looking young Chinaman" about his business troubles or when the "two men" journey across the border together, they appear to be not just "the smuggler and the would-be smuggled" but trusting, open friends (106).

Not only does cross-dressing in this story make possible a free companionship between a (Chinese) wo/man and a (white) man, but it also allows the Chinese heroine to express her love for a white man without having to play the role of a submissive Oriental doll-woman. When Tie Co tells Fabian in a "clear and sweet" "boyish voice," "I not like woman, I like man. . . . I like you," she is in effect declaring her love for the white man without his knowing (107). While the homoerotic overtone of this scene mocks the (white-male/Asian-female) heterosexual code in the Butterfly formula, it also reconstructs Asian female desire and refigures the Asian woman as a subject in her own right instead of a passive object of white masculine fantasy.

It is also precisely her gender performance that makes Tie Co's sacrifice distinctively different from the Butterflies' in the master plot. Although Sui Sin Far's heroine does sacrifice all for love, and her sacrificial act is admittedly a product of patriarchal culture, the transvestite plot ultimately recontextualizes the trope of Asian self-sacrifice. While the master trope serves to validate white masculine authority, Tie Co's sacrifice frustrates Eastern and Western men alike as a result of her gender parody. Not only can no Chinese man in Canada or New York explain "the mystery" of her gender ambiguity (109), but Fabian also fails, even after her death, to decipher her gender/sexual identity and to grasp the meaning of her sacrifice. As Tie Co continues to haunt his memories, he sometimes finds himself "pondering long and earnestly over the mystery of Tie Co's life—and death" (109). Far from being a spectacle exhibiting the beauty of Asian female sacrifice, Tie Co's death, beyond the white male protagonist's interpretation, deprives the hegemonic culture of pleasure and mastery and thereby suspends the white masculine fantasy of Asian feminine submission.

On the other hand, Sui Sin Far's resolution of the plot through her heroine's death also reveals an authorial attempt to resolve an irresolvable ideological and narrative impasse. As already noted, through the trope of gender-passing, the author replaces the Butterfly fantasy with a new fantasy in which an Asian woman is able not only to cross conventional gender boundaries but also to express her love for a white man without being reduced to an exotic, erotic object. However, given the social and cultural reality of her time, given the Orientalist, white male dominant culture within which the female character lives, the new fantasy cannot be sustained. For if the Chinese heroine is to fulfill her love, she will eventually have to reveal her sex as female and thus revert, inevitably, to her predetermined position within the established power structure. Therefore, because her sexual identity is female and heterosexual and yet she must continue to perform a male gender identity so as to maintain her subjectivity, death becomes for her the only way to claim love. As a woman, then, and as a Chinese woman in love with a white man, ultimately she cannot transcend the gender and racial boundaries in white patriarchy.

Nonetheless, although its narrative resolution underscores the perniciousness of hegemonic power and suggests Sui Sin Far's inability to envision an autonomous Asian female identity outside the hegemonic culture, "The Smuggling of Tie Co" represents a significant revision of the Butterfly story.

Clearly, its North American, Chinese-exclusion era setting separates this text from the Oriental exoticism of the "Oriental" narratives. More important, through the trope of gender-passing, Sui Sin Far creates a Chinese heroine who subverts the constrictive gender roles she is consigned to play in Eastern-Western patriarchy. In so doing, she destabilizes the established power relations and suspends the very fantasy that underlies the master narrative.

The tricksterism in the Eaton sisters' revisions of the Butterfly story demonstrates that nondominant discourses have the ability to challenge dominant production of knowledge. Although the Orientalist discourse attempts to essentialize the Asian woman as an exotic, erotic object, a sign of sexual and cultural submission, discursive instabilities ultimately reveal the ambivalence of Orientalist fantasies and provide the opportunity for challenging interventions. By refiguring the Asian woman and revising the trope of Asian female sacrifice, Watanna and Sui Sin Far have successfully appropriated the dominant discursive space and brought further dissonance and instability to Orientalist formations.

The complex relations between dominant and nondominant discourses as revealed here suggest that a cultural studies-rhetorical inquiry, such as this one, may become an effective critical and rhetorical tool. By exploring the power relations operating in discourse, the process through which knowledge is produced, and the ways in which a discourse is maintained and transformed, we are no longer limited to the study of the effects of individual rhetorical acts, but begin to see these acts in a larger context—as historically constituted and ideologically inscribed discourses, or as different conceptions of social and political conditions. Such an inquiry suggests pedagogical implications as well. It means that we commit ourselves to teaching writing as a sociopolitical act, the production of texts governed by ideologically coded cultural constraints. This requires an attempt to explore the social dimensions of various stylistic strategies and to engage students in cultural critique—challenging the established cultural codes by placing them against alternative codes. Once we foster an awareness of language as an arena of competing discourses that shape our knowledge and consciousness, we can enable students to develop a critical distance from "truth" or "objectivity" and to achieve new ways of speaking, thinking, and knowing.

Notes

I thank Laura Gray-Rosendale for her helpful comments on earlier versions of this essay and the late James A. Berlin for introducing me to cultural studies.

1. Elizabeth Ammons, introduction to *Tricksterism in Turn-of-the-Century American Literature: A Multicultural Perspective*, ed. Elizabeth

Ammons and Annette White-Parks (Hanover: University Press of New England, 1994), x.

2. As he explains in *The Archaeology of Knowledge*, trans. A. M. Sheridan Smith (New York: Pantheon, 1972), 224, discourse operates according to a principle of inclusion and exclusion, for a set of conditions and rules of discursive formation determines what governs statements, what statements are allowed in the first place, who is allowed to say them, and how certain statements, instead of others, are deemed appropriate and valid.

3. Ibid., 209, and Foucault, *History of Sexuality*, vol. 2, *An Introduction*, trans. Robert Hurley (New York: Pantheon, 1978), 102.

4. Annette White-Parks, "'We Wear the Mask,' Sui Sin Far as One Example of Trickster Authorship," in Ammons and White-Parks, 2.

5. Ibid., 3.

6. While Winnifred created a Japanese writing persona and wrote "Japanese" romance novels to play on Western Orientalist fantasies, Edith adopted a Chinese pen name and wrote sympathetic stories about Chinese immigrant men and women in North America to express her solidarity with the maligned people of her mother's race. See Amy Ling, "Creating One's Self: The Eaton Sisters," in *Reading the Literatures of Asian America*, ed. Shirley Geok-lin Lim and Amy Ling (Philadelphia: Temple University Press, 1992), 305–18; Yuko Matsukawa, "Cross-Dressing and Cross-Naming: Decoding Onoto Watanna," in Ammons and White-Parks, 106–25; and Annette White-Parks, "'We Wear the Mask': Sui Sin Far as One Example of Trickster Authorship," in Ammons and White-Parks, 1–20.

7. See Robert J. C. Young, *Colonial Desire: Hybridity in Theory, Culture and Race* (London: Routledge, 1995); and Ann L. Stoler, "Making Empire Respectable: The Politics of Race and Sexual Morality in 20th-Century Colonial Cultures," *American Ethnologist* 16 (1989): 634–60.

8. Some of the most popular Butterfly narratives of the time include Pierre Loti's *Madame Chrysanthème* (1888, Paris: Levy, 1893), a novel widely identified today as the prototype of the Butterfly story; Clive Holland's *My Japanese Wife: A Japanese Idyll* (Westminster: Constable, 1895) and its sequel, *Mousmé: A Story of the West and East* (New York: Frederick A. Stokes, 1901); and, most notably, John Luther Long's novella, "Madame Butterfly," in *Madame Butterfly* (New York: Century, 1898), 1–86; as well as its adaptations, including David Belasco's Broadway play, *Madame Butterfly* (1900–1905), and Giacomo Puccini's opera *Madama Butterfly* (1904).

9. Edward W. Said, *Orientalism* (New York: Pantheon, 1978; New York: Vintage, 1979), 3 (the page citation is to the Vintage edition).

10. Gina Marchetti, *Romance and the "Yellow Peril": Race, Sex, and Discursive Strategies in Hollywood Fiction* (Berkeley: University of California Press, 1994), 81.

11.   Homi K. Bhabha, "Signs Taken for Wonders: Questions of Ambivalence and Authority under a Tree Outside Delhi, May 1817," *Critical Inquiry* 12 (Autumn 1985): 154.

12.   Lisa Lowe, *Critical Terrains: French and British Orientalisms* (Ithaca: Cornell University Press, 1991), 5.

13.   Earl Roy Miner, "The Japanese Influence in English and American Literature, 1850–1950" (Ph.D. diss., University of Minnesota, 1955), 354.

14.   Michel de Certeau, *The Practice of Everyday Life*, trans. Steven F. Rendall (Berkeley: University of California Press, 1984), xix.

15.   T. Min-ha Trinh, *Woman, Native, and Other: Writing Postcoloniality and Feminism* (Bloomington: Indiana University Press, 1989), 38.

16.   Onoto Watanna, *A Japanese Nightingale* (New York: Harper, 1901), 21, 22, 26, 28.

17.   Henry Louis Gates Jr., *The Signifying Monkey: A Theory of Afro-American Literary Criticism* (New York: Oxford University Press, 1988), 47.

18.   Watanna, *Japanese Nightingale*, 148.

19.   Trinh, *Woman, Native, and Other*, 48.

20.   Ammons, Introduction, x.

21.   Rachel Blau Duplessis, *Writing beyond the Ending: Narrative Strategies of Twentieth-Century Women Writers* (Bloomington: Indiana University Press, 1985), 32.

22.   Sui Sin Far, "The Smuggling of Tie Co," in *Mrs. Spring Fragrance and Other Writings*, ed. Amy Ling and Annette White-Parks (Urbana: University of Illinois Press, 1995), 106.

23.   Judith Butler, *Gender Trouble: Feminism and the Subversion of Identity* (New York: Routledge, 1990), 139.

24.   Sui Sin Far, "Smuggling of Tie Co," 106.

25.   Butler, Gender Trouble, 138, 141. Although not from an exclusively feminist perspective, Marjorie Garber similarly argues that cross-dressing "puts in question identities previously conceived as stable, unchallengeable, grounded, and 'known'" and creates a "category crisis" that allows "border crossings from one (apparently distinct) category to another." *Vested Interests: Cross-Dressing and Cultural Anxiety* (1992, New York: Harper Perennial, 1993), 13, 16.

26.   Sandra Gilbert and Susan Gubar, *No Man's Land: The Place of the Woman Writer in the Twentieth Century*, vol. 2, *Sexchanges* (New Haven: Yale University Press, 1989), 343.

27.   For the sex ratio of the Chinese population in the United States and Canada in the early decades of Chinese immigration, see Sucheng Chan, "The Exclusion of Chinese Women, 1870–1914," in *Entry Denied: Exclusion and the Chinese Community in America, 1882–1943*, ed. Sucheng Chan

(Philadelphia: Temple University Press, 1991), 94; and Patricia E. Roy, *A White Man's Province: British Columbia Politicians and Chinese and Japanese Immigrants, 1858–1914* (Vancouver: University of British Columbia Press, 1989), xi.

28.   Chan, "Exclusion of Chinese Women," 94–95, 97–109.

29.   Andrew Parker et al., Introduction to *Nationalisms and Sexualities*, ed. Andrew Parker et al. (New York: Routledge, 1992), 10.

30.   Other examples include Sui Sin Far's autobiographical essay, "Leaves from the Mental Portfolio of an Eurasian," and several short stories, such as "Its Wavering Image," "Tian Shan's Kindred Spirit," and "The Americanizing of Pau Tsu."

31.   Sui Sin Far, "Smuggling of Tie Co," 106.

Works Cited

Ammons, Elizabeth. Introduction to Ammons and White-Parks, vii–xiii.

———, and Annette White-Parks, eds. *Tricksterism in Turn-of-the-Century American Literature: A Multicultural Perspective*. Hanover: University Press of New England, 1994.

Bhabha, Homi K. "Signs Taken for Wonders: Questions of Ambivalence and Authority under a Tree Outside Delhi, May 1817." *Critical Inquiry* 12 (Autumn 1985): 144–65.

Butler, Judith. *Gender Trouble: Feminism and the Subversion of Identity*. New York: Routledge, 1990.

Chan, Sucheng. "The Exclusion of Chinese Women, 1870–1914." In *Entry Denied: Exclusion and the Chinese Community in America, 1882–1943*, edited by Sucheng Chan, 94–146. Philadelphia: Temple University Press, 1991.

de Certeau, Michel. *The Practice of Everyday Life*. Trans. Steven F. Rendall. Berkeley: University of California Press, 1984.

Duplessis, Rachel Blau. *Writing beyond the Ending: Narrative Strategies of Twentieth-Century Women Writers*. Bloomington: Indiana University Press, 1985.

Foucault, Michel. *The Archaeology of Knowledge*. Trans. A. M. Sheridan Smith. New York: Pantheon, 1972.

———. *The History of Sexuality*. Vol. 1, *An Introduction*. Trans. Robert Hurley. New York: Pantheon, 1978.

Garber, Marjorie. *Vested Interests: Cross-Dressing and Cultural Anxiety*. New York: Harper Perennial, 1993.

Gates, Henry Louis, Jr. *The Signifying Monkey: A Theory of Afro-American Literary Criticism*. New York: Oxford University Press, 1988.

Gilbert, Sandra, and Susan Gubar. *No Man's Land: The Place of the Woman Writer in the Twentieth Century*. Vol. 2, *Sexchanges*. New Haven: Yale University Press, 1989.

Lowe, Lisa. *Critical Terrains: French and British Orientalisms*. Ithaca: Cornell University Press, 1991.

Marchetti, Gina. *Romance and the "Yellow Peril": Race, Sex, and Discursive Strategies in Hollywood Fiction*. Berkeley: University of California Press, 1994.

Miner, Earl Roy. "The Japanese Influence in English and American Literature, 1850–1950." Ph.D. diss. University of Minnesota, 1955.

Parker, Andrew, et al. Introduction. In *Nationalisms and Sexualities*, edited by Andrew Parker et al., 1–18. New York: Routledge, 1992.

Said, Edward W. *Orientalism*. New York: Pantheon, 1978; New York: Vintage, 1979.

Sui Sin Far. "The Smuggling of Tie Co." In *Mrs. Spring Fragrance and Other Writings*, edited by Amy Ling and Annette White-Parks, 104–9. Urbana: University of Illinois Press, 1995. First published in *Land of Sunshine* 13 (July 1900): 100–104.

Trinh, T. Minh-ha. *Woman, Native, and Other: Writing Postcoloniality and Feminism*. Bloomington: Indiana University Press, 1989.

Watanna, Onoto. *A Japanese Nightingale*. New York: Harper, 1901.

White-Parks, Annette. "'We Wear the Mask': Sui Sin Far as One Example of Trickster Authorship." In Ammons and White-Parks, 1–20.

12

The Alternative Feminist Discourse of Post-Mao Chinese Writers

A Perspective from the Rhetorical Situation

HUI WU

When a post-Mao Chinese female writer,[1] Wang An-yi, is asked if she is a feminist, she tells the interviewer, "They [feminists] would very much like me to be a feminist. But I really am not" (cited in Zheng, "Three Interviews," 165). Another writer, Dai Qing, simply declares that "Chinese women have no reason to be interested in feminism abroad" (cited in Zheng, "Three Interviews," 194). These writers' positions would surely raise the eyebrows of Western feminists, whose theory embeds itself mainly in the assumption that women share similar experiences—economic oppression, feelings of inadequacy, resistance to patriarchal subjugation, essentialized biology, and so on (e.g., Delmar; Fuss). What Western critics cannot understand is why Chinese female writers do not admit that they are feminists while constantly addressing women's issues in their fiction. After examining their works, some scholars conclude that gender equality and women's liberation are not major concerns for Chinese women themselves, and few of their works overtly challenge the conventional definition of feminine modes of behavior and thought (Diamond, 136; Croll, 116).

If we look more closely, however, Chinese female writers are strong fighters for women's rights and social status, although their rhetoric presents a feminist tendency different from that of Western feminists. To understand these writers' positions on gender politics, Western feminists and scholars need to avoid decontextualized representation of Chinese female writing and instead interpret their discourse as part of a particular rhetorical situation.

As Lloyd Bizter points out, "it is the situation which calls the discourse into existence" (Bitzer, "Rhetorical Situation," 301).[2] In other words, it is indeed difficult to understand why Chinese female writers deny that they are feminists until critics fully understand the rhetorical situation to which Chinese female writers respond.

Using the key component of rhetorical situation, *exigence*, to investigate the political condition post-Mao female writers intend to change, this chapter sheds light on the connections of rhetorical situation to the strategies and purposes of their discourse. I closely examine two main features—reclaiming femininity and regaining human integrity—in the work of post-Mao female writers to show that the constituent elements of the rhetorical situation need to be taken into consideration if we want to avoid misunderstandings of the post-Mao Chinese feminist rhetoric.

The Exigence for Post-Mao Feminist Rhetoric

An exigence, according to Bitzer, is "an imperfection marked by urgency; it is a defect, an obstacle, something waiting to be done, a thing which is other than it should be" ("Rhetorical Situation," 304). In his "Functional Communication," Bitzer further enlarges his observations about the relationship among exigence, the purpose of rhetoric, and the moral responsibility of the rhetor. He suggests,

> From among the mass of details comprising the total environment something is recognized as other than it should be, that is an exigence; and something else is recognized as a means of remedy or modification. These two constituents—exigence and remedy—are essential. . . . After all, the person must recognize the exigence and see the connection between the instrument or remedy and the exigence; *often the person will estimate accurately the propriety of his adjustment.* ("Functional Communication," 23)

Apparently, Bitzer notices a strong tie between the rhetor's perception of an exigence and the purpose of rhetoric, indicating that a discourse without aiming to modify a defective situation is not rhetoric. In this regard, "rhetoric is a mode of altering reality . . . by the creation of discourse which changes reality through the mediation for thought and action" ("Rhetorical Situation," 302). From this situational perspective, for example, the post-Mao Chinese female writing can be regarded as a moral response to an exigence wherein women have been denied the right to possess their bodies.

The term "post-Mao women writers" should be interpreted only within the boundary of its sociopolitical settings (see note 1 for the definition of the writers). The generation of post-Mao female writers was either born or grew up under the Red Flag, the symbol of Mao's leadership. People of this generation endured the worst famine in the world from the late 1950s to the early 1960s. They worshiped Mao only to be disillusioned as they witnessed the persecution of innocent people, including parents, friends, and even themselves, during the Anti-Rightist Campaign, the holocaust of intellectuals in the late 1950s, and then the Cultural Revolution (1966–78), when education, literature, traditional fine arts, science, and religion were all banned. During more than a decade of the Cultural Revolution, schools and colleges were shut down, and faculty and students were sent to the countryside to receive reeducation from factory workers and peasants whose lack of education was held as "uncontaminated knowledge of life." As a result, people of the Red Flag generation, while still in their teens, were forced to leave urban homes and were assigned heavy manual labor in the countryside or in factories. For example, the parents of Zhang Kang-kang, a female novelist, were persecuted in the 1950s and during the Cultural Revolution. When she was sixteen, she had to toil on the farm in *Bei Da Huang* (the Great Northern Wildness), one of the most impoverished and isolated areas in China. This life lasted eight years (R. Zhang, 478–94). Other female writers, such as Wang Xiao-ying, Wang An-yi, Zhang Xin-xing, and Lu Xing-er worked as strenuously as male manual workers in the countryside of Anhui and Heilongjiang provinces respectively when they were teenagers (Wei, 45, 271; Mei, 76; J. Li, 349; Zeng, 503).

Women of this generation were called "iron girls" who held up the "half of the sky," an icon used to claim that women were able to accomplish the physical tasks that men did (cf. Rofel, 244). As such, women took nontraditional tasks in the workplace, but their domestic duties were not reduced. The government even encouraged women to take care of all housework so men could be entirely engaged in socialist construction. As a consequence, while women were recognized in public as equal to men, at home they remained servants. The required double role placed a double burden on women. Furthermore, love, beauty, emotion, and courtship were forbidden topics. Femininity was put down as "petty bourgeois," and womanhood was reduced to a simple biological existence of daughter, wife, or mother with politics in command in the home as well as in public (cf. Honig and Hershatter, 4). This kind of women's liberation did not help them win respect from men, nor did it allow them to enjoy "gender equality." As a result, the women of the Red Flag generation were never acquainted with social courtesy from men. For instance, Chinese women had to elbow their way against men onto the crowded public transportation, and men never pulled out chairs for women nor held doors open for them. These now middle-aged women were ignorant of commodities that Western women used as daily necessities for sexual differentiation, such as cosmetics and gender-specific apparel. Not until the economic reform in the 1980s characterized by a tremendous interest in Western science and technology, ideology, and democracy as well as a growing interest in Western fashion, entertainment, and art forms, did Chinese women finally "have the right, the luxury to talk about the differences between men and women, to enjoy something that distinguishes women from men" (Wang An-yi cited in Zheng, "Three Interviews," 165). Only then were Chinese women's consciousnesses about their bodies awakened.

However, the gender awakening received incentives not so much from Western feminist thought as from Western Enlightenment and humanism that had heavy impact on the May Fourth Movement in China in the early twentieth century, a movement that defied suppression of individual freedom and abuses of women, such as foot-binding and enforced marriage. Post-Mao women's literature in the 1980s thus expresses a strong desire for women's rights to pursue individual longing and happiness. In this way, women's literature has helped Chinese women realize that the women's liberation in the Maoist fashion used "gender equality" to disfranchise women through a denial of biological and psychological differences and actually deprived women of human rights.

Chinese women have become aware that the State's rhetoric has used men as the standard to de-sex women in honor of Mao's call for socialist productivity. Using only male standards to promote sameness and gender equality consequently perpetuates gender inequality by depriving women of their humanity. This period of Chinese history, in its effects on women, was once seen by American feminists as a positive one (Honig and Hershatter, 339). These scholars argued that the woman's traditional role as a domestic servant was overthrown and women's contributions outside the home were finally recognized. However, through the experience as "iron girls," many Chinese women have realized that simply erasing gender differences does not lead to women's liberation. They are aware that if women's liberation merely means equality by assimilating women into the male world, then men still remain dominant and the norm, and women will automatically use male standards to judge themselves (X. Li, 372). The fact is that for more than four decades, Chinese women have lived supposedly without gender differences (Wang Anyi cited in Zheng, "Three Interviews," 166), and China has been a society where "woman" as a concept of human was virtually nonexistent (Zhang Kang-kang, 265).

Furthermore, women, whose right to their body was completely invalidated, were used as labor resources rather than valued as autonomous human beings. "More than forty years of mental and physical exhaustion caused by the extraordinary stress of a double role" has made Chinese women endure a heavy burden that "neither women in history nor contemporary men have experienced!" (X. Li, 374). Women's liberation without the guarantee of female humanity and dignity, according to Chinese women, is not true liberation. Dai Qing, a female novelist, recognizes that "Western feminism occurred with the development of productive forces" where people no longer have to rely on brute strength and can use their brains (cited in Zheng, "Three Interviews," 193–94). But in China, she points out, the trend is just reverse of what it is in the West (cited in Zheng, "Three Interviews," 193). Chinese women were involved defenselessly in manual labor under primitive conditions. A Chinese critic, Li Xiao-jiang, points out that the egalitarian distribution and structural liberation based on an underdeveloped economy restricted social development as well as women's own development (374). In other words, although confronting men physically and psychologically seems to promote gender equality, many Chinese women argue that the "equality" has been attained at women's expenses. They feel strongly that "the life of a beast of burden is certainly not the liberation which Chinese women have so painstakingly sought" (X. Li, 376).

The exigence dominated by the political and physical exploitation of women and social injustice at large under Maoism gives incentives to post-Mao female writers for arousing women's consciousness of their body, to draw public attention to gender politics, and, ultimately, to change the defective situation wherein human beings have had little freedom to make decisions concerning their own destiny. Using the perspective of the rhetorical situation to see post-Mao female writing as a moral response to a defective situation will enable us to form a contextualized perception of their discourse.

Reclaiming Femininity and Regaining Human Integrity as Moral Action

Post-Mao feminist rhetoric features two characteristics—reclaiming femininity and recovering the human character. Reasserting femininity functions as an emotional appeal to the audience that can share the writers' outcry against the officially encouraged desexualization of women and can understand the problems Chinese women encounter. Meanwhile, they regard women's problems as part of the human issues in China. Therefore, post-Mao female writing does not limit itself to concerns about women's issues but embraces authors' worries about undervalued human life at large. Chinese women's fate, post-Mao writers believe, is intertwined with that of the nation. To ensure women's liberation, then, the society in which governmental agendas are held above human life must be changed.

In reference to biological differences and social differences, many Chinese feminist critics believe that strengths and weaknesses of two sexes, as far as human needs are concerned, are "a given that could not be defined as positive or negative" (X. Li, 378). Li Xiao-jiang argues, "[biological] sex difference was not human-made, nor is it a gap that can be bridged by human effort. On this basis any sort of formal equality between men and women can only create inequality on an essential level" (378). What puts women in jeopardy is not essentialized biology, but the accompanying thought that feminine characters are inferior to those of the other sex. For this reason, the "'incurable' petty qualities of femininity," "the valuable human characteristics that have long been undervalued," should be given a good name (X. Li, 397). The rhetoric of women writers thus defies the deprecation of the feminine aspects of human nature to promote the "unconditional acknowledgment of the worth of individual human life" (X. Li, 379).

Appealing for respecting and valuing womanhood, post-Mao women's nonfiction shows middle-aged women who have been repulsively masculinized during the Cultural Revolution and expresses self-pity for not having a feminine life. In her memoirs, *Say "No" to Your Fate*, Zhang Kang-kang sadly deplores her position as a middle-aged post-Mao woman. She asks, What is left to the woman herself after her dedication to the country, her contributions to the workplace, her love for the husband and children, and her filial duties for parents (238)? Depriving us of "inborn feminine beauty," "tenderness," and "delicacy," Zhang Kang-kang writes, suffocates us to death (239). Exploring the sorrow of the women of her generation, Zhang Kang-kang shows her disapproval of the image of "liberated women" during the 1970s. She asserts that the masculinized persona holding revolution above emotions and "preferring" army uniforms to dresses mispresents the human nature. The women after Maoism, writes Zhang Kang-kang, do not have to do what men do, but should maintain self-confidence in order to realize what they desire (265)—"They do not want merely to be like men; they want to be different from and more powerful than men" (266). To Zhang Kang-kang, suppressing the female character is demeaning women's social status and self-worth.

Many Chinese women writers thus contend that the biological fact of being a woman is an asset, for her sensitivity makes her think at a more profound level than men. According to Ai Yun, feminism is not a theory against patriarchy but encouragement for woman to think with her body (2). Ai Yun's *A Woman's Narrative* depicts a typical Chinese female writer: she is sitting in a corner of a salon, listening to men. When the men are exchanging opinions excitedly, the female writer, enlightened by the subject, quietly leaves the room to write whatever she wants to (2). The female writer shows contempt to the endless arguments but captures the sparks of illuminating thoughts of her own by watching the debate. This scenario serves as an example of Ai Yun's belief that "language is revitalized by female innermost emotions" (Ai Yun, 2). In other words, womanhood constitutes the substance of a woman's writing, giving impulsive creativity and exquisiteness to her works.

The claim that "women's nature makes them especially suitable for certain types of work and certain types of literary styles, which are always defined in terms of difference from male style" sounds insidious in the West due to its implications of women's incapability of reason and language use (Thakur, 13). Conversely, women's peculiar styles and the subject matters about women that have been banned for decades are the characteristics that post-Mao women writers want to demonstrate, and only to their advantage. Handling the double burden has already verified women's talents and abilities in using discourse conventions sanctioned by a patriarchal and autocratic structure. Therefore, contemporary women writers are not intimidated by male discourse, nor do they need to imitate male writing in order to be accepted by the reading public (cf. L. Liu, 24; Leung, 136).[3] What they want to share with their readers are their peculiar rhetorical constituents: the finesse and instinctive insights male writers are unable to claim or offer. For example, much of post-Mao women's fiction and poetry, such as Zhang Jie's "Love Cannot be Forgotten," Wang An-yi's "When the Flutist Plays Solo," Zhang Kang-kang's "The Right to Love," Tie Ning's "The Red Shirt without Buttons," and Shu Ting's poem, "Ode to the Oak Tree," center on women's emotions, desires, self-esteem, and self-respect (L. Liu, 12). These works manifest an intimate feel of the pulse of life and insightful observations of characters' innermost feelings so they are popular with female readers and are highly admired by male writers and readers as well. Similar to the political goal of Western feminists for awakening women to their consciousness of sexual essentialization, Chinese female writers' desire to return to the feminine nature indicates their resistance to the deprivation of women's rights. They explore women's lives in order to criticize Maoist government's "disregard of women's femaleness and its distortion of sexual distinctions" (Zheng, "Maoism, Feminism," 138). This is why post-Mao women writers address femininity without fear of causing suspicion of essentialism.

The restoration of femininity, however, does not rule out women writers' concern that women's views of themselves may be distorted by the conventional definition of women's roles and patriarchal discourse. Thus, women's literature struggles against the male discourse and, at the same time, aims at increasing women's consciousness of their quality and self-worth (Zhang Kang-kang, 263–64). According to post-Mao women writers, the key to women's emancipation lies largely in women themselves. To make society recognize women's intellectual ability, women themselves should understand the importance of independence and create opportunities for social achievements. Almost all writers in their interviews, memoirs, and prose recognize that injustice to women caused by history and patriarchy has instilled in women a sense of sexual inferiority (Zhang Kang-kang, 263). Recalling their own dilemma of balancing career and family, many writers confide that being a woman is hard (e.g., Zhang Jie cited in Yang, 7; Shen Rong, "At Middle Age," *Sadness*; Ai Yun, 248). Some writers, such as Wang An-yi, defy the traditional definition of women's responsibilities by not bearing children. Nevertheless, besides pointing to society as responsible for women's disfranchisement, they think Chinese women themselves should stand up for their own liberty and fight off the restraints surrounding a feminine role to change the "fate." Zhang Kang-kang thinks that Chinese urban women in the new era are more challenging to their male counterparts than previous generations. They want more respect, independence, and self-esteem (262). But only criticizing male supremacy does not help women gain a quality life (Zhang Kang-kang, 263); a woman needs to look at herself critically to increase female integrity and to overcome the sense of biological inferiority. Much of their nonfiction encourages women to struggle for a quality life without relying on men. For example, Tie Ning's "A Type of Women" and Zhang Kang-kang's "Who Abandons Whom Nowadays?" criticize some women who take an easier path by depending on men, rather than developing their own potential, for their personal life goals. These women, who often compete among themselves for men's attention, still regard themselves as accessories to the male, the authors believe. Only when a woman proves her self-worth through professional and social achievements can she establish her self-esteem and conquer male chauvinism, egocentrism, and arrogance (Zhang Kang-kang, 263).

Nevertheless, post-Mao women writers separate men from the political system and consider men at a more personal level than Western feminist critics. To Chinese women writers, male supremacy reflects the traditional and stereotypic vision of women's roles as mother, wife, or daughter. It frequently indicates some men's problematic perspectives on women, which are often shown within the domestic domain or on person-to-person bases. Therefore, problems between genders are individual issues, thus personal and negotiable. However, the political system directed by Maoism is the major antagonistic force to the development of society, which intensifies women's problems and is hence a women's issue at the institutional and political levels. Viewed from this angle, Chinese women's anger at their sufferings, as Rey Chow notices, can never be pinned down to the narrowly sexualized category of "women" versus "men" only because "what is often assumed to be the central transaction between women and culture—women's heterosexual relation to men—has little relevance to the China crisis" (83). Accordingly, post-Mao female writing encompasses a concern that is broader than that of Western feminists: it refers to the political system and social tradition, not mere male domination, as the hindrance to female emancipation.

For instance, Shen Rong's fiction, "At Middle Age," is generally read in the West as an exposure of gender inequity in Mao's China. But Shen Rong herself points out in "To the Reader of 'At Middle Age'" that Dr. Lu, the female protagonist, symbolizes the sufferings of all intellectuals (including men) of "the new generation" who have received education under the Red Flag (*Sadness*, 217). The author praises Chinese intellectuals' devotion of "blood and flesh" to the "motherland" and to the following generations and shows sympathy toward this generation that has endured an unbearable workload and life hardships (*Sadness*, 217). While recognizing the misery women intellectuals, like Dr. Lu, have gone through, she adds, "their husbands and children have also made sacrifices" for the socialist country (*Sadness*, 217). Shen Rong's explanation of her purpose of writing indicates female writers' identification with "the same cohort," intellectuals (including males) who have experienced the Cultural Revolution as "*the* formative experience of their lives" (Zheng, "Maoism, Feminism," 134). "At Middle Age," in fact, depicts the common life of both genders adversely affected by the political system.

From a political point of view, a female character under the pen of a post-Mao Chinese female writer signifies a broader spectrum of social issues, which can never be studied separately from the general political environment in which she emerges. "The condition of women," Dai Qing believes, "*is* the condition of the country at large" (cited in Zheng, "Three Interviews," 194). Her remarks affirm the belief of most writers that women's problems are indicative of the general sociopolitical atmosphere of the country, because women's sufferings reflect the deteriorated human conditions. The solution to women's problems is embodied in the improvement of the political situation at large, and converting the exigence dominated by the derogation of human integrity can better women's situation. Chinese female writers thus feel compelled to launch a cause for creating a society that affirms the value of human life and brings about the freedom for individual independence, which, they think, is the major guarantee against the impediment to women's liberation.

Most post-Mao women writers, therefore, command the esteem of human values in the first place, which will in turn bring forth the esteem of womanhood. Women writers accordingly shoulder more responsibilities than male authors. While addressing women's issues, they also want to be, in Tie Ning's words, writers of "the third sex" (X. Ai, 26), who are bound to change the political situation for the public (e.g., Zhang Kang-kang, *Say No to Your Fate*; Shen Rong, *Sadness*; Dai Qing in Zheng, "Three Interviews,"

194). Ai Xiao-ming, a literary critic, observes that "a common tendency in the literature about women is that women writers consider gender issues a reflection of general social problems faced by the mass of people" (26). For example, the theme in Zhang Kang-kang's fiction signifies larger political issues that can lead to gender problems. She contends that her writing focuses on "human issues":

> My attention is drawn by the crises in life and in spirit faced by both men and women in the same world: distortion of human nature, humiliation, suppression of individuality, and restriction of thinking during the ten-year domestic turmoil, as well as by the spiritual emancipation and the modern ethics in the new era since 1978. All these determine prosperity or decline of my country. . . . My interest in these issues outweighs my concerns about women's fate. (261)

The conflicts faced by her characters reflect those faced by the country as a whole—loss of human dignity due to the control by the political institution. Zhang Kang-kang expresses her anger at a "rhetorical situation" hostile to addressing women's concerns. In the hope that enhancing esteem of human values will bring about women's liberation, Zhang Kang-kang's criticism is directed at the social system that sabotages human integrity through limiting people's rights to quality life.

The emancipation of women in the Chinese sociopolitical context, therefore, means more than coping with women's predicaments; it includes arousing people's consciousness of human worth. Li Xiao-jiang's words illustrate well the connection of China's political and economic conditions to women's issues:

> Because human liberation and women's liberation are multidimensional, no matter in which direction one exerts effort during the development, all paths are viable; any one of them may bring progress. For instance, the development of society and the economy can lessen human dependence on nature, thus alleviating the stress of double roles for women. Alleviating contradictions between classes and encouraging social stability will help advance political democratization and give free rein to individuality, thus establishing the conditions for female self-worth. A choice of professions will measure people's level of initiative; this is the premise for women's economic independence. (380)

Not until the concept of humanity becomes respected and women are valued as autonomous individuals can women's liberation be truly achieved. Post-Mao women writers are fighting for the ideal that women should be first recognized as humans whose bodies stand independent of political institutions and whose qualities and differences, as components of human integrity, should be affirmed and highly regarded.

Conclusion

If "I am not a feminist" serves as a claim in post-Mao women writers' rhetoric, the recognition of the unique sociopolitical context then forms the unstated premise of their reasoning: "Chinese women's studies received more impetus from contemporary political and intellectual ideologies in China than from Western feminism" (Zheng, "Maoism, Feminism," 136). Being deprived of womanhood by Maoist feminism marks the experience of Chinese women, which finds no parallel in the West. Underlying this recognition is Chinese women writers' awareness of the cultural separation from Western feminists and of the different rhetorical situation that "cannot be sufficiently explained entirely by theoretical models derived from the experience of Western women" (L. Liu, 23).

First, most Chinese women writers cannot read in foreign languages, and, until recently, sources in Chinese systematically introducing Western feminism have been scarce. The Chinese versions of Simone De Beauvior's *The Second Sex* and Virginia Woolf's *A Room of One's Own* still remain the major works of reference. For example, Zhang Kang-kang says, "I am not familiar with the definition of women's literature in Europe. Does it refer to women's works or any subject matters about women's life including male authors' works?" (260). Wang An-yi states that her knowledge about Western feminism has been obtained from conversations with Western feminists, and not from her own reading because she refuses to read translated works due to the "distance between the original and the translation" (cited in Zheng, "Three Interviews," 165). Obviously, post-Mao women writers' gender consciousness is mainly originated from the Chinese sociopolitical context. Maybe this is why they deny being feminists because they do not think they fully understand the theory. The denial may also affirm Chinese women writers' unwillingness to accept a label whose substance is not familiar to them. On the other hand, it signifies that their approach to Chinese gender problems is hardly influenced by Western feminism, which has developed in a completely different social context (see Dai Qing cited in Zheng, "Three Interviews," 193–94).

Second, post-Mao writers think, not without limitation, that "one of the premises of [Western] feminism is to deny the distinction between men and women. They think that women and men are the same" (Wang An-yi cited in Zheng, "Three Interviews," 165). This type of "gender equality," as

Wang An-yi interprets, sounds similar to the ideology Maoism has imposed on Chinese women. Her understanding and interpretation of Western feminism as sharing the attributes of an oppressive regime is also explanatory of post-Mao writers' denial of being feminists.

Third, most Chinese women writers recognize that gender differences *are* historically and "socially constructed," but they believe that these differences are not changeable and should remain unchanged because "both the female and male are human beings with independent, and not subordinate, characters" (L. Liu, 12). Valuing women's distinct qualities and capabilities is affirming the human character. Therefore, womanhood should receive as much respect as manhood. Chinese women writers hope to create a society in which both genders "exist harmoniously" and "the abilities of men and women get along with one another" (X. Li, 380). This is "an important measurement for gauging society's degree of civilization and the social guarantee for women's development" (X. Li, 380). Although they are not clear in what way and to what extent women can exist harmoniously with men without being dominated by the latter, the hope implies that gender relations in China are not polemic when both sexes are enforced to conform to the demand from the political institution. Women's problems, according to post-Mao female writers, are a continuum of the human issues affected by the defective political reality, which varies from the political situation of Western women.

Envisioned from a situational perspective, women writers in the post-Mao period have been trying to develop a rhetoric that fits a cultural milieu in which their audience's life experiences and mores are embedded. The discourse of post-Mao female writers, shaped by their unique personal history distorted by the state-sponsored desexualization of women, satisfies the urge of Chinese women to reclaim femininity. Understanding the situation at hand enables these writers to discover fitting responses to the exigence wherein humanity has been suppressed. Post-Mao female writers' indifference to Western feminism, therefore, denotes their understanding of China's distinct political condition and their perception of womanhood and gender relations. As these women writers have learned in consequence, erasing femininity as a process in reaching gender equality would lead to gender inequality and disintegrate women's liberation. Hence post-Mao feminist rhetoric presents women as autonomous human beings (not only as females) whose different qualities are as valuable as and even more so than those of men, and as revolutionaries who are determined to fight for women's rights and human values in society. The above analysis shows that post-Mao Chinese feminist discourse stems from a rhetorical situation different from those to which Western feminists respond, hence possessing different rhetorical features. However, although their stress on returning to femininity sounds essentializing, their rhetorical purpose—to restore women's rights as human rights—is not dissimilar to those of Western feminists (Okin). Post-Mao feminist rhetoric actually confirms most values that Western feminists uphold, such as independence and liberty from political and economic oppressions. Post-Mao women writers' rhetoric thus must be looked at from the problematic situation wherein women's lives have been subjected to the political agenda of an authoritarian government. Understanding the cultural constraints on this rhetoric can further help us perceive woman not as a single, deterministic category, but rather as the nexus of diverse experiences.

The above study of the alternative post-Mao feminist rhetoric provides a model for the epistemological understanding of feminism in a cross-cultural context. The analysis of the impact of the exigence on the post-Mao female writing proves that the theory of rhetorical situation can be applied, persuasively and effectively, in cross-cultural and interdisciplinary communication criticism. The rhetorical criticism of the post-Mao women writing strengthens the viewpoint put forward by Lisa Ede, Cheryl Glenn, and Andrea Lunsford, that the epistemic status and heuristic values of rhetorical theory provide guides to explore the borderlands of rhetoric and feminism and "offers feminism a vibrant process of inquiring, organizing, and thinking, as well as a theorized space to talk about effective communication" (401).

Notes

I would like to thank the Center for East Asian Studies at the University of Kansas for awarding me a travel grant that enabled me to include secondary sources in Chinese in this essay.

1.   Post-Mao women writers are authors whose literary works have gained popularity since the end of Mao Ze-dong's regime (1949–76). Chinese critics also call them post–Cultural Revolution writers. These women writers fall into two categories: those who graduated from college before the Cultural Revolution (1966-1978) and those who graduated from college in the 1970s and 1980s after they had served as factory workers or peasants during the Cultural Revolution from 1966 to 1978 (cf. Thakur, 91).

2.   Lloyd Bitzer refers to the rhetorical situation as an exigence that strongly invites utterance. There is a twofold implication in Bitzer's treatise. First, a problematic occurrence, or the exigence, induces a work of rhetoric. Second, a rhetorical work is like a moral action because it aims to solve the problems, change the defective reality, or overcome the obstacle. Put another way, a situation invites a rhetorical response, but the meaning of the response is bestowed on by the rhetor in proportion to his or her perception of the situation (see Bizter, "Rhetorical Situation," 300–304). Although

Bitzer's position that a rhetorical situation determines the existence of a discourse has been challenged and modified by other critics of rhetoric (e.g., Pomeroy; Consigny; Hunsaker and Smith; Vatz), the case of post-Mao female writing confirms Bitzer's proposition.

3.   I must point out that Zhang Kang-kang's article, "We Need Two Worlds," in *Say "No" to Your Fate* (Shanghai Knowledge Press, 1994) does not contain the analogy of the handicapped athlete to explain her point of women writers' fear of being trivialized by the male literature. Apparently, the edition Lydia Liu refers to must be different from this one (24).

Works Cited

Ai, Yun. *nü ren zi shu* (A Woman's Narrative). Shanghai, China: Shanghai Knowledge Press, 1997.

Ai, Xiao-ming. "dang dai zhong guo nü zuo jia de cuang zuo guan huai he zi wo xiang xiang" (The Concerns and Imagination of the Contemporary Chinese Women Writers). *guangdong she hui ke xue* (Guangdong Social Science) 2 (1997): 128–34. *fu yin bao kang zi liao: zhong guo xian dai, dang dai wen xue yan jiu* (Newspaper and Journal Digest: Modern and Contemporary Chinese Literature Studies) 6 (1997): 21–27.

Bitzer, Lloyd. "The Rhetorical Situation." *Philosophy and Rhetoric* 1 (1968): 1–14. *Rhetoric: Concepts: Definitions, Boundaries*, edited by William A. Covino and David A. Jolliffe, 300–10. Boston: Allyn and Bacon, 1995.

———. "Functional Communication: A Situational Perspective." In *Rhetoric in Transition: Studies in the Nature and Uses of Rhetoric*, edited by Eugene E. White, 21–38. University Park, Pa.: Pennsylvania State University Press, 1980.

Chow, Rey. "Violence in the Other Country: China as Crisis, Spectacle, and Woman." In *Third World Women and the Politics of Feminism*, edited by Chandra T. Mohanty et al., 81–100. Bloomington: Indiana University Press, 1991.

Consigny, Scott. "Rhetoric and Its Situations." *Philosophy and Rhetoric* 7 (1979): 175–86. *Landmark Essays on Rhetorical Invention in Writing*, edited by Richard Young and Yameng Liu, 59–67. Davis, Calif.: Hermagoras, 1994.

Croll, Elisabeth. *Chinese Women since Mao*. New York: Zed, 1983.

Delmar, Rosalind. "What is Feminism?" In *What Is Feminism: A Re-Examination*, edited by Juliet Mitchell and Ann Oakley, 8–33. New York: Pantheon, 1986.

Diamond, Norma. Review of *Revolution Postponed*, by Margery Wolf. *Journal of Asian Studies* (November 1985): 136–37.

Duke, Michael S., ed. *Modern Chinese Women Writers: Critical Appraisals.* New York: M. E. Sharpe, 1989.

Ede, Lisa, et al. "Border Crossing: Intersections of Rhetoric and Feminism." *Rhetorica* 13 (1995): 401–41.

Fuss, Diana. *Essentially Speaking: Feminism, Nature, and Difference.* New York: Routledge, 1989.

Honig, Emily, and Gail Hershatter. *Personal Voices: Chinese Women in the 1980's.* Stanford: Stanford University Press, 1988.

Hunsaker, David, and Craig R. Smith. "The Nature of Issues: A Constructive Approach to Situational Rhetoric." *Western Speech Communication* 40, no. 3 (1976): 144–56.

Leung, Lai-fong. "In Search of Love and Self: The Image of Young Female Intellectuals in Post-Mao Women Fiction." In *Modern Chinese Women Writers*, edited by Michael S. Duke, 135–51. New York: M. E. Sharpe, 1989.

Li, Jing. "Lu Xing-er Zhuan" (Biography of Lu Xing-er). In *zhong guo dang dai qing nian n zuo jia ping zuan* (The Biographical Commentary on Contemporary Chinese Female Writers), edited by Lu, Qing-fei et al., 349–67. Beijing, China: Chinese Women's Press, 1990.

Li, Xiao-jiang. "Economic Reform and the Awakening of Women's Consciousness." Trans. S. Katherine Campbell. *Engendering China: Women, Culture, and the State*, edited by Christina K. Gilmartin et al., 360–82. Cambridge, Mass.: Harvard University Press, 1994.

Liu, Lydia. "The Female Tradition in Modern Chinese Literature: Negotiating Feminisms across East/West Boundaries." *Genders* 12 (1991): 22–44.

Lu, Qing-fei. Preface. In *zhong guo dang dai qing nian n zuo jia ping zuan* (The Biographical Commentary on Contemporary Chinese Female Writers), edited by Lu, Qing-fei et al., 1–17. Beijing, China: Chinese Women's Press, 1990.

Mei, Ping. "A Brief Biography of Wang An-Yi." In *zhong guo dang dai qing nian n zuo jia ping zuan* (The Biographical Commentary on Contemporary Chinese Female Writers), edited by Lu, Qing-fei et al., 75–93. Beijing, China: Chinese Women's Press, 1990.

Okin, Susan Moller. "Feminism, Women's Human Rights, and Cultural Differences," *Hypatia* 13 (1998): 32–52.

Pomeroy, Ralph S. "'Fitness of Response' in Bitzer's Concept of Rhetorical Discourse." *Georgia Speech Communication Journal* 4 (1972): 42–71.

Rofel, Lisa. "Liberation Nostalgia and a Yearning for Modernity." In *Engendering China: Women, Culture, and the State*, edited by Christina K. Gilmartin et al., 226–49. Cambridge, Mass.: Harvard University Press, 1994.

Seven Contemporary Chinese Women Writers. Preface by Gladys Yang. Beijing: Panda, 1983.

Shen, Rong. "At Middle Age." In *Seven Contemporary Chinese Women Writers*, 121–206. Beijing: Panda, 1983.

———. *zhong nian ku duan* (Sadness at Middle Age). Shanghai: Shanghai Knowledge Press, 1994.

Thakur, Ravni. *Rewriting Gender: Reading Contemporary Chinese Women*. London: Zed, 1997.

Tien, Ning. "A Type of Woman." In *Visiting Rodin*, 88–91. Changchun, China: Jilin People's Press, 1996.

Vatz, Richard E. "The Myth of the Rhetorical Situation." *Philosophy and Rhetoric* 6, no. 3 (1973): 154–61.

Wei, Yu-chuan. *Brief Biographies of Modern and Contemporary Chinese Female Writers*. Beijing, China: Chinese Women's Press, 1990.

Yang, Gladys. Preface. In *Seven Contemporary Chinese Women Writers*, 5–9. Beijing: Panda, 1983.

Yue, Meng. "Female Images and National Myth." In *Gender Politics in Modern China*, edited by Tani E. Barlow, 118–36. Durham, N.C.: Duke University Press, 1993.

Zeng, Zhen-nan. "Biography of Zhang Xin-xing." In *zhong guo dang dai qing nian n zuo jia ping zuan* (The Biographical Commentary on Contemporary Chinese Female Writers), edited by Lu, Qing-fei et al., 503–19. Beijing, China: Chinese Women's Press, 1990.

Zhang, Kang-kang. *ni dui ming yun shuo, "bu"* (Say "No" to Your Fate). Shanghai: Shanghai Knowledge Press, 1994.

Zhang, Ren. "Biography of Zhang Kang-kang." In *zhong guo dang dai qing nian n zuo jia ping zuan* (The Biographical Commentary on Contemporary Chinese Female Writers), edited by Lu, Qing-fei et al., 478–519. Beijing, China: Chinese Women's Press, 1990.

Zheng, Wang. "Three Interviews: Wang Anyi, Zhu Lin, Dai Qing." In *Gender Politics in Modern China: Writing and Feminism*, edited by Tani E. Barlow, 158–208. Durham, N.C.: Duke University Press, 1993.

———. "Maoism, Feminism, and the UN Conference on Women: Women's Studies Research in Contemporary China." *Journal of Women's History* 8, no. 4 (1997): 126–52.

13

When Worlds Collide

Rhetorics of Profit, Rhetorics of Loss in Chinese Culture

JEFF SCHONBERG

L iteracy can provide people with a number of benefits, but like a gun, it can also provide death and destruction. I reached this conclusion while looking over my field notes and photographs obtained from my work among an agricultural community of animistic cave-dwellers in 1996 in the People's Republic of China.[1] But a number of literacy advocates tell me I am wrong. Alex Inkeles and David Smith argue that personal literacy is directly proportional to such individual traits as empathy, innovativeness, and rationality (66). They do not consider that personal literacy could also be directly proportional to such traits as elitism, revisionism, and recklessness. Peter Laslett declares that literacy, if "transmitted through carefully controlled institutions created for that purpose and supervised closely, could be a powerful force" (213) for focusing national concerns on maintaining social order, instilling morality, and training citizens for government positions. He does not state that literacy can disrupt social order, threaten established religious precepts, or stimulate unemployment. Finally, Emmanuel Todd asserts that high literacy rates directly affect both a society's international economic influence and its members' consumption of goods and services (7). However, he does not show that high literacy rates also negatively affect a subculture's ability to maintain traditional economies and consumptive practices.

My quiet university office undermines further the spiritual crises, social conflicts, economic upheavals, and personal fears associated with Chinese literacy movements that my notes and photographs depict. The filled bookshelves, the desk cluttered with student papers awaiting my comments, and administrative memos concerning program review and assessment responsibilities, and a computer, a printer, and piles of labeled and unlabeled disks attest to my status as a believer in Todd's, Laslett's, Inkeles's, and Smith's descriptions. Was my fieldwork then faulty? Does literacy result purely in selective advantages, thereby establishing an undeniable, linear trend of improvement? If my fieldwork was not faulty, however, something else was creating an ambiguity that screened the reality of literacy programs in this area of China. Could my descriptive apparatus itself be suspect? Could my calculus relegate such concepts as "cultural disharmony" or "religious chaos" to the status of epiphenomena because of my own allegiances to literacy? Was it, in other words, ignoring a vital rhetorical concept and thus losing the distinction between social gain and cultural loss?

Following the discursive trail of business interactions by both the Chinese government's rhetoric of gain and the cave-dwellers of Li Shan Mountains' rhetoric of loss provides answers to the questions concerning the acuity of my fieldwork and my sense that literacy movements in rural China have a decidedly dual and rhetorical nature. For following this path creates a new picture of Chinese rural literacy movements not simply as ramified means to sets of desired ends but as manifestations of *kairos*. More specifically, to maintain the distinction between sociological and cultural processes, I will argue that literacy in rural China is the point of ambivalence between difference and fear that rhetorically charges both the government's conquest narratives and the cave-dwellers' terror narratives. This depiction of literacy removes the ambiguity adhering to the reality of these literacy movements by revealing two realms for rhetorical analysis. The first is the Chinese government's narratives as they culminate in feelings of gain derived from conquering economic and social inertia. The second is the cave-dwellers' religious and economic resistance to the government's narratives manifested in the didactic narratives adults tell each other to relieve the psychological stress created by a loss of cultural identity and a loss of the ability to make religious, familial, and individual decisions.

The PRC's Rhetoric of Gain

Current literacy movements in the PRC trace their spirit of conquest to Mao Zeong's "Third Speech at the Hangzhou Conference," delivered on May 10, 1958. He predicted that "by the end of the century . . . on the average, everybody [in China] will have 1,000 tons of steel and 2,000 to 3,000 catties of grain and feed, and the majority of people will have a college education" (*Miscellany*, 111). The context for Mao's statement lies partly in the

rhetorical power of the World Bank's Gross National Product (GNP) ratios used to describe the amounts of energy China consumed to produce one dollar of GNP in the early 1960s through the mid-1990s and partly in the Chinese government's attempt to rhetorically conquer social problems by quantifying the notion of a "quality life." The theme tying these apparently disparate discourses together is the provincial and federal government's belief in school-based literacy as the primary means of modernizing the economy and thus increasing its efficiency.

According to the World Bank's GNP estimates, China's 1960 economy was 2.5 times more inefficient than India's and 7 times more inefficient than Japan's, a record of unequaled inefficiency. By 1978, China's economic efficiency was comparable to pre-Soviet collapse Poland, but by 1996, the country's efficiency growth was once again decreasing; it was now nearly 1.5 times more inefficient than Mexico and post-Soviet collapse Russia. China's efficiency growth, in other words, could not be maintained at the levels seen in the late 1970s.[2]

The emblematic power of the World Bank's ratios warranted the Chinese government's arguments directly attributing high levels of agricultural, economic, and textual illiteracy among rural citizens as the primary causes of economic and social inefficiency. These arguments appeared in political addresses and journal articles. For example, in a speech to the National People's Congress, reprinted in the *People's Daily* of June 17, 1994, Chen Muhua, the vice chair of the National People's Congress Standing Committee, proclaimed that both adults and children living in rural areas must become textually literate to support "socialist modernisation in an all-around way" (*Miscellany*, 1). An echo of this rhetoric of gain in which literacy results in modernization through conquering economic and resource inefficiency barriers reverberates in Yu Youhai's "U.S. $1,000 by the Year 2000":

> Ideas are the critical input in the production of more valuable human and nonhuman capital. But for ideas to live on after the [originators] are gone, both the young and the old must be able to partake in those ideas. Especially in the interior [of China], more children and adults must become able to use these ideas to solve practical problems [concerning] water and energy use, health, and land use. They must, in other words, become increasingly more literate. (16–18)

The context for Mao's earlier rhetoric of gain is echoed again in the Chinese government's attempts to promote a relationship between a vague notion of a "quality life" and modern socialism. Through family narratives published in both the *People's Daily* and in pamphlets produced by the various committees of the People's Congress depicting the adequacy and makeup of nutrition, improvements of life expectancy, opportunities for intellectual advancement, and consumption of goods and services, government claims evoke again the spirit of modernization through conquest. The July 11, 1996 edition of the *People's Daily*, for example, includes a story about two families living in Henan province, both of whom included pregnant daughters-in-law. One family's patrilineal grandparents, following traditional religious doctrine, consulted a fortuneteller about the time of birth for the expected grandchild. For a fee of 500 yuan, the grandparents expected information telling them what kinds of blessing ceremonies needed to be prepared for the mother. When told that the baby would be born at a time associated with bad luck, the unhappy grandparents forbade the son and daughter-in-law from revealing the birth date to the other inhabitants of their village. As a result, no blessing celebrations could be planned, and no "special foods," selected for their nutritional value and beyond the family's ability to pay for them, could be obtained. Both the malnourished mother and child died during the birth.

The second family's paternal grandparents, however, had read a government-prepared pamphlet concerning neonatal health and sought the services of a local medical clinic for information about the time of birth. When told what dietary supplements the daughter-in-law needed prior to birth, the grandparents arranged the blessing ceremonies according to these needs. The properly nourished mother had an easy birth, and the infant was expected to grow into a healthy child (7–8).

Transforming the apomnemonysis of these families' narratives to an apologue for modernization provided strategies for conquering two obstacles that hindered the Chinese government's literacy campaigns. First, the government was able to equate the second family's use of "proper nutrition," the baby's "easy birth," and its status as a "healthy child" with the paternal grandparents' ability to read a neonatal health pamphlet. More important, the three-part equation supports the government's claim that targeting the 140 million rural denizens over the age of fifty who cannot read or write will result in increased live-birth rates and expanded opportunities for further literacy programs in the areas of agriculture and goods and services consumption. As Lu Jiehua, associate professor in the Institute of Population Research at Beijing University, notes in an article in the July 11, 1998 issue of the *People's Daily*, "According to the theory of human resources . . . an individual's life quality is determined primarily as a return on medical investment. The research results attest to the need for the government to enhance medical care in rural areas through improving literacy rates among the older people and enrollment levels for formal education among the youth" (*Miscellany*, 6–7).

Second, equating the deaths of the mother and baby in the first family with the "feudal thinking" status of traditional religious doctrine supports the Chinese Association for Science and Technology's perception of traditional religious practices as barriers to governmental literacy programs and these programs' ability to disseminate "applied technology, modern medicine, and farming skills" (*Miscellany*, 10). Moreover, identifying rural women who cannot read or write as those most interested in "superstitious practices" personifies additional targets for these programs. Zhang Zhenglun, an Association official and member of the People's Congress, specifically addresses this target in his February 3, 1999 announcement that "special efforts [literacy campaigns] are underway to upgrade rural women's social positions and to safeguard their interests and rights" (*Miscellany*, 10).

In the July 11, 1996 issue of the *People's Daily*, other articles appear concerning China's inability to increase its meat, egg, and dairy output without raising the share of its grain harvest used as animal feed. In addition, the issue includes articles concerning rising school dropout rates in rural areas. These articles undercut the evocative power of modern socialism's use of literacy programs as the weapon of choice for conquering its enemies. As this erosion of intent grew increasingly common throughout the later half of the decade, a third group of pamphlets wtih a focus on literacy as the primary source of "ingenuity"—that is, ideas applied to solve practical social and technical problems—was produced by the federal government, published by the provincial governments, and disseminated by local Party officials to rural village populations. Nonetheless, rural resistance to these efforts to increase both childhood and adult literacy increased in several provinces,

H   L
 | |
particularly among the [nUŋ mIn] population near Luoyang in Henan province. The sources of this resistance are both religious and economic, and both manifest themselves in the didactic narratives adults tell each other as a primary means of relieving the psychological stress created by a loss of cultural identity and a loss of the ability to make religious, familial, and individual decisions.

Rural Communities and Their Rhetoric of Loss

Within the larger population of Buddhist farming families living in the limestone caves in the Li Shan Mountains east of Luoyang and west of the village of Xinshin is a group of 140 animist families who have lived in the area for forty-eight generations (approximately 2,200 years). Faced with a growing push to send their schoolage children a distance of about 30 kilometers to the Xinshin village school for political, economic, and literacy instruction, the adult family members have responded to the provincial and federal governments' rhetoric of gain with their own rhetoric of loss. Reflective of pronounced social strain and severe psychological tension, this rhetoric is rooted in the complex beliefs and rituals that had effectively brought the previous generations safely through floods, droughts, blights, and civil disturbances. To understand these families' resistance to the governments' various attempts at increasing mathematical, agricultural, and language-based literacy levels, we need to understand a range of social and cultural characteristics that have developed over the years these families have resided in this area.

The religious tradition of these 140 families is an animistic tradition similar to a number of other cultural groups living farther south and west in Sichuan and Yunnan provinces. This tradition fused with Confucianism's filial piety and Buddhism's "noble eightfold path" during the Chou (1027–256 B.C.) and Han (202 B.C.–220 A.D.) dynasties, and resulted in a balanced synthesis of beliefs and rituals cohesively binding local spirits and demons, Buddhist gods, and Confucian obedience.

The central rituals in this synthesis are the daily supplications to and conversations with local and ancestral spirits. These prayers are intended to maintain stable relationships with those entities residing in the bean and corn fields, the hills and streams and trees surrounding the fields, and the animals and insects common to the area, thereby ensuring the success of crop, fish, and meat production as well as ensuring the family members' continued health and well-being. Similarly, the conversations with ancestral spirits create a system of checks and balances concerning appropriate behaviors, agricultural methods, and family tradition; violations of any of these place in jeopardy the family members' health and feelings of well-being. According to the oldest adult members of these families, all of the spirits draw sustenance from the prayers and conversations, as long as the petitioners maintain a humble attitude toward the spirits, as long as the prayers are made at the right times and geographical locations, and as long as the petitioners actually act on the words of the spirits. Children under the age of twelve,

therefore, are formally instructed by adult family members in [dzEn tzə], the "propriety of spirit speech." Prayers made by those older than twelve are constantly monitored by family elders to make sure propriety is maintained.

Living family members draw assurance from their belief that their agricultural efforts will be met with increased crop, fish, and meat production and from the knowledge that they are behaving appropriately and following correctly the traditional agricultural methods. The result of these rhetorical cycles is twofold: the spirits are appeased, and both inter- and intrafamily feelings of solidarity are strengthened.

Yet, over the past fifty years, the synthesized religious system and the solidarity within and among these families have been progressively undermined by population and agricultural losses, ecological damage, and changes

in economic and political doctrines. The goals of the Communist Party and a renewed feeling of Chinese nationalism among the economically and politically sophisticated urban residents of Luoyang and Zhengzhou strengthened the notion that illiterate societies like this one were representative of "feudal thinking" and were therefore removable. More specifically, these
          H   L
rural societies were branded as [nUŋ mIn], or "peasants," a title which in the cities means "illiterate." On the other hand, within these families there arose a more self-conscious sense of identity, a sense that continues to protect the material of the religious system. The contrast between the urban identity
M   H   H   L
([tUn dze], literally "comrade" but now meaning "literate"), and the [nUŋ mIn] forms the major cultural distinction in this part of Henan province.

    In governmental circles on the local, provincial, and federal levels, as
          H   L
well as in the [nUŋ mIn] families, this contrast plays a crucial role. For federal economic planning committees, the contrast between literate and nonliterate warrants the government's argument that, because of its reluctance to follow the government's agricultural, health, and educational policies, the
H   L
[nUŋ mIn] society is "overly consumptive of . . . intellectual and physical energy sources"[3] and therefore should be displaced in favor of a more efficient, more literate society. On the provincial government level, however, the contrast warrants an argument not of exclusion but of inclusion: for modern socialism to further evolve, all the people must become literate. The local government argument echoes the provincial argument: for the village—that is, the economic locus used by outlying societies as their principal market—to prosper, all the people must become literate. More important, on all the governmental levels, literacy emerges as an important point of social reference rather than a simple contrast in levels of education. Literacy becomes a symbol of the nation's perception of itself as the awakening economic "lion," of Henan province's perception of itself as just as vital to Chinese socialism as Jiangsu province, and of Xinshin's perception of itself as an economic hub.
                                                                  H   L   M
    For the animist families, the distinction between [nUŋ mIn] and [tUn
H
dze] becomes even sharper, for the contrast emerges as the primary symbol of social identity. Friendships, potential mates, and notions of behavioral
                                                      H   L
propriety are all strongly influenced by what it means to be [nUŋ mIn] as
                            M   H
opposed to what it means to be [tUn dze]. The contrast between literate and

nonliterate, however, also evokes memories within the [nŪŋ mĪn] of past animosities that are continually reawakened by face-to-face encounters in

the marketplaces with old adversaries. Add to these memories the [nŪŋ mĪn]'s understanding that their traditional forms of life are being steadily dissolved by those same adversaries, and the result is the generation of tremendous levels of tension. During the 1970s, for example, residents of Xinshin, inflamed with the spirit of the Cultural Revolution and under the direction of provincial political agents, destroyed spirit and ancestral shrines as a means of removing "antirevolutionary" symbols. Twenty years later, the terror inspired by those acts is reaffirmed when the [nŪŋ mĪn] become the recipients of the literacy program's rhetorics of gain carried by the same villagers, now in positions of economic, political, and educational power, who destroyed the religious shrines.

One of these terrifying relationships forms out of the decline of the communist collective and the growth of the household as the dominant free market unit of production. Under the direction of the collective, families were provided with seed, told what and how much to grow and how much soil and water could be used. Moreover, the collective controlled storage and distribution of the products as well as the income each family derived from their efforts. Primarily responsible now for all agricultural production, from acquiring seed and fertilizer to processing, transporting, and marketing, the household is evolving into a far more complex unit, requiring new skills in production and management. As a result, children are bearing more responsibility for the continued economic success of the family, for they are the ones who are the primary recipients of the new production and marketing skills incorporated within the various literacy movements. The distance from the caves to Xinshin, however, makes attending the village school risky; [nŪŋ mĪn] children must leave their homes for school dormitories, inviting the wrath of both ancestral and local spirits. Moreover, the free market production and management techniques learned in the Xinshin school and brought back to the family often contradict the traditional methods so firmly ensconced within the synthesized religious system. As a result, the already stressful life of the [nŪŋ mĪn] families becomes more so; undernourished spirits cause diseases, and children who are in school cannot assist with the work required by bean fields, rice paddies, eel and fish ponds, or goat herds. In addition, the

labor pool consisting of children educated in the newest agricultural methodologies as well as other skills learned through literacy programs must migrate
to larger cities to find employment.

One means used by the [nUŋ mIn] families to deal with these stresses
involves creating a rhetoric of loss aimed at appeasing the anger of spirits
left unhappy and underfed by the growing absence of [dzEn tzə]. Moreover,
the rhetoric of loss reinvokes traditional family cohesive strategies, expunges
feelings of terror and difference, and comes to terms with the increasing number of [haI dze mEn me IU], children who are both spiritually and physically
absent.

The texts creating the [nUŋ mIn]'s rhetoric of loss take up a majority of
the time needed for both familial and spiritual dialectics, a change reflective
of the transitory nature of the [nUŋ mIn] culture. According to [nUŋ mIn]
adults over the age of sixty, prior to 1949, the year the Communist Party
consolidated its political control over China, the idea of rhetorically framing
a sense of loss for either ancestral and local spirits or family members was
completely unknown. Since the late 1950s, however, more and more time
has been spent with this rhetoric of loss. By 1996, the amount of time given
to [dzEn tzə] was significantly less than the time spent rhetorically appeasing
those spirits.

Such was the situation on the morning of July 24, 1996, when Liu Ma
Ling arrived at a water spirit's shrine along a small stream in the foothills
below his family's cave at about 5:30 A.M. Mr. Liu's traditional method of
prayer epitomized [dzEn tzə]: he would calmly and undemonstratively request
the spirit's assurance that the beans irrigated by this stream would continue
to flourish, the eels in the pond filled by this stream would continue to multiply, and the goat herds watered by this stream would continue to grow in size
and number. Thus, the traditional prayer's momentum would carry Mr. Liu's
beans, goats, and eels through the possibilities of drought, blight, and dis-
ease without risking a large amount of emotional investment. For according
to the tradition invoked by [dzEn tzə], overly emotional supplications could,
at best, cause the water spirit to provide Mr. Liu with more attention than
needed, thereby lessening the amount given to other families and creating
interfamily disharmony. At worst, the water spirit could become angered by
the surplus of emotion and withdraw its assurances.

This morning, however, Mr. Liu was neither calm nor undemonstrative. Several days earlier, the administrator of the Xinshin primary school had sent Liu and his wife a message, saying that their nine-year-old son, Bao, had to be moved into the school dormitory by September 1 to continue his education. This date was in the middle of the harvest period for the current bean crop, the weaning period for the goats, and the eel transportation period to the market in Xinshin. Although a combined journey to Xinshin could transport both eels and son, Mr. Liu had been counting on his son's assistance with the beans and goats. Bao, however, looked forward to returning to school. He could already read and write better than the majority of the village children in his class. Although he did not particularly like mathematics, he understood how to count money, how to decide whether to choose between an expensive and an inexpensive fertilizer, and how to measure the amount of diesel fuel needed to run the school's electrical generator. Mr. Liu, therefore, was highly agitated. He was afraid of what the water spirit would do when Bao could no longer say his prayers at the shrine, and he was afraid that once Bao's basic education was completed, he, like other families' children, would leave the family to look for a job in a city. Moreover, Mr. Liu knew his prayer was no longer one that would bring sustenance to the water spirit; for instead of asking the spirit for its protection, he was beseeching it not to harm his agricultural or familial investments.

The water spirit's cataplexic response to Mr. Liu's request had a twofold

$$\overset{H}{|} \quad \overset{L}{|}$$

effect. First, because the [nUŋ mIn] believe emotional catastrophes are caused by the suddenness with which stress or frustration appears, the shock of the water spirit's immediate reply sent Mr. Liu's already unsteady emotions into a further decline. Caught between the choice of either abandoning his religious belief in the local spirits or accepting the doom promised by the spirit, Mr. Liu's feelings of terror coalesced into an act of sheer frustration: he stormed into the bean field and began pulling up his bean crop. His wife and son, having witnessed this destruction of the bean plants and heard his screams, had gathered a number of the families living closest to the Liu home for support.

When he finally arrived home about 2:30 P.M., still feeling the mixture of fear, frustration, and anger over the prophecy of disorder and decay, Mr. Liu found the second of the immediate effects of the water spirit's response: to Liu's dismay, thirty-three distraught neighbors and one very confused foreigner had gathered outside the family's doorway. Upon Mr. Liu's arrival, the gathering split into two groups: the quiet, almost sullen male neighbors, a once again distraught Mr. Liu, and Bao squatted under a large tree about 5 meters from the doorway, while the nervous, whispering female neighbors and Mrs. Liu stood by the small pen of goats. Tension began to rise, the men began to mutter about various afflictions from which Mr. Liu could be suffering ("We can't even grow vegetables anymore without someone running afoul of something these days," one older man about seventy told me. "Too many changes have occurred, and nobody respects the elders, the ancestors, or the spirits anymore."). Meanwhile, the afternoon blended into the evening. Finally, about 7:00, Li Zhou Hwang, a forty-year-old neighbor of Mr. Liu who had been squatting on the periphery of the rough circle of men surrounding Liu, decided to do something about the situation. He rose to his feet, crossed the circle, and clasped Mr. Liu's shoulder. And Mr. Liu, aroused somewhat from the depths of his catatonia, began a sequence of narratives whose marked feelings of powerlessness lay in the narrator's inability to act in defiance of either the spiritual or the secular forces' definitions of order and in the narratives' subsequent evocation of a rhetoric of loss. (See appendixes 1, 2, and 3 for the complete texts of the narratives.)

"The word-using animal," wrote Kenneth Burke, "not only understands a thou-shalt-not; it can carry the principle of the negative a step further, and answer the thou-shalt-not with a disobedient No" (186–87). But the cost of that "disobedient No" is reflected by the ratio between Disorder and Order; a narrative that proceeds from obedience to disobedience, for example, changes the proportions of the ratio, leaving the act-agent relationship empty. As a result, notes Burke, the actor can no longer act but is instead "being moved, like a billiard ball tapped with a cue and behaving mechanically in conformity with the resistances it encounters" (188). The narrative's audience, therefore, is drawn toward the narrator by its identification with him and is at the same time repelled from him by his connection with disorder and mechanistic behavior. Within this vortex of emotions, religious faith and a stable social identity counteract the centrifugal forces of terror and difference and provide the means of reestablishing the audience's shaken solidarity. Yet, when the power of religion and social identity are undercut by greater external forces, the audience is left in a void, moved only by what Burke calls "resistances." Its members can only cling to the traditional meanings of the symbols that have guided them through life and can only evoke those meanings through a rhetoric of loss.

The [nUŋ mIn] audience present on this particular evening found themselves marooned in this Burkeian void, and the three narratives produced by Mr. Liu evoke the traditional meanings of [nUŋ mIn] religious symbols by first making those symbols concrete in narrative 1 (appendix 1) and then undercutting the symbols' power for his audience in narratives 2 (appendix 2) and 3 (appendix 3), thus creating the rhetoric of loss. In the first narrative, an anamnesitic introduction locates the personified "Lobster Head" in a spiritual time "before the ancestors," that is, before humans, as well as in a differentiated society. The developing theme of the fish's devotion to the

water spirit's demands reconfirms the dominant position of the [nUŋ mIn]'s spiritual history as the core of their social identity. Moreover, the fish's sym-

bolic representation of the [nUŋ mIn] is made readily apparent through the

narrator, Mr. Liu. His name, [liu], means "heavenly fish," and it signifies a small carp found occasionally in the Yellow River, the main water source for

the [nUŋ mIn].[4] Finally, "Lobster Head" is differentiated from other members of the larger society by its physical appearance, position in the universe of the Yellow River, and relationship with the water spirit, characteristics

which the [nUŋ mIn] point to as key differences between themselves and the Han who dominate the Chinese urban and village populations. Suspended in a "muddy slush" between heaven and earth, only the beneficent intrusion of the water spirit through a dream provides meaning to "Lobster Head" as well

as the [nUŋ mIn]. Apprehending this meaning, however, takes commitment:

both the fish as protagonist in one aspect of this allegory and the [nUŋ mIn] as protagonists in the alternative aspect of this allegory must be willing to maintain their separate "illiterate" identities in the face of the dominant population's identity as the "literate" soldiers of modern socialism. "Lobster Head" must distance himself in both time and geography from the other fish in the

river; the [nUŋ mIn] must hold on to their family-centered behaviors, traditions, and agricultural methods to distance themselves from the dominant social identity. Yet, there is a cost for this continued spiritual belief: Lobster Head's individual desires must be eschewed for the water spirit's directives, and contentment and harmony may only be maintained in the shadow cast by

promised punishment. Similarly, individual desires among the [nUŋ mIn] must reflect the spirits' directives; outside influences can only lead to punishment.

By itself, the "Lobster Head" narrative affirms the symbolized meanings

on which the [nUŋ mIn] social relationships and religious system rely. Meaning comes from the spirit world's intrusions into the human world, while contentment and harmony are maintained by real punishments for transgressions. The second and third narratives, however, undermine the affirmative power of the first narrative by apocarterestically sundering the spirit world from meaning (narrative 2) and then by separating the [nUŋ mǐn] from spiritual influence and moving the power to punish from the spirits to man (narrative 3).

Within the fable-like second narrative produced by Mr. Liu, the dream framing the mother's request for an apple comes not from a spirit but from her weakened physical condition. As a result, her definition of healing cannot come from appeasing an angered spirit or petitioning a spirit to take action; instead, healing derives from the only source available to the mother: modernized agricultural and medical methods. But the mother is not the protagonist; rather, her "good" daughter and her symbolic act of begging in the village represents for the [nUŋ mǐn] the process through which literacy movements have affected the spiritual core of their identity: the future generations, lacking the traditional spiritual identity because of their reliance on modern means of agricultural production and storage, are forced to beg for assistance from the same villagers responsible for destroying the [nUŋ mǐn] religious shrines during the Cultural Revolution. Feelings of chaotic terror have thus replaced feelings of calm spirituality. Even though the mother feels well enough to return to work, because her cure comes from the hands of the village medical personnel through her daughter, rather than through the directions of a local or ancestral spirit, the family, and by extension the [nUŋ mǐn], is spiritually doomed.

Narrative 3 functions rhetorically in a similar way. Because agricultural failure stems now from a lack of modern methodology, the family is once again separated from the spirit world and thus the family's source of traditional meanings. The only solution to the family's resulting economic problem the father can offer is a concrete representation of this spiritual separation: he must separate himself from his family and home to seek work in a factory in Luoyang. The father, however, is unequipped to function successfully in this literate world. Thus, he falls back on traditional meanings which, because of his physical and spiritual separation from their sources, are doomed to failure: an agriculturally related pursuit (selling fruit) and a spiritual pursuit (fortune telling). Adrift in a world that is becoming darker and colder, deception and theft—both attributes the [nUŋ mǐn] attach to urban life—are the protagonist's only choices for sustenance. Yet, these too lack meaning. The police do not punish him for his acts, and the food and shelter offered by temporary refuge become the stimuli of both a desirous dream and a final act of deception. Loss thus begets disappearance, sickness, and death, the reply given to Mr. Liu by the water spirit earlier that day.

What results from these separations of act and agent, from the feelings of terror and difference, is a society reduced to fish in a meaningless "muddy slush." The social structural forms in which the [nUŋ mIn] participate become dissonant, and contentment derives from individual desires. More generally, the social forms become those of the urban centers as a result of the differentiated, literate, urban occupational structure's displacement of the agricultural structure as the symbol of a successful life. The rural animist religious forms buffering the [nUŋ mIn] identity become indistinguishable from those of literate urban consumers as a result of the redefining of modern socialism. Finally, the [nUŋ mIn] become impotent entities facing a darker, colder, but literate future.

Conclusion

After examining the above narratives, I returned to my question concerning the accuracy of my fieldwork. I had discovered that the disruption of this nonliterate society by literacy movements dating from the early 1960s could be traced to a single source: an incongruity between the [nUŋ mIn] religious and social frameworks of meaning and the [tUn dze] economic patterns of social interaction. More specifically, the incongruity focused on the differences between the [nUŋ mIn] and the [tUn dze] definitions of appropriate ways of using social and cultural energies. Current literacy research paradigms are often unable, however, to describe this kind of incongruity for several reasons. First, the paradigms fail to discriminate between meaningful integration of such matters as identity and functional integration of goal-seeking actions. In other words, research methodologies often cannot distinguish between cultural and sociological processes. Kathleen Gough's comparative study of literacy in China and India, for example, concludes that literacy must be studied as an "enabling factor" in each country and identifies specific functional categories of inquiry: large-scale organizational and accumulative processes for knowledge, storage and retrieval systems of knowledge, and the field-dependent definitions of knowledge as they are used in such areas as science and the arts (55–56). Further investigations of these functional categories may develop possibilities for how "the overall development of [China's and India's] technology and social structure[s] [as well as] the character of [their] relations with other societies" will make use of these categories to achieve goals (56). Yet, these investigations cannot address the rhetorically represented conflicts between the societies' use of the categories and the meanings associated with religious, familial, and individual identities. Such conflicts thus become epiphenomena.

Second, current literacy research paradigms often fail to realize that cultural structure and social structure are not related reflexively. That is, cultural structures and social structures are not completely reliant on a dialectical relationship for each to exist. Instead, they exist as independent, yet interdependent variables. Walter Ong's definition of rhetoric as an "art" comprised of "a body of sequentially organized, scientific principles" applied to spoken persuasion and produced by writing, for example, supports his argument that a rhetorical tradition was "distinctive of the [literate] west . . . in contrast with [the oral] Indians and Chinese, who programmatically minimized [rhetoric]" (109, 111). What Ong's statement confuses, however, is the difference between forms of social organization and cultural patterns. Specifically, he sees the Western social institution represented by the Greek rhetor and the lack of such an institution in India and China as behavioral incarnations of cultural patterns that either value or devalue persuasion or exposition. What results from this confusion is an inability to describe or evaluate the dynamics of incongruity that develop when cultural patterns collide with changes in social organizations. The rhetorics of loss and gain formed by people caught within this incongruity are thus relegated to the status of epiphenomena. In other words, my fieldwork was not faulty; rather, the research paradigms into which I was trying to fit my discoveries were unable to ask the questions concerning the relationships between literacy discourses and counterdiscourses I was attempting to outline.

What literacy researchers need is a research paradigm that accounts for

$$\overset{\text{H}}{\underset{\big|}{}} \quad \overset{\text{L}}{\underset{\big|}{}} \qquad \overset{\text{M}}{\underset{\big|}{}} \quad \overset{\text{H}}{\underset{\big|}{}}$$

both the notion that people like the [nŬŋ mĭn] and the [tŬn dze] want to live in worlds based on meanings they can grasp and the notion that this common desire is often undercut by the behaviors sanctioned and demanded by social structures. Deborah Brandt, in her recent study of the various economic sponsors of literacy affecting "ordinary people," provides, perhaps, a starting point for developing such a paradigm. She concludes her study by observing that "as we assist and study individuals in pursuit of literacy, we also recognize how literacy is in pursuit of them. When this process stirs ambivalence . . . we need to be understanding" (183). Researchers should, in other words, enlarge Brandt's focus on "individuals in pursuit of literacy" to include not only the individual "pursuing" in various ways the socially sanctioned goals achieved through literacy but also those individuals who, as members of disempowered cultures, often become the "prey" of those who sanction the goals. Both groups' rhetorics become important suggestions of how a conflict between society and culture "stirs [the] ambivalence" between gain and terror, between difference and similarity, between loss and gain. Additionally, researchers must remember that these contrasting senses of reality lying behind the goals societies attain through literacy movements—increased economic profits, increased labor efficiency, and increased problem-solving capabilities—provide the contexts for ambivalent discourses. Michael Taussig addresses the power of such contrasts in his discussion of Joseph Conrad's experience with the terror generated by the expanding rubber industry in the Congo: "There were three realities there: King Leopold's, made out of intricate disguises and deceptions, Roger Casement's studied realism, and Conrad's [which, according to Karl Frederick] fell midway between the other two, as he attempted to penetrate the veil and yet was anxious to retain its hallucinatory quality" (Taussig, 10). Seeing the power, however, requires, according to Michel Foucault, an understanding of how power is produced "within discourses which are in themselves neither true nor false" (Foucault, 118). Narrating our visions of contrastive contextual power behind social uses of literacy movements thus requires an understanding of the potential counter-discourses created by the intricately constructed webs of meaning forming

the realities of such groups as the [nUŋ mIn] and the [tUn dze]. The spider metaphor is vital here; it provides a means of understanding literacy as not simply a linear mechanism but as the *kairos* for a branching network of symbolic possibilities.

Appendix 1

Many years ago, before the ancestors came here, the water spirit gave a beautiful fish a wonderful dream about a tall, ornate dragon gate along the Yellow River. In the dream, the fish jumped over the gate and became the water spirit's favorite. After awakening, the fish remembered his dream and became determined to find the dragon gate and fulfill his dream.

The Yellow River was a full of dirt and grit then as it is now, and because the fish was smaller than the other fish who lived in the river, he could not swim through the thick water as fast as the others. In fact, he could not even float like the other fish. Instead of floating effortlessly, letting his fins balance him in the muddy slush, he had to move his tail mightily, staying all the while close to the surface. Thus, the other fish laughed at him and called him "Lobster Head" since his head was always pointed toward the surface of the river while his tail was pointed toward the murky bottom.

After swimming for many days, the beautiful fish found himself tired, hungry, and, because he was far from home, very scared. With the last of his energy, he fought his way to the river's surface and pushed his head into the air. Before him stood the magnificent dragon gate. Awestruck, he stared at the clouds covering the top of the gate and asked himself, "How could you ever hope to jump over the top of that?" But remembering his dream, he swam as fast as he could toward the gate. Gathering his muscles, he jumped as high as he could, but the top of the gate remained far above him.

"I give up," the fish whimpered. "I'd better go back home."

The memory of his dream, however, returned to him and renewed his determination to jump over the dragon gate. So over and over and over again the fish jumped. And over, and over, and over again he failed. Feeling disappointed and defeated, he turned to go home.

As he slowly swam, his head pointed up and his tail pointed down, the dream haunted him. And once again, he could hear the other fish taunting him. These thoughts made him stop and think about what waited for him at home because of his failed attempts.

Filled with a new sense of determination, the fish returned to the dragon gate. He prepared himself by praying for the water spirit's approval. Then he jumped.

To his complete surprise he found himself looking down on the clouds covering the top of the dragon gate. Then, suddenly, he was back in the muddy slush of the river on the other side of the gate.

A voice trumpeting "Congratulations!" filled all the fish's senses as the water spirit appeared before him. "But," warned the spirit, "do not think you can jump over all the dragon gates just because you jumped over this one. If you try to jump over them, you will end up in disgrace. Instead, be happy with what you have done and live happily here with me as my favorite."

Still amazed by his jump, the beautiful fish swam, reveling in his accomplishment. Soon, however, he came to an ever grander, more ornate dragon gate, far superior to the one he had conquered. But the fish was content. He had fulfilled the dream given him by the water spirit. The new dragon gate, therefore, did not bother him.

Appendix 2

A little girl who was a very good daughter took very good care of her ill mother. One day, the mother said to the girl, "How wonderful it would be if I could have an apple." It was winter, however, and apples were not growing on the trees. And only the people who lived in the village had a way to store apples picked in the fall for the winter. So the mother's request was really nothing more than a wish created by her illness.

The little girl didn't say anything in response to her mother's request. Later that day, though, she took a basket from the house, walked to the village, knelt on the ground by some large buildings, and raised the basket above her head. "My poor mother wants apples," she told passers-by. "Please, please, give me some apples to make my mother feel better."

The girl spent the next two days kneeling on the ground and begging for apples. The evening of her third day in the village, her pleas were answered by two women who dispensed [dzoːŋ yao] (herbs, natural remedies) to the sick. "Take these apples and make sure your mother eats all of them," the women told the girl. "If she eats them all, she will soon be able to go back to work."

Excited, the girl took the apples, thanked the women, and ran home. She sat next to where her mother lay and offered her the apples. After eating one, the mother claimed she felt much better. But remembering what the women in the village told her, the daughter pointed out how much better her mother would feel if she ate all the apples. Finally, after eating the rest of the apples, the mother felt well enough to back to the field where she worked.

Appendix 3

There was once a family of farmers who lived on the other side of the Li Shan Mountains. The family included a father, a mother, a daughter, and the father's mother. After several hard years, the father decided to stop raising rice and begin raising goats and beans. The goats, however, got sick and died, and the beans never grew very well. The father, threfore, decided to leave the family and move to the city to become wealthy by working in the tractor factory. His mother, wife, and daughter, however, didn't want him to leave. They pleaded with him to stay and plant rice again because he was a farmer, not a factory worker. The father did not listen to his family's entreaties. In fact, he became very angry with them. Gathering his clothes and his bowl, he shouted defiantly, "You'll change your minds when I come back with money and an apartment in the city!" Then he left his family and traveled to the city.

Unfortunately, the farmer could not get work at the tractor factory. So he tried to get other jobs. The same result. With no other possibilities open to him, he went back to what he knew—farming—to get a job selling fruits on one of the market streets. But the customers complained that all his fruits were rotten. Next he got a scrap of cloth, drew some strange-looking figures on it, and tried telling fortunes. But one of his clients grew angry over the prediction given him and beat the farmer. Finally, he was left with no other choice but begging. Not once during this time did he think about going back to his family.

The winters in the city are colder than they are here. Because the farmer had no warm clothes and did not have any money or food or a place to live, he decided to spend the night in a jail. "The jail will be warmer than the street, and the policemen will give me food and clothes," he reasoned. "Besides, staying in the jail will be easier than trying to find another job or going home."

The farmer, however, did not know how to get into the jail. So he began watching the people around him. He saw how the sellers in the markets cheated the customers when the measured the weights of meat and noodles. He saw how one store owner stole sleeping mats from another store owner so that the second one would not make more money than the first one. The farmer knew these actions were forbidden, but he learned that these actions were typical of how people in the cities lived.

Spotting an umbrella left outside a door, the farmer took it. Suddenly, the owner of the umbrella came out of the door and saw the farmer holding the umbrella.

"That is my umbrella!" shouted the owner at the farmer.

"I know," replied the farmer. "I just want this umbrella."

"But that umbrella is mine," sputtered its owner.

"I know this umbrella is yours," repeated the farmer. "But I want it!"

"Do you want me to take you to court so I can prove the umbrella is mine?"

"No," stated the farmer. "Going to court would take too long, and the court is not close by." The farmer returned the umbrella to its owner and walked further down the street.

Pretty soon, the farmer saw two policemen standing on a corner. "If I fight with the policemen, maybe they will put me in jail," thought the farmer. He approached the policemen and asked if they would either fight him and then take him to jail or if they would just take him to jail because he had tried to steal an umbrella.

"Did you really steal the umbrella?" asked one of the policemen.

"Yes, I did," answered the farmer.

"Why did you steal the umbrella?"

"I made a mistake a long time ago," answered the farmer. He then explained how he had given up farming and left his family to come to the city because he wanted money.

"Will you change your ways and go back to your family and farm?" asked the other policeman.

"Yes," grumbled the farmer. "I have learned my lesson."

Night was coming on, and as the light faded, the farmer felt colder and colder. One of the policemen asked the farmer if he had a place to stay.

"No," answered the farmer. "Besides, I'm hungry and cold."

"If we let you stay the night in our office, will you go back to your family tomorrow?" asked the other policeman.

"Yes, I promise!" the farmer assured them.

That night, while the farmer slept in the first warm place he had been in for many days, he dreamed about the food, the blanket, and the clothes the policemen had given him. In the dream, he had many different foods to eat, had many clothes, and had a warm bed softer than any he had ever slept on. The farmer awoke from his dream and thought to himself, "I will never have these things if I go back to the farm." Seeing that the policemen were asleep, he quietly walked out the door into the night. Determined to make lots of money, he walked quickly around the corner and disappeared into the dark streets.

No one ever saw the farmer again. His mother died, not knowing what had happened to her son. His wife grew old and sick and had to rely on neighbors for food and clothing. And his daughter grew up, but because she had dreams like her father had, she was scorned by the other families. She disappeared too, and we don't know what happened to her.

Notes

1.   The fieldwork was conducted in the Li Shan Mountains between the city of Luoyang and the village of Xinshin, Henan province, People's Republic of China.

2.   The figures produced by the World Bank are important, for to the government of the PRC they represent the Western economic world's perception of the PRC's political status. For example, in 1960, the PRC needed to expend 1.75 kg of oil equivalent to generate one dollar of GNP. By 1978, this figure had been reduced to 1.23 kg of oil equivalent per dollar of GNP; the government of the PRC could, therefore, present a picture of economic and social success to the world. Between 1978 and 1996, however, the ratio had only improved slightly to 1.10 kg of oil equivalent per dollar of GNP. When compared to the Mexican (0.60 kg of oil per dollar of GNP) and post-Soviet collapse Russian (0.70 kg of oil per dollar of GNP) economies, both of which had had been severely criticized by the World Bank to the extent that the respective governments had been threatened with economic sanctions, the symbolic power of the PRC's continued efficiency improvement lost considerable strength. As a result of this rhetorical embarrassment, the government of the PRC had to once again rely on arguments substantiating their literacy movements as a means of increasing the strength of their waning symbols of economic and social power.

3. This specific statement, quoted directly, was made by a member of the People's Congress during an interview with him on July 23, 1996.

4. The spiritual theme is further emphasized by the name [liu]. According to tradition, this carp could only be captured by fishermen supplying the emperor and his family, could only be physically touched by cooks specifically selected by the emperor, and could only be eaten by the emperor and his family. As the emperor was an important part of the Buddhist cosmology, the fish's spiritual significance, both within the narrative and for the

[nUŋ mIn], increases.

Works Cited

Brandt, Deborah. "Sponsors of Literacy." *College Composition and Communication* 49 (1998): 165–85.

Burke, Kenneth. *The Rhetoric of Religion: Studies in Logology*. Berkeley, Los Angeles, and London: University of California Press, 1970.

Foucault, Michel. "Truth and Power." In *Power/Knowledge: Selected Interviews and Other Writings, 1972–1977*, 109–33. New York: Pantheon, 1980.

Frederick, Karl. *Joseph Conrad: The Three Lives*. New York: Farrar, Strauss and Giroux, 1979.

Gough, Kathleen. "Implications of Literacy in Traditional China and India." In *Perspectives on Literacy*, edited by Eugene R. Kintgen, Barry M. Kroll, and Mike Rose, 51–70. Carbondale and Edwardsville, Ill.: Southern Illinois University Press, 1988.

Inkeles, Alex, and David Smith. *Becoming Modern*. Cambridge, Mass.: Harvard University Press, 1974.

Laslett, Peter. *The World We Have Lost*. New York: Scribner, 1966.

Miscellany of Mao Tse-tung Thought, 1949–1968. Washington, D.C.: JPRS, 1974.

"Modernizing Socialism." *People's Daily*, June 17, 1994, 1.

"Nutrition and Birth." *People's Daily*, July 11, 1996, 7–8.

Ong, Walter. *Orality and Literacy: The Technologizing of the Word*. New York and London: Methuen, 1982.

Taussig, Michael. *Shamanism, Colonialism, and the Wild Man: A Study in Terror and Healing*. Chicago: The University of Chicago Press, 1987.

Todd, Emmanuel. *The Causes of Progress: Culture, Authority and Change*. Oxford: Basil Blackwell, 1987.

Yu, Youhai. "U.S. $1,000 by the Year 2000." *People's Daily*, June 17, 1994, 15–20.

Contributors

Valentina M. Abordonado, the mother of Andrew, Ashley, Andrea, and Andre Alan Abordonado, is an assistant professor of English at Hawaii Pacific University. She has collaborated with Phyllis on a feminist analysis of Aristotle and has coauthored a chapter on gender and linguistic variation in written communication with Duane Roen and Chere Peguesse in *Composing Social Identity in Written Language.* Abordonado's current scholarly interests include gender and writing, feminist pedagogy, and computers and writing.

Shane Borrowman is a graduate student at the University of Arizona, where he is completing a Ph.D. in rhetoric, composition, and the teaching of English. His work has appeared in *College Teaching, Inland,* and *Washington English Journal.* Currently Borrowman is the associate editor of *Rhetoric Review* and is working on his dissertation, which explores the connections among composition, social memory and history, and the television media's continuous reinterpretation of the Vietnam War.

Daniel F. Collins teaches at Cape Fear Community College in Wilmington, North Carolina. He received his Ph.D. from Indiana University of Pennsylvania, where he was introduced to multicultural rhetorical traditions. Collins is currently editing a book entitled *Teaching After the End* with Derek Owens.

Kathleen A. DeHaan is an assistant professor of communication at the College of Charleston, South Carolina, with a Ph.D. in rhetoric from Northwestern University. She has also worked in the corporate and not-for-profit sectors. DeHaan's research interests include immigrant letter writing, identity construction, and organizational communication. She has presented papers on these subjects at numerous national conferences as well as at the International Society for the History of Rhetoric Conference, in Amsterdam, The Netherlands, July 1999. DeHaan teaches communication theory, rhetoric, rhetoric and identity, speechwriting, and organizational communication.

Theresa Enos is professor of English and director of the rhetoric, composition, and the teaching of English graduate program at the University of Arizona. Founder and editor of *Rhetoric Review,* she teaches both graduate and undergraduate courses in writing and rhetoric. Her research interests include the history and theory of rhetoric and the intellectual work and politics of rhetoric and composition studies. She has edited or coedited seven books, including the *Encyclopedia of Rhetoric and Composition: Communication from Ancient Times to the Information Age* (1995) and has published numerous chapters and articles on rhetorical theory and issues in writing. She is the author of *Gender Roles and Faculty Lives in Rhetoric and Composition* (1996) and immediate past president of the National Council of Writing Program Administrators.

Laura Gray-Rosendale is an assistant professor of rhetoric and former chair of The Commission on the Status of Women at Northern Arizona University. She teaches graduate and undergraduate classes in cultural studies, the history of rhetoric, gender studies, and composition theory. Gray-Rosendale's work has appeared in *Signs: A Journal of Women and Culture, CONCERNS,* the *Journal of Basic Writing, Dialogue,* and *Composition Forum,* and can be found in anthologies such as *Getting a Life: Autobiography and Postmodernism, Miss Grundy Doesn't Teach Here Anymore: How Popular Culture Has Changed the Composition Classroom, The Personal Narrative: Writing Ourselves as Teachers and Scholars, Multiple Literacies for the Twenty-First Century, Questioning Authority,* and *The Literacy Standard.* Her book, *Rethinking "Basic Writing": Exploring Identity, Politics, and Community in Interaction,* is published with Lawrence Erlbaum Associates.

Sibylle Gruber is an assistant professor of rhetoric at Northern Arizona University, where she teaches graduate and undergraduate courses in literacy studies, rhetoric and cultures, computers and composition, and the theory and history of composition studies. She is the editor of *Weaving a Virtual Web: Practical Approaches to New Information Technologies.* Gruber's work on cybertheories, feminist rhetorics, composition, and cultural studies can be found in journals such as *Computers and Composition, Computer Supported Cooperative Work, Journal of Basic Writing, Works and Days, The Journal of the Assembly on Computers in English,* and *The Information Society;* and books such as *Feminist Cyberspaces: Essays on Gender in Electronic Spaces* and *Global Literacy Practices and the WWW: Cultural Perspectives on Information Distribution, Interpretation, and Use.*

Barbara Heifferon is an assistant professor at Clemson University and mother of two daughters: Elizabeth, a student at the Fashion Design Institute in Los Angeles; and Leah, a student at Georgetown University. She was a cardiopulmonary technologist for a number of years before deciding to teach writing. Her interests include medical rhetoric, writing across the curriculum, service learning, multimedia, and liberatory pedagogy. She coedited two students' guides to composition (Burgess, 1997, 1998), and has published in *Theorizing Composition* (Greenwood, 1999) and *Science and Engineering Ethics*. She is currently guest-editing a special edition of *Technical Communication Quarterly* on medical rhetoric.

John B. Killoran, assistant professor of English language and literature, is currently tending a nascent writing program at Brock University in Ontario, Canada. Since 1996, he has worked to develop the professional writing and computer communications course. The course has both informed and been informed by his research on computer-mediated communication, specifically individuals' homesteading on the Web. His dissertation based on this research was successfully defended in 1999.

Jacqueline J. Lambiase is an assistant professor of journalism at the University of North Texas, where she teaches technology and writing classes. Her research interests include Internet discourse, feminist theory, and sexually oriented appeals in advertising. Her professional experience includes print media and media relations jobs in both Texas and Maryland. Lambiase's collaborative work on examining sexually oriented appeals has appeared in *Journalism and Mass Communication Quarterly* and the forthcoming *Sexual Rhetoric: Media Perspectives on Sexuality, Gender and Identity*. An essay on Internet rhetoric appears in the recently published *Rhetoric, the Polis, and the Global Village: Proceedings of the Rhetoric Society of America's 30th Anniversary Conference, 1998*.

Anthony J. Michel is a doctoral candidate in the American Studies Program at Michigan State University. His emphases include rhetoric, cultural criticism, and contemporary U.S. fiction. Michel is now working on a dissertation on rhetorical approaches to Cold War and post–Cold War narratives.

Huining Ouyang is an assistant professor of English at Edgewood College, Madison, Wisconsin. She teaches ethnic American literature, literary criticism, and English composition.

Duane H. Roen, co-parent of Nicholas and Hanna Roen, currently directs Arizona State University's Center for Learning and Teaching Excellence. Most recently, he served as director of the composition program at Arizona State University. Roen has also served as director of the writing program at Syracuse University and as director of rhetoric, composition, and the teaching of English at the University of Arizona. With Stuart Brown and Theresa Enos, he coedited *Living Rhetoric and Composition* (Erlbaum, 1999). He coedited, with Gesa Kirsch, *A Sense of Audience in Written Communication* (Sage, 1990). With Donna M. Johnson, he coedited *Richness in Writing:*

Empowering ESL Students (Longman, 1989). He also coauthored, with Stuart C. Brown and Robert Mittan, *Becoming Expert: Writing and Learning in the Disciplines* (Kendall/Hunt, 1990) and *A Writer's Toolbox* (Allyn and Bacon, 1997). He has authored or coauthored more than 130 chapters, journal articles, and conference papers. Roen's current scholarly interests include teaching portfolios, outcomes assessment, collaborative writing, gender and written language, and audience.

Phyllis Mentzell Ryder is an assistant professor of English at the George Washington University. Her research analyzes the relationships among rhetoric, cultural studies, and composition classes, with a particular focus on the rhetoric of education in the United States. She has published in the *Journal of Advanced Composition*, and has collaborated with each of the authors of her chapter on other articles and book chapters: with Valentina on a feminist analysis of Aristotle, with Barbara on a definition of the term "deconstruction" in Mary Kennedy's *Theorizing Composition* (Greenwood, 1999), and with Duane on a chapter on audience in *Evaluating Writing* (National Council of Teachers of English, 1999). She presented a critical analysis of the rhetoric of midwifery at the Conference on College Composition and Communication in 1998. She and her husband, Eric Mentzell, have one son, born with the help of midwives in Tucson, Arizona.

Jeff Schonberg, assistant professor of English at Angelo State University in San Angelo, Texas, has been working as a language research consultant with the Henan and Shaan Xi provincial governments, Northwest University in Xi'an, and Zhengzhou University in Zhengzhou, The People's Republic of China, since 1994. An active presenter at CCCC, NCTE, and other rhetorical and linguistic conferences, Schonberg is currently working on two book-length manuscripts, the first dealing with linguistic and rhetorical changes in south-central China, and the second on Plato's influence on the rhetorical nature of anthropology.

Catherine F. Smith is associate professor of writing and English at Syracuse University, where she teaches advanced composition, professional and technical communication, and discourse studies. She has published various book chapters and articles on issues related to gender, discourse analysis, and public discourse. Smith's current scholarly interests are historical rhetoric, public policy discourse, and writing for the World Wide Web.

Hui Wu is a lecturer in rhetoric and composition at the University of Central Arkansas. Her research interests include comparative rhetoric, contemporary Chinese women's rhetoric, and ESL composition instruction. Wu has published various articles on Chinese rhetoric and composition.

Index

Aaron, Daniel, 162
Abbott, Don Paul, 29
Abordonado, Valentina M., 6, 33, 257
Abortion, 97, 116
Activism, 84
Adam, Ian, 183
Aesthetics, 178–79
African American, 147, 159, 164, 170–71, 173, 175, 182
Afrocentric rhetoric, 10, 185, 188–91, 193, 195
Agency, 8, 18, 22, 64, 67, 120, 141, 144, 146, 150, 159, 175, 186, 190, 194, 202
Aggression, 7, 78, 83–84, 114
Agonism, 9, 10, 186, 187–88, 191–92
Agriculture, 238
Ai, Xiao-ming, 227–28, 232
Ai, Yun, 224–26, 232
Alcoff, Linda Martin, 49
Alienation, 151, 153
Allee, Marjorie Hill, 162
Alliteration, 151
Alternative rhetorics, 5–7, 57, 67, 88, 185, 190
Ambiguity, 119, 204, 212, 236
Ambivalence, 11, 44, 206, 208, 213, 236, 249, 250
American, 9, 11, 12, 23, 27, 31, 50, 51, 72, 75, 93, 97–98, 102, 113, 146, 150–51, 156, 158–59, 162,
163–65, 172, 182, 185, 188, 190–91, 198, 203–04, 206–09, 213, 216, 217, 222, 259
Ammons, Elizabeth, 203, 216–17
Anaphora, 151
Anderson, Teresa, 89
Andrews, Richard, 198
Anthropology, 260
Anti-military, 123
Antithesis, 44, 151
An-yi, Wang, 219, 221–22, 225–26, 229
Anzaldúa, Gloria, 11, 90
Apposition, 151
Aristotle, 1, 95–96, 109, 111–12, 118, 125, 257, 260
Armstrong, Peggy, 49
Asante, Molefi Kete, 189, 191–92, 198, 200
Asian, 6, 201–02, 204–05, 207–13, 232
Assonance, 151, 153
Audience as a rhetorical construct, 191
Authorial stance, 209
Authorial subject position, 9, 169, 174
Authoritative text, 18, 176

Bailey, Margaret Lewis, 29
Baker, Augusta, 163
Baker, Houston A. Jr., 162
Bakhtin, Mikhail M., 143, 163
Barlow, Tani E., 234
Bassett, Jon E., 163

Todd, Emmanuel, 235–36, 255
Transgression, 246
Transvestite, 212
Treichler, Paula, 91
Tricksterism, 10, 204, 213
Trimbur, John, 50, 198
Trinh, Minh-ha T., 72, 91, 183, 207, 209, 217
Trojan War, 111, 114, 120
Tuana, Nancy, 126
Turkey, 205

Unemployment, 65, 154, 235
UNIFEM, 7, 78, 85–89

Vanderstel, David G., 73
Vatz, Richard, 234
Vaughn-Roberson, Courtney, 165
Videon, Carol, 94, 109
Villanueva, Victor, 12
Virtual spaces, 88
Visual imagery, 180
Visual rhetorics, 9, 168, 172, 174, 177–78, 180–81
Vitanza, Victor J., 16
Von Rad, Gerhard, 31
Vora, Erika, 192, 200

Wahlstrom, B.J., 144
Walker, Alice, 92
Wang, An-yi, 230
War, 7, 23, 25, 31, 77–78, 81–82, 84–85, 89, 102, 111–12, 114
Warschauer, Mark, 13
Watanna, Onoto, 10, 203–04, 206–09, 213, 217
Watson, John Selby, 110
Webber, Joan, 31
Wei, Yu-chuan, 221, 234
Weise, Elizabeth R., 125
Weitz, Rose, 51
West, Cornel, 91
White, Eugene E., 232

White, Hayden, 73, 261
White, James Boyd, 73
White-Parks, Annette, 204, 216–17
Will, George, 51
Willey, R. J., 186
Williams, Helen E., 165
Williams, J. Whitridge, 51
Williams, Jean C., 145, 147
Williams, Jeffrey, 51
Williams, Raymond, 200
Winterowd, Ross W., 51
Wintz, Cary D., 165
Wolf, Christa, 126
Women Activist Groups, 7, 77
Women's issues, 82, 84, 86–89
Women's rights, 7, 78, 84, 86, 88
Woods, M., 31
Woodyard, Jeffrey Lynn, 200
Woolf, Virginia, 30–31, 32, 229
World Wide Web, 75–76, 78, 88, 94, 127, 141, 143, 260
Worsham, Lynn, 12, 51, 165, 183, 202
Wu, Hui, 10, 219, 260

Xiao-Ying, Wang, 221

Yang, Gladys, 234
Yarbrough, Stephen, 13
Yates, Frances A., 32
Young, Iris Marion, 92
Young, James O., 165
Young, Richard, 232
Yu, Youhai, 255
Yue, Meng, 234

Zagreb, 85
Zeng, Zhen-nan, 221, 234
Zeong, Mao, 236
Zhang, Kang-kang, 226, 234
Zhang, Ren, 234
Zheng, Wang 219, 222–23, 225, 227, 229, 234
Ziegler, Dhyana, 200